Northwest Arkansas
Travel Guide
2015-2016

Lynn West

Cover Photo: *Crystal Bridges Museum of American Art*

For Don & Becky West, my parents

They Made Northwest Arkansas A Better Place

Special Thanks to:

Ryan West, Tyler VandenHeuvel, Kris Ashmore, Adam West, Jamei Hopper, Carla Chadwick, Priscilla Rudd, Sherry Thomas, Steve Gunter, Sharon Platz, Joan White, Bonnie VandenHeuvel, Tim Dills, Greg Caldwell, Kathy Cross, Nancee Helms, Stephnei Berry, Jay Wisely, Luanne Bachman, Terri Tolbert, Becky Ford, Chryl Hoyt, Kay Matthews, Terry Coberly, Janie Rodden, Dave Schloss, Jennifer Terry, JC Cross, Del Groh, Brenda Carr, Valerie West, Connie Welty, Rod Welty, Vincent West, Roger Thomas, Linda Boothe, Charles Rudd and Jim Ford

TABLE OF CONTENTS

HOW TO USE THIS GUIDE

How does this guide work? If you find a hotel, restaurant, specialty shop or any other place that you want more information about, simply click on the title. Clicking the title will take you directly to the business' website or Facebook page where you will find additional information.

WHY BUY THIS BOOK

Most of us don't have time to spend doing in-depth research on vacation destinations, and that is why I've spent the time finding all the first-rate accommodations, unique restaurants and exciting things to do in this scenic NW corner of Northwest Arkansas. The guide's easy-to-use layout helps you quickly find your way around ALL THE CITIES in the area, and doesn't just focus on one or two.

Using this guide will turn you into a savvy NWA traveler. You'll soon get the hang of all the guide features and discover a few little-known tricks that will help you stretch your vacation dollars while letting you have a wonderful, fun-filled vacation.

Regardless of which NWA city you decide to stay, this book will give you plenty of pertinent advice and answers to your questions.

WHAT THE LOCALS SAY...

We've listened to the locals who live in the area and solicit the boutiques, specialty shops, restaurants and other businesses every day and passed along what they've said about them. They aren't paid to give a "good recommendation," they are simply telling it like it is!

ITINERARIES AND DAY TRIPS IDEAS

We've included some fun-filled sample itineraries and day trips to make sure you get the most out of NWA. These aren't official tours, just suggested places to stay, play and dine.

ACCOMMODATIONS

We separated the hotels in to 2 and 3 star ratings. I also created a specific section for bed and breakfasts, cottages, cabins, resorts, treehouses and rv parks.

RESTAURANTS

We used the $ symbol to designate restaurant prices. One $ is considered budget, $$ is considered mid-range and $$$ carries an upscale designation.

DEALS AND TRAVEL TIPS

Want to know the best deals and save money? Easy! Check out our website at NWATravelguide.com. It has a section for daily deals at restaurants throughout Northwest Arkansas. For example, if it is Monday, click on Monday to see what restaurants offer discounts, happy hours and other savings.

NWATravelGuide.com also includes exclusive deals on accommodations, rental cars and attractions in the Northwest Arkansas area. Specials are for every price range from budget to luxury.

… Now, let's travel to NWA!

NORTHWEST ARKANSAS

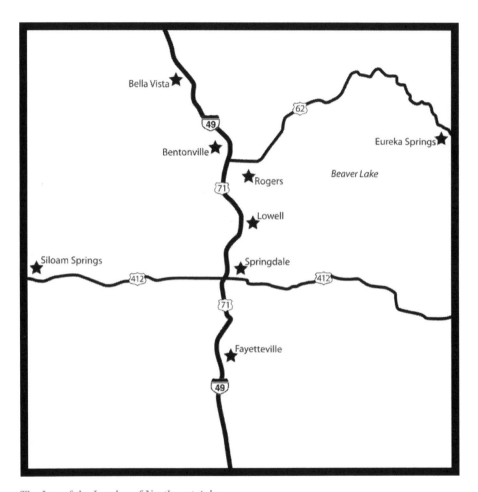

The Lay of the Land... of Northwest Arkansas

Approximately 3.2 million visitors per year make the trip to Northwest Arkansas, and there are no signs of the traffic slowing down. If you are asking why, you've never been to the area! There are tons of amazing things to do in Northwest Arkansas.

The Northwest corner of Arkansas is home to a number of towns and smaller communities, which together are commonly referred to as Northwest Arkansas or NWA. Bentonville, Bella Vista, Eureka Springs, Fayetteville, Lowell, Rogers, Siloam Springs and Springdale are the cities covered in this recently researched and up-to-date area guide.

The NWA area is a unique picturesque part of the state and has many different communities; some simple farming communities; some more complex, sophisticated bustling business centers. Always noted for its natural beauty and cleanmountain air, NWA has grown to encompass a huge variety of attractions.

What you will find in NWA is an area filled with friendly people and a fascinating history alongside a thriving business community. Who could have imagined that Walmart, the world's largest corporation, would incubate and establish itself utilizing this tiny corner of the state as its base? In addition, J.B. Hunt and Tyson Foods are also headquartered out of NWA.

NWA invites its visitors to enjoy:

- Awe-inspiring Museums - **Crystal Bridges Museum of American Art**, a dazzling, world-class 1.2 billion dollar museum.

- Bustling Vibrant Business Community - More than 300 Fortune 500 businesses have operations in NWA

- Breathtaking Natural and Manmade Wonders - **Beaver Lake, Ozark Mountains, Hiking & Biking Paradise**

- Architectural and Historical Treasures - The Entire **Downtown of Eureka Springs**, Civil War Cemeteries Town Courthouses **Bentonville Film Festival** – The first and only film competition in Arkansas and the world, for that matter, to offer digital and retail home entertainment distribution for its winners.

- Championship Level Bicycle Walking & Hiking trails - Award-winning bicycle friendly communities, Fayetteville, Rogers, Bentonville

- Award-winning Chefs and Culinary Districts - Bentonville, Fayetteville, Eureka Springs, Siloam Springs, Local & eclectic food

- Vibrant Entertainment Districts - Downtown & Dickson St. in Fayetteville, Downtown in Eureka Springs

- Hundreds of Festivals and Special Events - The Walmart AMP, Bikes, Blues & BBQ Festival, Arts and Crafts Festivals

- Metropolitan Level Upscale Shopping - Downtown Rogers, Fayetteville, Eureka Springs

- Countless Unique Boutiques and Little Out-Of-The-Way shops - Eureka Springs, Fayetteville, Springdale

- Antiquing at Its best - Fayetteville, Siloam Springs, Springdale, Eureka Springs

- **Accommodations to Suit Every Preference** - Everything from luxurious inns, to quaint peaceful B & B's, to the prestigious 21c Museum Hotel.

- **National and Collegiate Sports** Programs - LPGA Championship, University of Arkansas Razorback Sports, Come call the Hogs

- **America's Favorite Farmer's** Markets - Fayetteville, Bentonville, Rogers

In recent years, NWA has gone through an extensive metamorphosis and anyone will find a long list of many wonderful activities nestled amongst the posh accommodations to enjoy.

For this traveler, my list of things to do in Northwest Arkansas include stopping by the fabulous Crystal Bridges American Art Museum, the Botanical Garden of the Ozarks, the Cherokee and Choctaw casinos, the Compton Gardens, and the Museum of Native American Artifacts. These are only a few of the attractions that you will enjoy during your stay in the NWA area.

NWA Climate

Another reason to travel to the NWA area is its temperate climate. Visitors relish in NWA's mild weather and four distinct seasons. If you like your fall weather to be blazing with color, your spring weather to be dazzling with daffodils, winter's weather to be moderate, and your summer days to be bright and warm, you will love NWA. The average overall temperature for the area is 58 degrees Fahrenheit.

Ways to Get to NWA

Flying:

Northwest Arkansas Regional Airport (XNA): The NWA Regional Airport is referred to as XNA, and while it is located in Bentonville, it's a hub for all Northwest Arkansas communities. It is served by five airlines: Allegiant Air, American/American Eagle, Delta Airlines, United Airlines and U.S. Airways

Express. XNA is small enough that you won't spend hours getting in and out of the facility, yet large enough that you can fly nearly everywhere from XNA. For more information call (479) 205-1000 or visit www.flyxna.com.

Branson Airport: Branson Airport is a smaller airport served by Branson Air Express and Buzz Airways.

Tulsa International Airport: Tulsa International Airport is served by seven airlines: Allegiant Air, American/American Eagle, Delta Airlines, Southwest Airlines, Sun Country Airlines, United Airlines and U.S. Airways. Oftentimes you'll find a great bargain flying in and out of Tulsa since Southwest Airlines utilizes this airport. You can opt to fly in to Tulsa and rent a car to drive to NWA, as Tulsa is about a one-and-a-half to two-hour drive to Bentonville. It's not a bad drive, but XNA is far easier and quicker.

Smaller Airports

Bentonville Municipal Airport/Louise M. Thaden Field: This airport accommodates private charter, air charter and single/twin engine planes.

Rogers Municipal Airport: Rogers accommodates private and corporate aircraft, including jets and single/twin engine planes. Aircraft maintenance and charter services are available. For more information, call (479) 631-1400 or visit www.rogersarkansas.com/airport.

Fayetteville Executive Airport/Drake Field: This airport serves mainly general aviation aircraft comprising of corporate, business charter, military, pilot training and recreational flyers.

Driving:

Albuquerque, New Mexico: 704 miles, approximately 11 hours
Branson, Missouri: 93 miles, approximately 1 hour 45 min
Dallas, Texas: 398 miles, approximately 6 hours
Kansas City, Missouri: 268 miles, approximately 3 hours 30 min
Kingwood, Texas: 463 miles, approximately 8 hours
Little Rock, Arkansas: 203 miles, approximately 3 hours 15 min
Long Beach, California: 1558 miles, approximately 23 hours
Memphis, Tennessee: 336 miles, approximately 5 hours 30 min
Oklahoma City, Oklahoma: 225 miles, approximately 3 hours 45 min
St. Louis, Missouri: 329 miles, approximately 5 hours
Tulsa, Oklahoma: 118 miles, approximately 2 hours

Transportation Once in NWA:

NWA is still in its infancy as far as mass transit is concerned. A rental car is the most efficient way to travel around town and from city to city.

Fortunately, there are many rental car companies located at XNA and Tulsa International airports and in many of the area's towns. Keep in mind that it is wise to book your transportation well in advance during the week of the Walmart stockholders meeting, during the numerous arts and crafts festivals, and during the Arkansas Razorback games.

If you do not wish to rent a car, taxicabs are available and the Ozark Regional Transit provides public transportation throughout Bentonville, Fayetteville, Rogers and Springdale. Find out when any Ozark Regional Transit bus is due to arrive at a scheduled stop via the RouteShout app for smartphones and Internet users.

Additionally, many area hotels offer chartered bus or shuttle service to and from XNA and the smaller area airports. Just make certain that your book your charter ahead.

See Appendix A for a complete list of car rental and limousine services.

BENTONVILLE

Crystal Bridges Museum of Art

The quote "big city amenities with a small town feel" aptly characterizes Bentonville, a city that is quickly answering the question: "Where is Bentonville, Arkansas anyway?" No longer a "small town," Bentonville is the home of the globally ranked Crystal Bridges Museum of American Art, the 21c Museum Hotel, award winning restaurants, art galleries and festivals of every kind.

Today, Bentonville is an epitome of opposites. This rapidly growing town of 38,000 is home to Walmart Stores, Inc. Yes, the largest retailer in the world founded and kept its home office in Bentonville, a most unlikely place. Headquarters for businesses even half this size are typically reserved for cities like New York City, Los Angeles and Chicago.

It isn't uncommon to be standing in line at the local Bentonville Walmart store with the buyer of bedding, sporting goods, women's apparel, or jewelry. These buyers and other head Walmart buyers are responsible for spending billions of dollars worldwide.

Likewise, as a visitor to Bentonville, you could be eating your dinner right next to one of Walmart's top executives and never know it. Walmart is not only a force throughout the world, but it also has a tremendous presence in its own hometown.

Speaking of Walmart, another unlikely entity found in Bentonville is the new, world-renowned Crystal Bridges Museum of American Art. The museum was founded largely through the efforts and financial support of Alice Walton, the youngest heir to the Walmart fortune.

With an endowment of $1.2 billion by the Walton Family Foundation, Crystal Bridges has almost instantly joined the ranks of some of the richest museums in the country. Though only opened in November of 2011, it has attracted over 1 million visitors and is listed amongst the top museums in the world. The bedrock of Middle America is not typically where museums of this stature are located.

World-class art is housed in a magnificent structure regarded around the globe as an architectural masterpiece. The museum's glass-and-wood design, with its gently curving pavilions, is nestled around two spring-fed ponds. Designed by Moshe Safdie, Crystal Bridges is regarded as America's newest cultural institution.

There is much excitement in the air regarding the Bentonville Film Festival slated for May 2015. This unprecedented festival champions women and diversity in film and is sponsored by some of the largest corporations in America including Coca Cola and Walmart. Academy Award Winning actor Geena Davis and ARC Entertainment are launching the festival with founding sponsor Walmart and Presenting Sponsor Coca Cola. May 5 -9 will see the first and only film competition in Arkansas and the world , for that matter, to offer digital and retail home entertainment distribution for its winners.

Bentonville retained its charming small town feel until the Crystal Bridges opening in 2011. It has since morphed into a booming cultural municipality, with a trendy downtown square littered with independent upscale restaurants and unique galleries, boutiques, and specialty shops of every kind. Bentonville hotels are popping up throughout the area making for a comfortable and pleasurable stay.

There are many hiking and biking trails around the downtown and museum areas. Have a bite to eat at one of the old or new restaurants in Bentonville, AR, and then take a leisurely stroll around the quaint and beautiful town square.

MAP OF BENTONVILLE

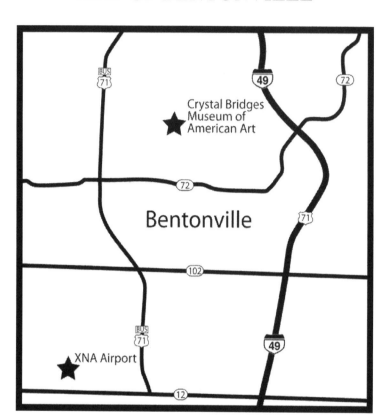

Neighborhoods

There are three main neighborhoods in and around Bentonville where the majority of the Bentonville, AR restaurants and hotels are located. There is the quaint downtown square area offering several amenities only blocks away from Crystal Bridges.

Closer to the Walmart home office there is another neighborhood where several Bentonville hotels and additional restaurants and fast food establishments are available for your resting and dining pleasure.

Finally, there is an area close to I-49, which divides Bentonville and Rogers, AR. This neighborhood has a plethora of restaurants, many of which are upscale independent, exclusive Bentonville, Arkansas restaurants sitting alongside fine dining national chain restaurants.

What the Locals Say...

There are plenty of things to do in Bentonville, AR, but let's take a listen to what the locals have to say about their hometown. After all, they engage in Bentonville life every day!

The Crystal Bridges Museum of American Art is the big "can't miss" attraction. You don't have to be a professional artist or an art critic in order to enjoy the incredible magnificence of this museum. You'll note that I speak of it often throughout this guide and with good reason!

The locals also say that Bentonville's Compton Gardens is a must-see, as well as the new 21c Museum Hotel's art collection. This beautiful and fascinating art collection is on display to the public 24/7. You don't have to be a staying at the 21c to peruse the collection.

The Walmart Museum is located in downtown Bentonville, and the locals say that everyone should see this fascinating center. Even if you are not a big fan of Walmart, you will appreciate the size and scope of this worldwide mega corporation. See the history of Walmart and its founders in this interactive museum center.

Another treat is to visit the actual Walmart store in Bentonville. It might seem odd to add this to your list of things to do in Bentonville, AR, but you won't have a better experience at any Walmart Center than you will have at the store in Walmart's hometown. It's something to see, and hey, you can stock up on the things that you forgot to pack!

The Farmer's Market is located in downtown Bentonville on Saturday mornings from 7:30 a.m. to 1 p.m., March through November. The locals shop here and you'll see why if you take the time to head downtown and visit it!

There are also several can't-miss restaurants in Bentonville and the surrounding areas (please see the restaurant listings in this guide for exact locations). The locals love to eat out, and they recommend:

- The Station Café on the downtown square for delicious burgers and great strawberry milkshakes.
- Fred's Hickory Inn, or just "Fred's on N. Walton Blvd" as they call it, where you will enjoy some of the best hickory-smoked BBQ you'll ever taste. Make sure to have a side of the spaghetti and meatballs.
- Tavola Trattoria for *AMAZING* Italian food.

- Does Eat Place for the best brews and steaks in town.

- Crumpet Tea Room for great chicken salad.

- The Hive located at 21c Museum Hotel, which specializes in artfully prepared food with local flavors in mind. Try the grilled quail appetizer and rabbit dumplings.

- The River Grille Steakhouse for terrific food and the Bleu Sky Bar, which is a fantastic local hangout for great drinks, some fun, and relaxation. The locals love Bleu Sky's happy hour.

- The Pressroom for coffee and afternoon cocktails. It has a super fun atmosphere, and the locals say it's just a good place to "chill."

- Table Mesa for cocktails, especially their "Cheap Dates" and "Moscow Mules." The locals rave about Table Mesa's lunches and say the service is always fantastic.

- Crepes Paulette, one of the most popular food trucks in the downtown square area. It serves delicious crepes for kids and adults. Kids will even stand quietly in line waiting on these crepes. Now that says a lot!

- Yeyo's Mexican Grill is another food truck you'll find in the downtown square area. According to the locals, it serves some seriously delicious Mexican cuisine.

- Glasgow's Cafe is also known for its Mexican fare and casual atmosphere. This restaurant has been a local favorite for years.

- Tusk and Trotter is a favorite Friday afternoon hangout where the girls get together with their friends for what the locals call their "HRT." Nope, doctors aren't sitting in the Tusk and Trotter handing out "scrips" for hormone replacement therapy. The prescription for this HRT is the best kind around – hanging out with friends for some fun and much-needed R&R! Try their infused vodkas and Tank 7 beer on tap.

- Beef 'O' Brady's serves up terrific food and has some kind of sporting event going all the time.

- Gravette is a Bentonville bedroom community just some 17 miles from Bentonville on Hwy72. Gravette is home to the Hard Luck Cafe. Steven, the owner, serves up great American food. Everyone raves about the fresh, fresh food in this place. The locals say it's well worth the short drive.

- Centerton is just a 5-mile drive west on Hwy 72. You'll find Jim's

Centerton Cafe in this tiny community. The locals drive to Centerton to eat at Jim's for two reasons: You can get a wonderful weekend breakfast and catch some local flavor while listening to the older men gossip!

- Bella Vista, which I speak of in greater detail in this guide, is another Bentonville bedroom community where you'll find Gusanos Pizzaria, a favorite for miles around. The locals say this restaurant is perfect for families.

I've talked a lot about Bentonville's downtown area, which the locals refer to as "Bentonville Square." Bentonville Square is the hub of activity and really something unique. Special events such as The Farmer's Market and First Fridays, as well as other festivals and events are common around this picturesque setting; gourmet food trucks and delightful restaurants will spoil any visitor with their delicious meals; specialty shops offer an eclectic display of items. Bentonville Square has it all!

Outdoor beauty is in abundance in Bentonville, and the locals encourage visitors to be sure to take advantage of the many biking, running, and walking trails in and around Bentonville. There are benches all along the trails should you want to stop and take a rest to listen to the little creeks flowing by.

Bentonville parks are well kept for locals and tourists alike, and they offer plenty of activities to keep you in the warm Bentonville sunshine. You'll find tennis, basketball, volleyball, skateboarding, and swimming among other Bentonville park fun.

The locals say that First Fridays, located on Bentonville Square, is *THE* place to be if you're in town on a Friday night. From March through November, 5 p.m. to 9 p.m., the square transitions into a huge block party complete with live music, kid's activities, food, and gallery openings.

Itineraries and Day Trips

Bentonville Itinerary #1

If you are in town on a Saturday from April through October, begin your day at the Saturday Farmer's Market on Bentonville Square. Vendors sell everything from coffee to delicious pastries to every imaginable type of produce. The market also features chef demonstrations and live music.

Other days of the week, check out The Hive at 21c Museum Hotel, and if you are a morning coffee person, be sure to grab a coffee at the Pressroom.

Once you've had a bite to eat, rent a bike at Phat Tire right off the square. Take a bike ride on some of the amazing trails around the city. Rentals include a helmet, a quick fit and suspension set-up, flat pedals, SPD, Crank Brother, SPD-SL, or you can BYOB... Bring Your Own Bike!

After your bike ride, come back to the square and grab some lunch at the Station Cafe, famous for its delicious burgers, or hit the Crepes Paulette food truck.

Browse the art galleries around the square in the afternoon or visit the Walmart Museum, which shows the history of the big box giant and its founder, Sam Walton.

Take a walk on one of Bentonville's beautiful walking trails. There are 3.5 miles of trail around and through the beautiful 120-acre Crystal Bridges Museum of America Art site.

Round out your day with dinner at Fred's Hickory Inn where you will sample some of the best smoked barbecue you've ever put in your mouth!

Bentonville Itinerary #2

Get up early and eat breakfast at the Village Inn Restaurant, known for its made-from-scratch buttermilk pancakes and extra friendly service.

Head on over to the Crystal Bridges Museum of American Art and take a guided tour of the fabulous permanent collection, which is on view year-round. Walmart sponsors FREE general admission.

While you are there, take a break from viewing the world-class art and dine at Eleven, the restaurant within the museum. Eleven features the modern

American comfort food found in the Ozark Mountains, which is the "high South and lower Midwest" region.

In the afternoon, you may be tired from being on your feet, so take a break and a few minutes rest. Grab some coffee at the Pressroom and drink it on Bentonville Square where there are many trees and plenty of comfortable places to sit.

For dinner try Table Mesa, a boutique style restaurant featuring multicultural offerings that make good use of delicious seasonal ingredients. Locals gather at Table Mesa and the staff is ultra-friendly.

In the evening, make it a point to attend one of the events on the square. First Friday on the Square occurs on the first Friday of every month from March through November. There are FREE food samples, live music and tons of unique activities. Vendor booths are set up all over the square and the crowd is lively. Regardless of where you are from, you will have a terrific and memorable time.

Bentonville Itinerary #3

For breakfast, try the Hive at 21c Museum Hotel, which features refined country cooking created by chef and Arkansas native, Mathew McClure.

After breakfast, view the art collection in the hotel. Regardless of where you stay in Bentonville, make it a point to see this hotel's collection of art, which is available 24/7.

Hop on over to Bentonville Square and shop some of the art galleries and boutique shops on the square and down the side streets.

Afterward, get some deep relaxation at the Studio Salon and Day Spa. Relax to your heart's content by escaping life's day-to-day stress for an hour… an afternoon… all day!

Eat lunch at the Red Onion Espressoria where the Grilled Atlantic Salmon is to die for and the staff is efficient and friendly to every customer who comes through the door.

Check out the calendar to see if any of Bentonville's festivals are in progress. The arts and crafts festivals are some of the best in the world. If no festivals or special events are in progress, visit the Museum of Native American History, the Peel Mansion and Heritage Gardens or the Compton Gardens.

For an afternoon treat visit Bizzy B's Bakery or head on over to Bentonville Square and get some coffee or an afternoon drink at the Pressroom

Try Tavola Trattoria specializing in creative Italian American cuisine for dinner. Customers rave about this place: "Love this place…" and "The Pizza Tavola makes my heart flutter…" are just a couple of the nice comments I've heard about this lovely little restaurant.

As an alternate to Tavola Trattoria, take in Tableside Theatre, a company of writers, actors and directors that bring live theater to restaurants and events. You get a great dinner and a show for $52.

Bentonville Day Trips

Eureka Springs, AR

Eureka Springs, AR, less than an hour's drive from Bentonville, is a quaint mountain village nestled in the beautiful Ozark Mountains. Its downtown area, with its winding up and down streets and Victorian architecture, offers activities for every member of your group.

Eureka Spring's Historic Downtown Shopping District features over 100 unique specialty shops of every description from family-owned candy factories to more than 20 top art galleries to fantastic antique shops. Visit Caroline's Collectibles to see live bunnies actually working; they give you your receipts and change!

If you are a history buff, you will love Eureka Springs. It has the largest collection of Victorian architecture in the region. The beautiful Victorian homes have been painstakingly preserved to maintain the details of yesteryear. For example, you will see historically accurate pastel colors used on all gingerbread decoration.

Since the 1800s, artists creating in every artistic medium have called Eureka Springs home. There are more than 400 working artists in the area. Sculptors, painters, weavers, jewelers, woodworkers and woodcarvers are just some of the artists who have settled in Eureka. Make it a point to visit the Art Colony on N Main Street where you can see artists at work and their creations on display.

Outdoors people and adventure seekers of all types can spend the day participating in area-favorite activities. Hiking, biking, fishing, spelunking, horseback riding, rock climbing, zip-lining, motorcycle touring and golfing are just some of the outdoor activities that are located in the Eureka Springs area.

Eureka Springs is the perfect romantic getaway. Stay at the Crescent Hotel with its old world charm yet modern conveniences. Dine at the Crescent Hotel Crystal Dining Room or make reservations at Ermilio's or Local Flavor Cafe, all excellent choices for romantic dining.

Eureka is home to *The Great Passion Play*. Save an evening to enjoy this inspirational activity. The play has a cast of 170 actors and dozens of animals. It is billed as America's #1 Attended Outdoor Drama. See the Bible come to life on a 550-foot-long multi-leveled stage.

Eliminate the stresses of life by relaxing in Eureka Springs. Visit a day-spa where experts spoil you with services sure to relax and rejuvenate. Available services include saunas, massage, steam cabinets, facials, weight rooms, aromatherapy, Ayurveda medicine, reflexology and exercise facilities.

Eureka Springs is known for its many weekend, weeklong and month-long events. Park your car and let the Eureka Springs Trolley Service take you from place to place. Many destinations have front door service from the trolley.

Tulsa, OK

Unless you are a businessperson, Crystal Bridges Museum of American Art is what most likely brought you to NWA. While you are visiting the area, save a day to make the one-and-a-half-hour drive to Tulsa and visit the Gilcrease Museum and many other area attractions.

Tulsa is also home to the new BOK Center, designed by Cesar Pelli. It is a state-of-the-art venue for national sporting events and major concerts.

Tulsa is Oklahoma's second largest city, and it is well known for its bustling shopping and entertainment districts. For example, the Blue Dome Entertainment District offers nine blocks of unique shopping opportunities, eateries to tempt even the most discriminating taste buds, indie boutiques, local pubs and trendy nightspots. It is fast becoming the place to be in Tulsa.

Visitors to Tulsa should always catch a live show, because Tulsa is known as one of the top 10 music entertainment cities in the U.S. The biggest names in music come to Cain's Ballroom with their energetic sounds; Tulsa's Brady Theater attracts acts like the Deftones and Tenacious D.; the Tulsa Performing

Arts hosts the Tulsa Ballet and international talent.

While in Tulsa visit the Gilcrease Museum, which celebrates the American West, American Indian legend, and the U.S. frontier lore. Wander through the vast galleries filled to the brim with more than 10,000 works of art, including an unparalleled anthropology collection. Before you leave, take the time to stroll through the eleven different themed gardens.

If you long for a full-fledged shopping spree, there is no destination more capable of satisfying your retail urge than Utica Square. Fashion and home decoration enthusiasts alike enjoy the higher-end boutiques, department stores and unique specialty shops.

If the exhilaration of trying your hand at blackjack, winning at the slots or showing a royal flush at the poker table is more in line with your idea of fun, then the excitement of gambling is alive and well in Tulsa's Hard Rock Hotel and Casino.

Take your entire family to visit the highly rated Tulsa Zoo. Let the kids see African lions, South American jaguars and Malayan tigers as you stroll through more than 80 acres of wild exhibits. Ride the popular Safari Train and visit the memorable walk-through caves, interactive petting areas, recreated Masai village, pre-Colombian ruins and much, much more.

Tulsa will keep you entertained from daylight until the wee hours of the morning. Take a day trip to Tulsa and you will definitely be back for more!

If you are unfamiliar with NWA, you may wonder about the accommodations available and the highlights and top spots in Bentonville .Don't worry! There are plenty of hotels in Bentonville, AR from which to choose.

Not only are several Bentonville, AR hotels within easy access to XNA, many are also equipped with business centers or conference rooms right on the premises. Some also supply a FREE copy of *The Wall Street Journal*. Every imaginable business convenience is made available to guests who need access to these types of amenities.

These facilities are set up with complimentary high-speed Internet access, telephones, printing services and audio/visual equipment. Many Bentonville hotels provide catering, with your choice from a menu for breakfast or lunch, to be served at your meetings.

Most hotels are equipped with laundry facilities, pools, fitness rooms, gift shops and valet service. If you prefer to make your own light meals or snacks, you will also find suites that provide a microwave and a mini-refrigerator. The Bentonville, AR hotels and motels often supply coffee makers, irons and ironing boards, and hair dryers.

You will find that some of the accommodations include secure storage spaces, a shipping and receiving department, and access to the business center 24 hours a day.

Hotels offering every amenity imaginable are already plentiful, but the opening of the beautiful 21c elevated the area hotel experience to even new heights.

ACCOMMODATIONS

If you are unfamiliar with NWA, you may wonder about the accommodations available and the highlights and top spots in Bentonville. Don't worry! There are plenty of hotels in Bentonville, AR from which to choose.

Not only are several Bentonville, AR hotels within easy access to XNA, many are also equipped with business centers or conference rooms right on the premises. Some also supply a FREE copy of *The Wall Street Journal*. Every imaginable business convenience is made available to guests who need access to these types of amenities.

These facilities are set up with complimentary high-speed Internet access, telephones, printing services and audio/visual equipment. Many Bentonville hotels provide catering, with your choice from a menu for breakfast or lunch, to be served at your meetings.

Most hotels are equipped with laundry facilities, pools, fitness rooms, gift shops and valet service. If you prefer to make your own light meals or snacks, you will also find suites that provide a microwave and a mini-refrigerator. The Bentonville, AR hotels and motels often supply coffee makers, irons and ironing boards, and hair dryers.

You will find that some of the accommodations include secure storage spaces, a shipping and receiving department, and access to the business center 24 hours a day.

Hotels offering every amenity imaginable are already plentiful, but the opening of the beautiful 21c elevated the area hotel experience to even new heights.

Let's take a look at the Bentonville, AR accommodations:

Hotel Amenities

Breakfast: B	Internet: I	Pool: P
Business Center: BC	Meeting Rooms: MR	Restaurant: R
Fitness Center: FC	Pet Friendly: PF	

Hotels, Bentonville, AR with 3 Star Accommodations

21c Museum Hotel 200 NE A Street, Bentonville, AR 72712 (479) 286-6500 BC, FC, I, MR, PF, R	Hilton Garden Inn Bentonville 2204 SE Walton Blvd, Bentonville, AR 72712 (479) 464-7300 BC, FC, I, MR, P
Best Western Plus Castlerock 501 SE Walton Blvd, Bentonville, AR 72712 (479) 845-7707 B, BC, FC, I, MR, P	Laquinta Inn and Suites 1001 SE Walton Blvd, Bentonville, AR 72712 (479) 271-7555 B, BC, FC, I, MR, P, PF
Comfort Suite 2011 SE Walton Blvd, Bentonville, AR, 72712 (479) 254-9099 B, BC, FC, I, MR, PF	Simmons Suites Bentonville, AR 3001 NE 11th Street, Bentonville, AR 72712 (479) 254-7800 B, BC, FC, I, MR, P
Courtyard - Bentonville 1001 McClain Road, Bentonville, AR 72712 (479) 273-3333 B, BC, FC, I, MR, P, PF	Springhill Suites 2304 SE Walton Blvd, Bentonville, AR 72712 (888) 287-9400 B, FC, I, MR, P
Doubletree Bentonville AR - Suites by Hilton 301 SE Walton Blvd, Bentonville, AR 72712 (479) 845-7770 BC, FC, I, MC, P, R	Wingate by Wyndham 7400 SW Old Farm Blvd, Bentonville, AR 72712 (479) 418-5400 BC, FC, I, MR, P, PF

Hotels, Bentonville, AR with 2 Star Accommodations

Days Inn 3408 S Moberly Lane, Bentonville, AR 72712 (479) 271-7900 B, BC, I, MR, P, PF	Motel 6 215 SE Walton Blvd, Bentonville, AR 72712 (479) 464-4400 I, PF, P
Econo Lodge 3609 Moberly Lane, Bentonville, AR 72712 (479) 271-9400 B, BC, FC, I, MR, P, PF	Super 8 2301 SE Walton Blvd, Bentonville, AR 72712 (479) 273-1818 B, BC, I
Holiday Inn Express Hotel and Suites 2205 SE Walton Blvd, Bentonville, AR 72712 (479) 271-2222 B, BC, FC, I, M	TownePlace Suites by Marriott 3100 SE 14th Street, Bentonville, AR 72712 (479) 621-0202 B, BC, FC, I, FC, P, PF, R
Microtel Inn and Suites 911 SE Walton Blvd, Bentonville, AR 72712 (479) 271-6699 B, FC, I, MR, PF	

Bentonville, AR Extended Stay Accommodations

South Walton Suites - Spa 1120 S Walton Blvd #100, Bentonville, AR 72712 (479) 845-4600 BC, I, FC, R,	Value Place Extended Stay 1201 Phyllis Street, Bentonville, AR 72712 (479) 254-1002
Suburban Extended Stay Hotel 200 SW Suburban Lane, Bentonville, AR 72712 (479) 268-4400 BC, I, PF	

Bentonville, AR Bed and Breakfast

Downtown Bentonville Cottage	Victoria Bed and Breakfast
Downtown Bentonville, 72712	306 N Main Street, Bentonville, AR
(479) 802-8222	72712
	(479) 273-3232

Bentonville, AR Vacation Rentals

Laughlin House	
102 NW 3rd Street, Bentonville, AR	
72712	
(479) 268-6085	

THINGS TO DO AND SEE

If you've been reading my guide from the first page, you already know that there are tons of amazing things to do in Bentonville, AR. If you skipped to this page, no problem, I'm going to talk about them again!

Business brings many to Bentonville. The Walmart and Sam's Club headquarters are located in Bentonville, as are the offices for the many vendors that supply the retail giants.

The Walmart Visitor's Center is located on the town square in the old original Walmart variety store and historically traces the origin and growth of this unsurpassed American business success story.

Sam Walton's old pickup truck is on display in the center, along with many other fascinating pieces of Walmart and Sam Walton memorabilia. During Walmart's shareholder's meeting, typically held in June, the center is mobbed, so plan ahead.

Today, a vast majority come to Bentonville to see the world-class attractions. Within walking distance of downtown Bentonville and close to many of the Bentonville hotels, is the recently opened Crystal Bridges Museum of American Art spearheaded by Alice Walton, daughter of Walmart founder Sam Walton.

This beautiful and unique repository already ranks among the top museums in the world and will eventually house famous American art totaling in the hundreds of millions of dollars.

Its breathtaking setting includes two creek-fed ponds, nature trails and a sculpture garden. The grounds will also include room for public events and concerts. The complex proper will have 217,000 square feet of galleries, several class and meeting rooms, and a library.

Visitors from around the world and all across America are visiting this amazing world-class art museum. Crystal Bridges alone is reason enough to visit the Northwest Arkansas area.

Art/Culture
Galleries
AbstractED Artwork - Erica Edwards
207 SW F Street, Bentonville, AR 72712
(479) 381-4950

Arend Arts Center
Live on Stage
1901 SE J Street, Bentonville, AR 72712
(479) 254-5161
A part of the Bentonville Public School System, the Arend Arts Center is an important center for both school and community arts in NWA. The Benton County Symphony performs there annually, as do many professional artists like pianists Vladimir Zaitsey and Rosario Andino.

Art
by Becky Christenson
2204 SE 14th Street, Bentonville, AR 72712
(479) 273-0668
Art features the work of artist Becky Christenson who specializes in one-of-a-kind designs including sculptures, paintings, ceramics and other original works.

Art Seen 107 Gallery
107 SE3rd Street, Bentonville, AR 72712
(479) 619-9115
Art Seen 107 Gallery is a gallery specializing in contemporary art.

Big Red Gallery
Rich and Sandra Anderson
Larry and Sherri Rice
9400 E McNelly Road, Bentonville, AR 72712
(479) 451-8866
Big Red Gallery offers their customers the largest selection of Limited Edition Prints, Limited Edition Canvas, Limited Edition Giclee Canvas and Originals in Northwest Arkansas.

Modern Canvas Studios and Gallery LLC
1902 SW 14th Street, Bentonville, AR 72712
(479) 200-1081

Norberta Philbrook Gallery
114 W Central Ave, Bentonville, AR 72712
(479) 876-8134

Sharon S Simmons Creative Spc
113 S Main Street, Bentonville, AR 72712
(479) 273-3137

Theatre for Youth (TRIKE Theatre)
107 NW 2nd Street, Bentonville, AR 72712
(866) 331-3681

Two25 Gallery
225 S Main Street, Bentonville, AR 72712
(479) 936-6805

Woodburnt Treasures
12706 C P Rakes Road, Bentonville, AR 72712
(479) 795-1112

Universal Art Images
1613 NE Greenbrier Road, Bentonville, AR 72712
(479) 657-2730

Museums
Amazeum (Opening 2015)
209 NE 2nd Street, Bentonville, AR 72712
(479) 696-9280
Family discovery center and museum

Crystal Bridges Museum of American Art
600 Museum Way, Bentonville, AR 72712
(479) 418-5700
Mon-Thurs 11a.m. to 6 p.m., Wed - Fri 11 a.m. to 9 p.m.
Sat-Sun 10 a.m. to 6 p.m., Closed Tuesday
Named for the natural spring that feeds the Museum's two ponds and the unusual bridge construction that is a part of the overall design, Crystal Bridges saw more than 160,000 worldwide visitors within the first four-and-a-half months of its opening.

Designer Moshe Safdie was selected not only for his commitment to the use of social, cultural and geographic elements that elucidate an area, but also for his designs that respond to human needs and goals.

The 120-acre museum park features six galleries, a restaurant, research library, sculpture trail, classrooms and a grand hall for special events.

American art from five centuries is represented here, including works by John Singleton Copley, Winslow Homer, Thomas Eakins, Andy Warhol and Georgia O'Keeffe.

Cost of admission is FREE. However, if you opt to become a Museum Member, you can get 10% off 21c Museum Hotels best available room rate.

The Walmart Museum
105 N Main Street, Bentonville, AR 72712
(479) 273-1329
Sam Walton's original variety store, now The Walmart Museum, chronicles the history of the Walton family, particularly Sam Walton, the founder of Walmart, and the meteoric rise of the big-box retailer on the world's stage. It features interactive displays and one-of-a-kind exhibits, making it an interesting and fun activity for families and Walmart employees to enjoy.

The Museum of Native American History
202 SW O Street, Bentonville, AR 72712
(479) 273-2456
View America's past by visiting one of the South's most comprehensive collections of Native American Artifacts. Make it a point to see this unique museum while in the area.

1875 Peel Mansion and Heritage Gardens
400 S Walton Blvd, Bentonville, AR 72712
(479) 273-9664
The Peel Mansion and Heritage Gardens, built by Colonel Samuel West Peel and his wife Mary Emaline Berry Peel, is a wonderful example of a Civil War-era home. It is available for tours and events.

Art
Painting with a Twist
1401 SE Walton Blvd, Bentonville, AR 72712
(479) 254-1997

Parks and Trails

Bentonville Trail System
The Bentonville Trail system is made up of three looped trails that connect and meander through three beautiful parks: Lake Bella Vista, Memorial Park and Park Springs Park. There are also seven linear bikeways and pedestrian paths. For the mountain bikers, there is an all-terrain bike trail. Additionally, there are numerous on-road bike routes. In all, there is a network amounting to over 20 trail miles.

The Bentonville Trail system is made up of three looped trails that connect and meander through three beautiful parks: Lake Bella Vista, Memorial Park and

Park Springs Park. There are also seven linear bikeways and pedestrian paths. For the mountain bikers, there is an all-terrain bike trail. Additionally, there are numerous on-road bike routes. In all, there is a network amounting to over 20 trail miles.

Crystal Bridges Trail (1 mile)

Along the western edge of the Crystal Bridges 120-acre property is a beautiful shaded multi-use trail. With a distance of 1.5 miles, you'll find stunning sculpture gardens along the trail and there is also an overlook to the Crystal Bridges

North Bentonville Trail (2.2 miles)

2400 N Walton Blvd, Bentonville, AR 72712

Traversing through natural wooded areas is the North Bentonville Trail. The trailhead is located on N Walton Blvd and is composed of a 10-foot-wide concrete linear trail and a jogging path. Parking and restrooms are available at the trailhead.

Park Springs (Funky Town) (.75 mile)

300 NW 10th Street, Bentonville, AR 72712

A beautiful, peaceful nature trail that includes a natural spring and wooden bridges.

Slaughter Pen Mountain Bike Trail (14.03 miles)

208 NW A Street, Bentonville, AR 72712

(719) 359-7071

This exceptional mountain bike trail is 5.18 miles long and designed especially for mountain bike enthusiasts. Slaughter Pen is an unusual and challenging single-track trail.

Special features of Slaughter Pen include drops, jumps and log rides. There is also a free ride area that includes a wall ride, tabletop jumps and bermed turns. There is a trail for everyone from beginners to advanced bikers. Parking and restrooms are available at 2400 N Walton Blvd, which is just south of Bark Park.

Additional Trails

- Arkansas Missouri Trail (.75 mile)
- Bella Vista Lake Trail (1.75 miles)
- Downtown Trail (1.1 miles)
- Enfield Trail (.2 mile)
- Memorial Park Fitness Trail (1 mile)
- Moberly Trail (2 miles)
- NE J Street Trail (1.2 miles)
- South Bentonville Trail (2.55 miles)
- Tiger Blvd Trail (1.5 miles)
- Town Branch Trail (.77 mile)
- Wishing Springs Trail (1.6 miles)

For more detailed trail information at Bentonville Trail System or download a Bike Path Maps here

Parks

Compton Gardens and Conference Center

The Compton Gardens and Conference Center was the home of Dr. Neil Compton who passed away in 1999. Credited with saving the Buffalo National River, Compton was an avid naturalist and a local physician. The grounds around the home are now a beautiful 6.5-acre park composed of native woodland gardens. Today, the home/conference center is available for events, meetings, seminars, retreats, film and photo shoots, and tours.

Additional Parks

- Austin-Baggett Park
- City Square
- Dave Peel Park
- Durham Place Park
- Elm Tree Ballfields
- Enfield Park

- Gilmore Park
- Lake Bentonville
- Memorial Park
- NW A Street Park
- Old Tiger Stadium
- Orchards Park
- Park Springs Park
- Phillips Park
- Town Branch Park
- Train Station Park
- Wildwood Park

For more detailed information concerning Bentonville parks, be sure to click here to check out the City of Bentonville site.

Dog Parks
Bark Park
2400 N Walton, Bentonville, AR 72712

The Bark Park has two sections, one for large dogs and one for small dogs. There is a middle section with agility equipment.

Shopping
Antique/Vintage Shops
Rusted Brown
208 NE 3rd Street, Bentonville, AR 72712
(479) 640-6760

The Paisley Place
116 S Main Street, Bentonville, AR 72712
(479) 715-6610

True Treasures
10770 Hwy 72 West, Bentonville, AR 72712
(479) 795-9396

Boutiques
Blue Moon Market
113 N Main Street, Bentonville, AR 72712
(417) 825-6114

Elysian Boutique
106 SE A Street, Bentonville, AR 72712
(479) 464-9261

Klothe
203 NE A Street, Bentonville, AR 72712
(479) 254-1125

NA Martin, LLC
207 SE A Street, Bentonville, AR 72712
(479) 236-6667

Pink Pistol
114 W. Central, Bentonville, AR 72712
(479) 268-5484

Pink Tomato Boutique
810 NW 3rd St, Bentonville, AR 72712
(479) 553-7664

Posh Alley Boutique
112 W Central Ave, Bentonville, AR 72712
(479) 464-8000

The Perfect Choice
Suite 10, 1406 S Walton Blvd, Bentonville, AR 72712
(479) 273-2073

Vintage Crush Boutique
3401 SW 2nd St, Bentonville, AR 72712
(479) 268-5486

Specialty Stores
Bleachers
110 East Central Avenue, Bentonville, AR 72712
(479) 250-0296

Bloom
120 W Central Ave, Bentonville, AR 72712
(479) 273-1190

Rollie Pollie
112 E Central Ave, Bentonville, AR 72712
(479) 273-3386

Fresh French Home
709 SW A Street, Ste 5, Bentonville, AR 72712
(479) 271-2551

Meteor Guitar Gallery
128 W Central, Bentonville, AR 72712
(479) 268-1500

Overstreet›s Jewelry
103 NE 2nd Street, Bentonville, AR 72712
(479) 273-5424

Ramo d'Olivo
500 S.E. Walton Blvd, Bentonville, AR 72712
(479) 715-6053

Rush Running Co
2212 S Walton Blvd, Bentonville, AR 72712
(479) 464-7866

Shirley›s Flower Studio
120 S Main Street, Bentonville, AR 72712
(479) 464-7673

The Mustache Bentonville
113 W Central Ave, Bentonville, AR 72712
(479) 876-8248

The Spice and Tea Exchange
109 SE A Street, Bentonville, AR 72712
(479) 254-9900

Walton Blvd. Wine and Spirits
406 Razorback Drive, Bentonville, Arkansas
(479) 273-7200

Bike Shops
Mojo Cycling
2104 S Walton Blvd, Bentonville, AR 72712
(479) 271-7201

Phat Tire Bike Shop
125 W Central Ave, Bentonville, AR 72712
(479) 715-6150

Tattoo Shops
Cherry Bomb Tattoos & Body
2106 S Walton Blvd, Bentonville, AR
(479) 273-9271

Nevermore Tattoo Studio
1380 SW Westpark Dr #12, Bentonville, AR
(479) 444-8287

Odyssey Tattoo
2210 S Walton Blvd #2, Bentonville, AR
(479) 254-9270

Queen Bee Tattoo
2106 S. Walton Blvd, Suite C, Bentonville, AR 72712
(479) 273-9271

Spas
Accents Salon
1120 S Walton Blvd, Bentonville, AR 72712
(479) 271-8300

Acropolis Salon and Day Spa
2003 SW Regional Airport Blvd, Bentonville, AR 72712
(479) 271-9909

Elite Day Spa
2603 N Walton Blvd, Bentonville, AR 72712
(479) 271-9772

Escape Face and Body Spa
1101 Mallard Place, Bentonville, AR 72712
(479) 268-6868

Reflections
810 NW 3rd Street # H., Bentonville, AR 72712
(479) 273-3202

Studio Salon and Day Spa
710 Tiger Blvd, Bentonville, AR 72712
(479) 271-7277

WellQuest Medical and Wellness Corporation
3400 SE Macy Road, Bentonville, AR 72712
(479) 845-0880

Special Events/Festivals

Arts and Crafts Events

Arts, crafts, and the festivals to feature them are huge events in NWA. The various events attract more than 300,000 arts and crafts enthusiasts from all over the country. Festivals include:

- Long's Old Orchard and Farm Arts and Crafts Festival
- Ozark Regional Arts and Crafts Show
- Rogers Antique Show and Sale
- Rogers Expo Center
- Sharp's Show of War Eagle
- Spanker Creek Farm Arts and Crafts
- War Eagle Fair
- War Eagle Mill Antique and Crafts Show
- Bella Vista Arts and Crafts
- Craft Fair Around the Square
- Frisco Station Mall Arts and Crafts
- Hillbilly Corner
- Jones Center Arts and Crafts

Art and Culinary Festival

The month of June is devoted to the 2014 Bentonville Art and Culinary Festival. Beginning June 1 and running through June 30, you can enjoy programming featuring the arts in all forms. There is something for everyone. Pick from live music shows, special culinary events and chef demonstrations, film workshops and visual art shows, and creative children's activities.

Around The Bloc

Around The Bloc is held June through October on the third Thursday of the month. This fun-filled Thursday evening event is hosted by downtown merchants, culinary delights, art tours, Artist Alleyway and special retail experiences.

Backstage Downtown

Become acquainted with Backstage Downtown. This ticketed one-of-a-kind series features a culinary art and performance experience with cooking and music talent from throughout the region.

Bentonville Film Festival

The unprecedented festival champions women and diversity in film and is sponsored by some of the largest corporations in America including Coca Cola and Walmart. Academy Award Winning actor Geena Davis and ARC Entertainment are launching the festival with founding sponsor Walmart and Presenting Sponsor Coca Cola. May 5 -9 2015 will see the first and only film competition in Arkansas and the world, for that matter, to offer digital and retail home entertainment distribution for its winners.

Downtown Bentonville on the Square

Bentonville's downtown square is the central hub of activities. There are popular restaurants that line the square and the surrounding area. An old favorite, The Station Café, serves the best hamburger in NWA. Flying Fish, Tavola Trattoria, Tusk and Trotter, Table Mesa and the Pressroom are all upscale restaurants that serve delicious food in unique, cozy environments.

There are also mobile eateries that are available on the square for special events. These aren't your typical hot dog stands. You won't believe some of the tasty-treat delights that are in store for you when you sample some of the delicious foods from such vendors as Crepes Paulette, Big Rub BBQ and Greenhouse Grill.

Benton County Fair

The Benton County Fair is held from mid-to-late-August every year. The Fair is a true fall tradition and is enjoyed for the livestock shows, fair foods, special events and rides.

Bentonville Farmers Market

The Bentonville Farmers Market is now in its thirty-eighth year. From April 28 to October 27, the market treats patrons to a huge assortment of top quality local foods, meats, produce, and arts and crafts. The market is open on Bentonville Square from 7:30 a.m. to 1 p.m. every Saturday during the season. The Farmers Market is also open May 16 –Sept 19, from 10 am – 2 pm at Ernie Lawrence Plaza.

First Friday on the Square

Like block parties? You will love First Friday on the Square from March to November, the whole community converges upon downtown Bentonville Square to participate in a huge monthly block party. Enjoy delicious food, children's' activities, gallery openings and live music. Each month features a different theme.

First Friday Flicks

First Friday Flicks at the Lawrence Plaza are held after each First Friday event in downtown Bentonville Square. Movies start at 8 p.m., or pretty close to it, and are FREE to the public.

Notes at Night

Artists from all across the region perform at the different downtown venues. Notes at Night is a FREE music series offering a broad array of music styles. Come early, stay late, and have dinner in beautiful downtown Bentonville.

Pickin' On The Square

Have a fun-packed night on the downtown Bentonville Square. Enjoy Picking On The Square every Friday evening beginning May 2, 2014 from 6 p.m. until late. During each of the First Friday events, Picking On The Square moves to Dave Peel Park at 206 E Central Ave.

Slaughter Pen Jam Mountain Bike Festival

A popular mountain bike race and jam including bicycle trials, rides, a 10 K Run, bike parade, exhibitions, and a one-of-a-kind, 3-day adventure packed jam that the entire family can enjoy. Kick back, enjoy melt-in-your-mouth food, and listen to award-winning bluegrass musicians perform live. This mountain bike festival continues to get bigger and better every year.

Summer Concert Series

FREE to the public, the Summer Concert Series at Orchards Park runs the second and fourth Friday night of the month beginning in June.

Sports

Bentonville is home to several premiere sports venues, including softball, football, tennis, soccer, swimming and baseball. Click here for a complete listing of venues.

Bowling
Bentonville Bowling Center
902 NW 14th Street, Bentonville, AR 72712
(479) 273-2590

On Target Driving Range and Batting Cages
501 Airport Road, Bentonville, AR 72712
(479) 268-6220

Gyms
Planet Fitness
1001 SW Westpark Drive, Bentonville, AR 727212
(479) 802- 6080

Skating
Great Skate Place
1615 Moberly Lane, Bentonville, AR 72712
(479) 273-1800

Lawrence Plaza Ice Rink and Splash Park
213-299 NE A Street, Bentonville, AR 72712
(479) 464-7275

RESTAURANTS

New restaurants are popping up everywhere in Bentonville, AR. This little town, tucked away in the beautiful landscape of Northwest Arkansas, is on the fast track to becoming one of the most desirable places to live, visit, and, of course, dine! Combine restaurants, Bentonville, AR, and your appetite, and you're sure to find gustatory heaven!

Why? Bentonville is home to the headquarters of Walmart, the world's largest retailer, and all the supporting businesses that go with it. Couple that with the addition of the new Crystal Bridges Museum of American Art, which opened in the fall of 2011, and you have a small town with an amazing ability to attract visitors by the throngs from all over the world.

As I mentioned in the Bentonville's Neighborhood section of this guide, there are three main areas in and around Bentonville where the majority of the Bentonville, Arkansas restaurants are located. There is the quaint downtown Square area, the area close to Walmart's home offices, and the area close to I-49 that divides Bentonville and Rogers, AR.

For excellence and variety, Bentonville area restaurants now compare favorably to New York City, Chicago and Los Angeles. Regardless of your dining preferences, you can find a suitable and delicious meal in NWA.

Fred's Hickory Inn is the place to go for outstanding hickory smoked pit barbecue meals. There are many other delightful restaurants especially along Walton Blvd and around Bentonville Square.

RESTAURANT PRICES

$ - Budget	$$$ - Upscale

$$ - Mid-Range	

American

Cracker Barrel Restaurant 2307 SE Walton Blvd, Bentonville, AR 72712 (479) 268-5907 $$	Ruby Tuesday Restaurants 1402 S Walton Blvd, Bentonville, AR 72712 (479) 254-8230 $$
Denny's Classic Diner 2209 SE Walton Blvd, Bentonville, AR 72712 (479) 464-7010 $$	Village Inn Restaurant 2300 SE Walton Blvd, Bentonville, AR 72712 (479) 464-0777 $$
Great American Grill (Hilton Hotel Restaurant) 2204 SE Walton Blvd, Bentonville, AR 72712 (479) 464-7300 $$	Wing Stop 231 N Walton Blvd, Bentonville, AR 72712 (479) 271-8833 $
Hapa's Hawaiian Grill 2910 S Walton Blvd, Bentonville, AR 72712 (479) 273-3777 $	Zary's Acropolis Restaurant 905 NW 13th Street, Bentonville, AR 72712 (479) 273-3872 $$

Jay's Diner 3404 SE Macy Road, Bentonville, AR 72712 (479) 254-1182 $	

Asian

A Taste of Thai II 2106 S Walton Blvd, Ste A, Bentonville, AR 72712 (479) 273-6663 $$	Pho Thanh 206 S Walton Blvd, Bentonville, AR 72712 (479) 254-9127 $
Goldtown Sushi Korean BBQ 1100 SE 14th Street, Bentonville, AR 72712 (479) 273-1000 $$	Sho-Gun 3606 SE Metro Pkwy, Bentonville, AR 72712 (479) 464-0882 $$
Kobe Sushi and Grill 1311 S Walton Blvd, Bentonville, AR 72712 (479) 254-7899 $$	Sushi House 2501 SE 14th Street #5, Bentonville, AR 72712 (479) 271-0370 $$
Li's Home Cooking 1120 S Walton Blvd, Bentonville, AR 72712 (479) 845-4633 $$	Thai Fusion 1100 SE 14th Street #8 (479) 268-3243, Bentonville, AR 72712 $
Mama Fu's Asian House 700 SE Walton Blvd #12, Bentonville, AR 72712 (479) 254-8381 $$	Thai Kitchen 707 SW A Street, Bentonville, AR 72712 (479) 464-7288 $$

Orient Express II 1402 Shane Lane, Bentonville, AR 72712 (479) 254-2929 $$	

Bakeries

Bizzy B's Bakery 1501 SE Walton Blvd, Ste101, Bentonville, AR 72712 (479) 657-2557	Olde Tyme Donuts 2502 SW 14th Street #2, Bentonville, AR 72712 (479) 464-4855
Dunkin' Donuts 2309 SE 14th Street, Bentonville, AR 72712 (479) 876-8631	Sweet Dz Express Bakery 1912 S Walton Blvd, Bentonville, AR 72712 (479) 553-7273
Krispy Kreme Donuts 1502 SE Walton Blvd, Bentonville, AR 72712 (479) 273-0168	Pat's Bakery and Express Coffeehouse 1201 N Walton Blvd, Bentonville, AR 72712 (479) 271-5301
Litterelly Delicious Cakery 8401 Glory Drive, Bentonville, AR 72712 (479)	Wow Bakery 402 SW Countrywood Road, Bentonville, AR 72712 (318) 614-2463

Bars/Clubs/Pubs

Beef-O-Brady's 2500 SW 14th Street #108, Bentonville, AR 72712 (479) 268-4545 $	Bike Rack Brewery ~ Coming Soon 410 SW A street, Bentonville, AR (479)

Bentley's Irish Pub 911 SE 28th Street, Bentonville, AR 72712 (479) 876-8060 $$	Buffalo Wild Wings 2707 SE Moberly Lane, Bentonville, AR 72712 (479) 254-9464 $$
Bentonville Brewing Company (Coming Soon)	

Buffets

Flavors Indian Cuisine 3200 SW Regency Pkwy, Ste 8 Bentonville, AR 72712 (479) 254-1035 $$	Orlando's Place Cuban, Latin American & Brazilian 1100 SE 14th Street, Bentonville, AR 72712 (479) 271-0042 $$
Lin's Garden Chinese Restaurant 2101 SE Walton Blvd, Bentonville, AR 72712 (479) 271-6288 $$	

Burgers

Ron's Hamburgers and Chili 1702 S Walton Blvd #12, Bentonville, AR 72712 (479) 464-4420 $	The Station Cafe 111 N Main Street, Bentonville, AR 72712 (479) 273-0553 $$

BBQ

Billy Sims Barbeque 3500 Block of SE J Street, Bentonville, AR 72712 (479) 268-3568 $$	Smokin' Joe's Ribhouse 1204 S Walton Blvd, Bentonville, AR 72712 (479) 273-1685 $$

Dink's Pit Barbeque 3404 SE Macy Road #18, Bentonville, AR 72712 (479) 657-6264 $$	Smokin' Joe's Ribhouse 2504 E Central, Bentonville, AR 72712 (479) 254-8383 $$
Fred's Hickory Inn 1502 N Walton Blvd, Bentonville, AR 72712 (479) 273-3303 $$	Whole Hog Cafe 1400 SE Walton Blvd, Bentonville, AR 72712 (479) 271-6566 $$

Candies

Martin Greer's Candies 813 W Central Ave, Bentonville, AR 72733 (479) 254-6996	

Catering

Bentonville Butcher and Deli 1201 S Walton Blvd, Bentonville, AR 72712 (479) 464-9933	Main Event 120 W Central Ave, Bentonville, AR 72712 (479) 372-3999
Which Wich 1406 S Walton Blvd, Bentonville, AR 72712 (479) 268-5175	

Coffee

Coffee at Eleven (Crystal Bridges Museum) 600 Museum Way, Bentonville, AR 72712 (479) 418-5700 $	Starbucks Coffee Company 1401 S Walton Blvd, Bentonville, AR 72712 (479) 254-0943 $

Kennedy Coffee Roasting Company 2501 SE Moberly Lane, Bentonville, AR 72712 (479) 464-9015 $	Starbucks Coffee Company 913 SE Walton Blvd, Bentonville, AR 72712 (479) 464-9069 $
Pressroom (Coffee, Cafe and Bar) 121 W Central Ave, Bentonville, AR 72712 (479) 657-2905 $$	

Fast Food

Burger King 1700 S Walton Blvd, Bentonville, AR 72712 (479) 254-8966 $	Ron's Hamburgers and Chili 1702 S Walton Blvd #12, Bentonville, AR 72712 (479) 464-4420 $
Firehouse Subs 3511 SE J Street, Bentonville, AR 72712 (479) 273-5622 $	Sonic Drive In 208 S Walton Blvd, Bentonville, AR 72712 (479) 273-9406 $
Honey Baked Ham 1400 SE Walton Blvd, Bentonville, AR 72712 (479) 271-7838 $	Sonic Drive In 2502 SE 14th Street, Bentonville, AR 72712 (479) 271-7224 $
Jimmy John's Gourmet Sandwiches 805 S Walton Blvd, Bentonville, AR 72712 (479) 254-6700 $	SUBWAY Restaurants 813 W Central Ave #10, Bentonville, AR 72712 (479) 273-9606 $

KFC Bentonville 901 N Walton Blvd, Bentonville, AR 72712 (479) 273-3124 $	**SUBWAY Restaurants** 1708 SE Walton Blvd, Bentonville, AR 72712 (479) 876-8152 $
Lenny's Sub Shop 800 SE Walton Blvd, Bentonville, AR 72712 (479) 464-8181 $	**SUBWAY Restaurants** 2610 SE 14th Street, Bentonville, AR 72712 (479) 271-8133 $
Panda Express 319 S Walton Blvd, Bentonville, AR 72712 (479) 273-1191 $	**Wendy's** 814 S Walton Blvd, Bentonville, AR 72712 (479) 271-7232 $
Panera Bread 1320 SE Walton Blvd, Bentonville, AR 72712 (479) 271-8009 $	**Zaxby's** 3510 SE J Street, Bentonville, AR 72712 (479) 254-9565 $

Fine Dining

Doe's Eat Place 2806 S Walton Blvd, Bentonville, AR 72712 (479) 254-8081 $$$	**The Hive Restaurant** 200 NE A Street, Bentonville, AR 72712 (479) 286-6575 $$$
Fred's Hickory Inn 1502 N Walton Blvd, Bentonville, AR 72712 (479) 273-3303 $$	**Tableside Theater** (479) 381-5149 $$$

River Grille Steakhouse 1003 McClain Road, Bentonville, AR 72712 (479) 271-4141 $$$	Tusk and Trotter 110 SE A Street, Bentonville, AR 72712 (479) 268-4494 $$
Table Mesa (Bistro) 108 E Central Ave, Bentonville, AR 72712 (479) 715-6706 $$	

Food Trucks

Big Rub BBQ and Catering	Olde English Fish and Chips
Crepes Paulette Artfully delicious handheld crepes	Kind Kitchen (Gluten Free, Vegan and Vegetarian)
Yeyo's Mexican Grill	

French

Petit Bistro 2702 N Walton Blvd, Bentonville, AR 72712 (479) 464-9278 $$$	

Indian

Aroma 1100 SE 13th Court, Bentonville, AR 72712 (479) 271-2119 $$	India Orchard 3404 SE Macy Road #24, Bentonville, AR 72712 (479) 715-6650 $$

Curry Point - Indian Cuisine 2505 S Walton Blvd, Bentonville, AR 72712 (479) 464-4545 $$	

Italian

Doma Bella's Italian Eatery 439 Centerton Blvd, Centerton, AR 72719 (479) 795-0735 $$	Tavola Trattoria 108 SE A Street, Bentonville, AR 72712 (479) 715-4738 $$

Ice Cream ~ Frozen Yogurt

Braum's Ice Cream and Dairy Stores 1119 N. Walton Blvd, Bentonville, AR 72712 (479) 273-7913 $	Spark Cafe 105 N Main Street, Bentonville, AR 72712 (479) 273-1329 $
Braum's Ice Cream and Dairy Stores 2305 SE Walton Blvd, Bentonville, AR 72712 (479) 273-9696 $	Yum Yo's Frozen Yogurt 700 SE Walton Blvd, Bentonville, AR 72712 (479) 254-9866 $

Mediterranean

Khan's Grill 2410 SW 14th St, Bentonville, AR 72712 (479) 553-7670 $$	

Mexican

Acambaro Mexican Restaurant 301 S Walton Blvd, Bentonville, AR 72712 (479) 464-8171 $	Las Fajita's Mexican Grill 1402 SE Falcon Lane, Bentonville, AR 72712 (479) 464-8147 $
Azul Tequila Mexican Cuisine 1000 S E Walton Blvd, Ste 22, Bentonville, AR 72712 (479) 876-8788 $$	Sabores Mexican Cuisine 706 S Main Street # 6, Bentonville, AR 72712 (479) 254-8608 $$
Glasgow's 411 SE Walton Blvd, Bentonville, AR 72712 (479) 273-9958 $	Taco Bueno 1302 SE Walton Blvd, Bentonville, AR 72712 (479) 273-6694 $

Pizza

Eureka Pizza 1140 N Walton Blvd, Bentonville, AR 72712 (479) 271-9999 $	Little Caesars Pizza 206 SW 14th St, Bentonville, AR 72712 (479) 273-9999 $
Gusano's Chicago-Style Pizzeria 2905 S Walton Blvd #9, Bentonville, AR 72712 (479) 271-8242 $$	Marco's Pizza 2502 SW 14th St, Bentonville, AR 72712 (479) 268-5422
Jim's Razorback Pizza 226 N Walton Blvd, Bentonville, AR 72712 (479) 273-9224 $	Mazzio's Pizza 1117 N Walton Blvd, Bentonville, AR 72712 (479) 273-7701 $$

Johnny Brusco's New York Style Pizza 700 SE Walton Blvd #10, Bentonville, AR 72712 (479) 268-6748 $$	Pedaler's Pub Pizza 410 SW A street, Bentonville, AR 72712 (479) 595-9669 $

Sandwiches

Bentonville Butcher and Deli 1201 S Walton Blvd, Bentonville, AR 72712 (479) 464-9933 $	Jimmy John's Gourmet Subs 805 S Walton Blvd, Bentonville, AR 72712 (479) 254-6700 S
Crumpet Tea Room Express 1140 N Walton Blvd, Bentonville, AR 72712 (479) 271-8110 $$	Lenny's Sub Shop 800 SE Walton Blvd, Bentonville, AR 72712 (479) 464-8181 S
Firehouse Subs 3511 SE J Street, Bentonville, AR 72712 (479) 273-5622 $	McAlister's Deli 900 SE Walton Blvd, Bentonville, AR 72712 (479) 271-6263 $$
Flying Burrito 1401 S Walton Blvd, Bentonville, AR 72712 (479) 715-6570 $	Red Onion Espressoria 201 SE 14th Street, Bentonville, AR 72712 (479) 268-3157 $$
Honeybaked Ham and Cafe 1400 SE Walton Blvd, Bentonville, AR 72712 (479) 271-7838 $$	Which Wich 1406 S Walton Blvd, Bentonville, AR 72712 (479) 268-5175 S

Seafood

River Grille Steakhouse	The Flying Fish
1003 McClain Road, Bentonville, AR 72712	109A NW 2nd Street, Bentonville, AR 72712
(479) 271-4141	(479) 657-6300
$$$	$$

BELLA VISTA

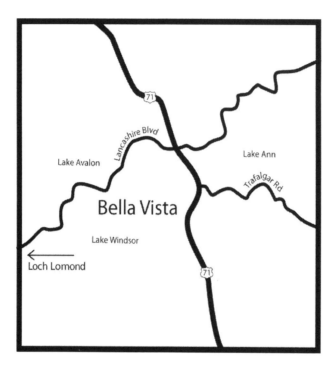

Bella Vista, AR is a Bentonville bedroom community, which has unique vacation opportunities not found anywhere else in NWA.

Just why do people come to Bella Vista to vacation? If you enjoy nature and the outdoors, you will love this village with its beautiful scenery, golf courses, tennis, swimming, fishing and other outdoor activities. To be specific, it has twelve tennis courts, eight lakes, seven golf courses, three swimming pools, three fitness/recreation centers and many trails throughout its 36,000 acres of rolling hills.

It is located on Hwy 71 at the end of I-49 between Bentonville and the Missouri state line. Bella Vista village covers approximately 65 square miles with a population of 27,347 according to the latest census.

Neighborhoods

Bella Vista's west side and east side are divided by I-49/I-49 and united by Highway 340/Lancashire. You have the highlands to the west and the east side is called the east side.

What the Locals Say...

Here are the good restaurants in Bella Vista according to Bella Vista residents themselves: El Pueblitos in the highlands is a great Mexican restaurant. For Italian try Gusanos just off I-49 and Riordan. Top China in the Sugar Creek Center and Duffers Cafe off Highway 340 West heading toward the Highlands are two other terrific places to eat.

ACCOMMODATIONS

While Bella Vista is a bedroom community to Bentonville, it offers travelers a very different type of accommodation experience. It doesn't have traditional hotels, but does provide a high level of natural beauty, peace and quiet, and an array of amenities not offered anywhere else in the NWA area. World-class bed and breakfasts, as well as vacation rentals where guests rent townhomes or individual homes, provide the main type of lodging in the village. Guests can enjoy access to golf courses, lakes, tennis courts, swimming pools, fitness/recreation centers and country club dining.

Bella Vista, AR Bed and Breakfast

The Inn at Bella Vista
101 Chelsea Road, Bella Vista, AR 72715
(479) 876-5645
The Inn at Bella Vista is a truly wonderful bed and breakfast featuring caring hosts and delicious breakfasts.

Bella Vista, AR RV Park

Blowing Springs Campground
725 RV Park Road, Bella Vista, AR 72715
(479) 855-8075

Bella Vista, AR Vacation Rentals

Bella Vista Vacation Rentals
430 Town Center NE, Bella Vista, AR 72714
(479) 855-1111
Rents townhomes and homes by the night, week or month

THINGS TO DO AND SEE

As I already mentioned, Bella Vista has twelve tennis courts, eight lakes, seven golf courses and many hiking and biking trails throughout the 36,000 acres of Bella Vista's rolling hills. All of these recreational activities can be accessed as a paid privilege when you rent a vacation home or townhome from vacation rental companies or an individual property owner.

Cultural activities are available in nearby communities. Broadway productions, exhibits and other activities are available at the Walton Arts Center in Fayetteville. View amazing art at the Crystal Bridges Museum of American Art in downtown Bentonville. Northwest Arkansas also offers several art galleries, studios and opportunities to see other diverse fine arts.

Shoppers are treated to quality handmade arts and crafts, antiques and fine arts during the fall and spring craft fairs in Bella Vista, Bentonville, Fayetteville, Rogers and Springdale.

While you are staying in the area, you can also discover the impressive Veterans Wall of Honor located between Bella Vista and Bentonville, which pays tribute to the veterans who gave their lives in military service. The stunning, unique memorial is a circular wall with 4,200 veterans' names on it along with 18 historical flags and cast bronze historical plaques.

While Bella Vista does have many lakes and golf courses, they are not open to the public at large. Only property owners and their guests are allowed to use them. However, if you stay in one of the many rental condos, you can access these facilities as a guest.

Festivals/Special Events

Bella Vista Arts and Crafts Festival
1991 Forest Hills Blvd, Bella Vista, AR 72714

The popular Bella Vista Arts and Crafts Festival is held annually on the third weekend of October. The proceeds from the Festival go entirely to support the arts, artists and artisans in Northwest Arkansas.

Simple Pleasures Event Center
13718 Rothbury Drive, Bella Vista, AR 72715
(479) 876-5959

Simple Pleasures is an Arkansas event center hosting weddings, receptions, parties and corporate events. Simple Pleasures' warm 1930s architecture and 18 park-like acres is a tranquil, relaxing setting for indoor and outdoor events.

Galleries
Wishing Spring Gallery
8862 W McNelly Road, Bentonville, AR 72712
(479) 273-1798

Movie Theater
Sugar Creek 10 Cinema
Sugar Creek Center
10 Sugar Creek Center, Bella Vista, AR 72714
(479) 855-7878

Museums
Bella Vista Historical Museum
1885 Bella Vista Way, Bella Vista, AR 72714
(479) 640-8336

Mildred B. Cooper Memorial Chapel
504 Memorial Drive, Bella Vista, AR 72714
(479) 855-6598

Veterans Wall of Honor
The Veterans Wall of Honor is located in a gorgeous park featuring large native trees, a paved walking trail and a lovely lake home to ducks and geese year round.
The beautiful and unusual circular wall was created to remind all visitors of the enormous sacrifices made by so many to preserve the freedoms we enjoy today.

Outdoors
Golf
Golf – 8 Golf Courses
Some of the most challenging and beautiful golf courses in Arkansas are found in Bella Vista. There are two executive 9-hole courses and six regulation 18-hole courses.

If you need to brush up on your stroke, the Tanyard Creek Practice Center and the Highlands Driving Range are available for those wanting to refine their game.

The courses offer multiple sets of tees to suit every golfer's skill level, and there are major retail golf shops available at the Kingsdale and Bella Vista Country Club facilities. In Bella Vista, members and their guests can enjoy golf almost year round and at a moderate cost to boot!

Berksdale Golf Course
Kingsdale Golf Shop
4 Kingsdale Lane, Bella Vista, AR 72714
(479) 855-812

Berksdale Golf Course, an 18-hole course, joins with the Kingswood Golf Course to create a 36-hole challenge called the Kingsdale Golf Complex.

The complex makes use of water, sand, trees and natural terrain to give the golfer a tricky round of play regardless of his or her skill level. Starting formats vary; check with the golf shop. This popular facility, while the most played, does not have a driving range.

Rental carts and clubs are available in the Kingsdale Golf Shop where you will also find an impressive collection of golfing merchandise.

Branchwood Golf Course
222 Glasgow Road, Bella Vista, AR 72715
(479) 855-8181

This 9-hole par-3 course operates out of the Branchwood Recreation Center. No carts are allowed on this beautiful course carved out of one of the many "hollers" in the area. The entire course off the white tees measures only 1,220 yards, with the longest hole being 153 yards.

Brittany Golf Course
Metfield Golf Shop
1 Euston Drive, Bella Vista, AR 72714
(479) 855-8160

The Brittany executive 9-hole course rounds out the 27-hole Metfield Golf Complex. Five par-3s and four par-4s make this an unusual course. The course plays 1,696 yards from the No. 3 tees, and 1,889 yards from the No. 2 tees. Both inexperienced and experienced players are challenged here. Starting formats vary; check with the golf shop.

The Bella Vista Country Club Golf Course
2271 Bella Vista Way, Bella Vista, AR 72714
(479) 855-8003

This is the oldest golf course in Bella Vista and is classic in its design. It gently rolls along U.S. 71 through the valley and its relatively flat terrain makes walking the course possible. There are four sets of tees to challenge everyone's skill level. Golf carts and rental clubs are available and starting formats vary.

The Dogwood Hills Golf Course
Metfield Golf Shop
1 Euston Drive, Bella Vista, AR 72714
(479) 855-8160

The Dogwood Hills Golf Course joins with the Brittany Golf Course to make up the 27-hole Metfield Golf Complex. Be aware that the course is a links-style course that does not allow you to return to the clubhouse until the 18th green.

Dogwood Hills Golf Course meanders through a woodland, rural area and Metfield's townhouses to provide a terrific and challenging golfing experience. While the terrain is fairly gentle, there are several long stretches from the greens to the next tee.

Starting formats vary; check with the clubhouse.

The Highlands Golf Course
1 Pamona Drive, Bella Vista, AR 72715
(479) 855-8150

Consisting of rolling terrain with many, many trees, the Highlands Golf Course opened in 1990. While offering extremely beautiful views, the course also presents plenty of opportunity for both challenging play and lost balls. There are four sets of tees to accommodate all skill levels, and there is a driving range right by the golf shop.

After 2 p.m., a golf cart is included in the green fee, and the driving range is closed on Monday's for maintenance. Starting formats vary; check with the golf shop.

The Kingswood Golf Course
Kingsdale Golf Shop
4 Kingsdale Lane, Bella Vista, AR 72714
(479) 855-8123

The Kingswood Golf Course combines with the Berksdale Golf Course to form the Kingsdale Golf Complex. More than 33 percent of the total rounds of golf played in Bella Vista are played at this popular links-style course. Note:

You will not return to the clubhouse until the 18th green.

Golf carts and rental clubs are available and the largest selection of golfing merchandise in all of Bella Vista can be found at the Kingsdale Golf Shop; there is no driving range at this course, however. Starting formats vary; check with the golf shop.

Scotsdale Golf Course
50 Scotsdale Drive, Bella Vista, AR 72715
(479) 855-8140

This course features a killer back nine with holes 11 through 15 taking you on a rollercoaster ride of demanding golf. The front nine moves through gently rolling terrain and offers a fair test of your skills, but it is definitely not as demanding as the back nine.

Rental carts and clubs are available, and after 2 p.m. a golf cart is included in the green fees. Starting formats vary; check with the golf shop.

Tanyard Creek Practice Center
10 Nature Trail Lane, Bella Vista, AR 72715
(479) 855-8133

PGA Golf Professional Mike Singletary hosts The Tanyard Creek Practice Center Golf Shop where you will find a huge selection of golfing equipment individually fitted to suit each golfer and his or her game. The equipment is offered either at or below Internet prices, and if you desire to perfect your game, there are three Class "A" PGA Golf Professionals that offer lessons at the center.

There are 28 uncovered and eight covered hard surface stations, which are heated for inclement weather and cold temperatures. Additionally, there are two indoor bays, a launch monitor to assist with club fittings, a practice area with chipping stations, and bunkers and a putting green.

Lakes
Lake Rayburn
Size: 47 Acres
Depth: 45 to 50 Feet
Restrictions: No Wake

Boat Access: North on U.S. 71. Exit onto Kingsland Road heading east. Take the first left, turn onto Lakeside Drive and follow it to the lake.

Lake Ann
Size: 112 Acres
Depth: 65 to 70 Feet
No Restrictions: Full sport lake
Water skiing, tubing, boogie board
Shoreline Mooring Rental: First-come basis
Shoreline Rack Storage: Canoes, jon boats

Lake Avalon
Size: 67 Acres
Depth: 40 to 50 Feet
Restrictions: No Wake
Heated boat dock for winter fishing
Shoreline Mooring Rental: First-come basis
Shoreline Rack Storage: Canoes, jon boats

Lake Norwood
Size: 35 Acres
Depth: 70 to 75 Feet
Restrictions: No Wake
Boat Access: East off Highway 340 (Lancashire Blvd)
and U.S. 71 behind Town Center
Shoreline Rack Storage: Canoes, jon boats

Loch Lomond
Size: 475 Acres
Depth: 80 to 85 Feet
No Restrictions: Full sport lake
Water skiing, tubing, boogie board
Marina docking is available
Motorized fishing boats available
for rent by the hour with POA ID card.

Lake Windsor
Size: 220 Acres
Depth: 75 to 80 Feet
No Restrictions: Full sport lake
Water skiing, tubing, boogie board
Shoreline Mooring Rental: First-come basis

Lake Brittany
Size: 35 Acres
Depth: 70 to 75 Feet
Restrictions: No Wake
Boat Access:

Walking Trails
Tanyard Creek Nature Trail
The Tanyard Creek Nature Trail features a 2.5-mile loop complete with a swinging bridge and a view from above of the Lake Windsor waterfall. It is located approximately 1.5 miles west of U.S. 71 on Highway 340 in Bella Vista.

Lake Bella Vista Trail
This marked, paved 1.75-mile trail features benches, picnic tables, a playground and a Disc Golf Course. The lake covers 22 acres and is approximately 8 feet deep. Located adjacent to U.S. 71, Lake Bella Vista Trail is perfect for bikers, hikers and dog walkers.

Dog Park

Bella Vista K9 Corral Dog Park
Glasgow Road and Scottsdale Drive, BV AR 72715

Shopping

Antiques/Flea Market
Bella Vista Flea Market and Antique Mall
2878 Bella Vista Way, Bella Vista, AR 72714
(479) 855-6999

RESTAURANTS

Bella Vista began in 1965 as a summer resort town, morphed into a retirement community, and has now rapidly grown to an incorporated city as of 2006.

Because Bella Vista is located just a few miles from Bentonville and Rogers, Bella Vista residents and vacationers often drive to those cities to experience exceptional and world-class cuisine.

Having said that, there's no need to leave Bella Vista to eat. There are several restaurants in and around Bella Vista Village where you will enjoy an excellent meal. Barnyard Café serves barbecue, burgers and seafood; Chen's Garden serves Chinese food; Las Fajitas of Bella Vista serves excellent Mexican food; Duffer's Café is known for its burgers and down-home American food.

Restaurant Prices

$ - Budget	*$$$ - Upscale*
$$ - Mid-Range	

American

Barnyard Cafe 12 Cunningham Corner, Bella Vista, AR 72714 (479) 268-6668 $	Duffer's Café 638 W Lancashire Blvd, Bella Vista, AR 72715 (479) 855-6094 $
DQ GRILL and CHILL RESTAURANT 1 Riordan Road, Bella Vista, AR 72714 (479) 855-2362 $	Sonic Drive-In 2 Sugar Creek Center, Bella Vista, AR 72714 (479) 855-9367 $

Asian

Chen's Garden 426 Town Center NE, Bella Vista, AR 72714 (479) 876-5556 $	Top China 32 Sugar Creek Center, Bella Vista, AR 72714 (479) 855-6868 $

Italian

Café Amici Bella Vista Country Club 98 Clubhouse Drive, Bella Vista, AR 72715 (479) 270-5040 $	

Mexican

El Pueblito 1705 Forest Hills Blvd, Bella Vista, AR 72715 (479) 855-2324 $	Las Fajita's 42 Sugar Creek Center, Bella Vista, AR 72714 (479) 855-7048 $

Pizza

Gusano's Pizzeria 19 Cunningham Corner, Bella Vista, AR 72714 (479) 876-6969 $$	Pizza Hut 30 Sugar Creek Center, Bella Vista, AR 72714 (479) 876-1705 $

Sandwiches

Papa Mike's 2 Kingsdale Lane, Bella Vista, AR 72714 (479) 855-8117 $	SUBWAY Restaurants 4 Cunningham Corner, Bella Vista, AR 72714 (479) 855-4822 $

EUREKA SPRINGS

Eureka Springs

Eureka Springs, Arkansas will astonish you with its rich history and its obvious determination to maintain the look and feel of yesteryear. Every member of your family is sure to have fun in this colorful little Victorian-era village. There really is something to suit everyone's pleasure in Eureka Springs, so bring the kids and the grandkids, too!

There are exciting vacation activities for the young, the young-at-heart and every age group in between. You will not be at a loss for things to do in Eureka Springs, Arkansas.

The downtown area of Eureka Springs is an eclectic collection of truly unique shops covering two levels of many buildings, so make certain you check for shop entrances upstairs, too. The shops are a joy to browse, and you will find everything from art galleries featuring sculpture, paintings and fine jewelry to quaint boutiques selling the local crafters' woodcarvings, pottery and weavings. You will definitely see extraordinary art that you never imagined existed in Eureka Springs.

Many people from surrounding towns, other states, and the entire world, in fact, come to Eureka Springs just for the plentiful and one-of-a-kind shopping opportunities. There are also a number of charming restaurants where you can get a tasty bite to eat, take a load off your feet and sift through your shopping bags marveling at the purchases you made that day.

If you are staying at one of the charming Eureka Springs downtown hotels, you can drop your bags off in your room once they become too heavy to carry, and then go shopping for some more Eureka Springs deals. You will be hard-pressed *not* to shop 'til you drop when visiting Eureka Springs!

In addition, Eureka Springs has been recognized as the Wedding Capital of the South; future brides take note! There is everything you need for your special day including innumerable hotels and venues ready to cater to your special day and all of your attending guests. The courthouse even stays open on Saturday to provide marriage licenses for prospective couples. What better place to hold your memorable event?

Eureka Springs is a breathtaking alpine village with a looping 5 miles of very steep and narrow winding streets lined with delightful Victorian-style cottages and charming B&Bs. Many cottages are authentically preserved to exacting standards for the "gingerbread" style of architecture and were originally constructed using local stone.

The trolley, reminiscent of yesteryear, is the main form of transportation, taking visitors throughout this charming village, including stops at the Eureka Springs Historical Museum and the Cornerstone Bank, both must-sees.

Art and cultural heritage enthusiasts will love Eureka Springs. It is not often that so many different major organizations have recognized the same city for its unique cultural opportunities. The National Trust for Historic Preservation has selected Eureka Springs as one of America's "Dozen Distinctive Destinations"; *American Style Magazine* has named it as a "Top Twenty-Five Arts Destination"; it has also been chosen as an America in Bloom award winner. The city in its entirety is on the National Register of Historic Places, making it one of the most popular tourist attractions in all of Arkansas.

If you like the outdoors, you will love the adventure opportunities in and around Eureka Springs. Fish in the crystal-clear trout streams, hike to Pivot Rock and the Natural Bridge rock formations, explore caves and waterfalls, or take a ride on a zip-line. There are plenty of Eureka Springs cabins ready to provide you with a wonderful night's rest after a day of playing in Eureka Springs' great outdoors.

Eureka Springs enjoys four distinctive seasons and is perfect for family outings or group travels. Many convention and meeting planners choose the area year after year for its outstanding hospitality and numerous Eureka Springs attractions.

MAP OF EUREKA SPRINGS

NEIGHBORHOODS

Eureka Springs Has Something For Everyone - Locals proudly boast that their town has something for everyone, and they aren't kidding! Bikers can live it up at the Pied Piper Pub and Cathouse Lounge; Christians love the Eureka Springs Passion Play; mountain bikers enjoy Lake Leatherwood; fishermen and fisherwomen take joy in the White River, Kings River, and Beaver Lake. The things to do list covers every base you can possibly think of!

The adorable village is noted throughout the world for its shopping, and I'm happy to report that the locals agree. They say that the downtown shops and galleries are "very cool". In fact, if you just walk into a few, you'll be pleasantly surprised.

After a fun day of shopping, mountain biking, or fishing, you're sure to be starving, and the locals are proud of all their local restaurants. Their favorites, however, include:

- KJ's Caribe Restaurant and Cantina
- Local Flavor Cafe
- Sparky's Roadhouse Café
- Mud Street Café
- Café Amore'
- Thai House Restaurant – a special local favorite
- FRESH – gourmet and organic food
- Sweet & Savory Cafe

Please see the restaurant listings for exact restaurant locations.

Turpentine Creek Wildlife Refuge Is Something Special – A great activity for the entire family and a local favorite is the Turpentine Creek Wildlife Refuge. This big cat rescue is a great activity for the entire family. In fact, some of the town's more unusual cabins are found on the property. You sleep while the cats wander around the grounds beneath your perch. You'll be hard-pressed to find an experience like this elsewhere in the world. Did I mention that the "Things to Do" list was going to be wonderfully eclectic?

Jim Fains Herbacy Offers Natural Potions and Vitamins – Where do the local residents go to get holistic healing for just about any ailment? Why Fains Herbacy, of course! According to the locals, Jim Fains Herbacy is a community treasure with a bonus of a knowledgeable and friendly staff. You'll find natural potions and vitamins to keep you feeling fit and ready for your entire stay and the rest of your life.

The Great Passion Play – Tourists and locals flock to this outdoor Christian attraction drama. The Christian play takes place in an outdoor amphitheater that includes special lighting and sound effects, live animals, and a cast of 150 Biblically-costumed actors. Be sure to take in the Bible Museum and Christ of the Ozarks as well.

The Farmers Market is an open-air market that meets on Tuesday and Thursday mornings from April through November, 7 a.m. to 12 p.m., at The

Village at Pine Mountain on U.S. 62 (aka E. Van Buren Street).The market sells locally grown produce, including organically grown goods, flowers, and plants. Depending on the growing season, you might also find herbs, honey, beef, chicken, breads, sweets, crafts, and more. Often, there is live music at this popular market. There is a covered space with chairs provided to sit and have coffee with your neighbors.

During the summer, there is also a Saturday morning market in the parking lot of Ermilio's Italian Home Cooking. Hey, not only a restaurant favorite, but also a great place to browse through yet another wonderful area market!

The locals are proud of the fact that their city is known as the Wedding Capital of the South. Almost every B&B can arrange for your wedding. Barbara Harmony officiates weddings and is said to give the sweetest ceremonies of anyone in the country. Susan Storch was mentioned as a very good wedding photographer. See, even the locals know that your special day will be made extra special if you have it in their little city.

Itineraries and Day Trips

Eureka Springs Itinerary #1 – for History Buffs

Arrive in Eureka early and tour the city via Eureka Van Tours or the Historic Tram Tour. Notice the Victorian architecture, especially the gingerbread decoration used on many of the B&Bs, cottages and other buildings. Eureka is home to the largest collection of Victorian architecture in the central U.S., and as I mentioned before, the downtown district is listed on the National Register of Historic Places.

Visit Eureka Springs Historical Museum located in the center of the Historical District; it is located in the 1889 California building. The museum is the place to learn about the colorful past of Eureka Springs through its authentic photographs, papers and other memorabilia documenting the city since its beginning.

Don't miss a chance to see the Crescent Hotel, just one of the five Eureka hotels predating 1906.Be sure to see the Downtown Cornerstone Bank, as well. The bank operates much as it did in years gone by; you can see the old brass teller cages, potbellied stove, original business machines and other working antiques.

St Elizabeth's Catholic Church in Eureka Springs is located between the Carnegie Library and the Crescent Hotel. Richard Kerens built the church and dedicated it to his parents in 1909. The church was built with St. Sophia's Church in Istanbul, Turkey in mind. There are 14 Stations of the Cross made of Italian marble along the right-hand side of the walk from the bell tower.

Eureka Springs Itinerary #2 – for Art Lovers

Take your time getting up and have a tasty, filling breakfast at your B&B, or maybe take a stroll down to the Mud Street Café, where from 8 a.m. to 11 a.m., it serves up the freshest food in town. According to the *Arkansas Times* Reader's Choice Awards, it also has the best coffee in the entire state of Arkansas.

Tour the local galleries, which are mostly located all along the winding streets of the downtown shopping area. There are more than 20 galleries in Eureka Springs supplied by an excess of 400 local artists. You may be fortunate enough to see some of the artists at work. Artists of every medium are represented. You'll find award-winning painters, potters, jewelers, sculptors of steel and stone, weavers, woodworkers, woodcarvers, scrimshanders, decoupers and tole painters.

Take a break from gallery hopping and visit the Keels Creek Winery at the beautiful Spanish-styled Keels Creek Art Gallery. The two massive stone fireplaces provide a perfect setting to relax and enjoy a glass of wine. There are both tasting and retail rooms at the gallery where you can taste and then purchase the perfect bottle of vino.

Grab a light lunch at one of the wonderful little restaurants along the main drag of Eureka Springs. Many have patio seating overlooking the bustling street below.

Relax and rejuvenate at one of Eureka Spring's state-of-the-art spas, such as the Serenity Spa and Salon located on the second floor of the Basin Park Hotel. Specialties include duet massage, wasabi body wrap, massage therapies, skin treatments, manicures, pedicures, foot maintenance and facials. If you prefer, you may simply sunbathe on the deck.

For dinner, have the meal of a lifetime at one of the award-winning restaurants in Eureka Springs. The Bavarian Inn features German, Eastern European and American cuisine; the Local Flavor features American, Italian and Vegetarian; the Port Orleans Rib and Steak features seafood, steak and Cajun/Creole. These are just a small sampling of the fine-dining restaurants in Eureka Springs.

Finish your day with Opera in the Ozarks located at Inspiration Point about 7 miles from Eureka Springs. Opera in the Ozarks began in 1950 as a school for young opera students; it continues that tradition today. Only internationally acclaimed productions are performed by the all-student cast.

Eureka Springs Itinerary #3 – Inspiration in America›s Victorian Mountain Village

Have breakfast at Myrtie Mae's where you will devour U.S. Grade A eggs cooked "eggsactly" as you like them. Breakfast is very reasonable; an All-American Breakfast is only $5.95.The feast includes two eggs cooked to order, served with bacon or sausage, hash browns, and toast or biscuits and gravy.

There is nothing like a visit to the Turpentine Creek Wildlife Refuge to inspire and uplift your spirits. This effort is humanity's best in action. The mission of the refuge is, "To provide lifetime refuge for abandoned, abused, and neglected 'Big Cats' with emphasis on Tigers, Lions, Leopards and Cougars." There are unusual lodging opportunities available on the grounds of the refuge. For example, you can sleep with the big cats roaming around below your cabin.

Discover the land of blue sky and laughing waters at Blue Spring Heritage Center. This amazing spring nurtured the Cherokee during the Trail of Tears. It pours 38 million gallons of water per day into the beautiful lagoon.

Thorncrown Chapel located on U.S. 62 West just a few miles from Eureka Springs is an amazing architectural achievement. Due to its majestic beauty yet simple design, critics have called it "one of the finest religious spaces of modern times." It stands 48 feet tall with 425 windows and over 6,000 square feet of glass. Thorncrown Chapel is available for daily visitation and weddings and conducts Sunday services. There is no admission fee but donations are accepted. Parking for RVs and buses is available. Groups get special treatment. A presentation is given and one of the Thorncrown musicians will sing an inspirational song.

Christ of the Ozarks Statue is located on the grounds of *The Great Passion Play*. Gerald K. Smith erected the monumental statue of Jesus Christ in 1966 as a "Sacred Project." It stands seven stories high and measures at 65.5 feet, which is 20 meters for you metric folks!

The Great Passion Play is billed as America's #1 Attended Outdoor Drama and casts over 170 Biblically costumed actors alongside 20 different animals. It is staged in an outdoor amphitheater utilizing a multi-level stage. Since 1968, the last days of Jesus Christ's life on earth have been performed deep in the beautiful Ozark Mountains. This is a must-see performance even if you are not a Christian.

Eureka Springs Day Trips

Branson, MO

Save a day or two to visit beautiful, family-fun oriented Branson, Mo. Nestled in the heart of the Ozark Mountains and only 49 miles from Eureka Springs, Branson is a natural choice for a fabulous one-day or two-day trip. Bring the whole family; there is something in Branson for everyone.

Branson is acclaimed for its amazing 100-plus live shows, including the China Acrobats; 60s, 70s and 80s music acts; the Charlie Daniels Band; the Charley Pride show and oh so many more. You can purchase tickets four different ways: Wait until you get to town to purchase your tickets, call the theater direct, purchase tickets online or use a travel professional. Branson Tourism Center is not only the largest ticket seller, but it also enjoys an excellent reputation. Buy tickets early as many shows sell out.

Be sure to visit Silver Dollar City where there are 30 thrilling rides, including the Fire in the Hole, the Powder Keg, Wildfire, the Giant Swing and Outlaw Run, the world's newest and most exciting wood rollercoaster. There are a million things to do and see in Silver Dollar City. You can easily spend a day there, so watch your time; you don't want to be late for the show!

Daring outdoor activities in the Branson area include: biking, canoeing, kayaking, camping, trout and bass fishing, trap and skeet shooting, horseback riding, hunting, spelunking, rock climbing and zip-lining. Beaches and public parks are also plentiful in Branson.

Offering a wide range of pricing and amenities, Branson has more than 150 hotels from which to choose should you decide to spend two or more days there. Select one of the four-star resort hotels where gourmet breakfast is served as you sit comfortably in your room watching the sunrise over beautiful Table Rock Lake. Or choose from the many different lodging establishments along the famous U.S.76. Many have family-style restaurants, swimming pools, water parks and miniature golf, and many are golf-front condos. Most stay open year round and offer reduced rates during the winter months.

Branson restaurants include family-style, steakhouse, seafood, fine-dining, eclectic, chain, buffets and banquet facilities for weddings and other special events. No matter your eating preference, Branson restaurants will sate your appetite. Choose from a wide range of cuisine, including American, Chinese, Italian, Japanese, Mediterranean, Mexican and many more. Many restaurants deliver right to your hotel, resort or campground.

You won't be disappointed with your one-day or two-day trip to Branson filled with daytime and evening excitement and fun.

ACCOMMODATIONS

Lodging is varied in Eureka Springs, but it is probably best known for its many wonderful bed and breakfasts. Outstanding B&Bs are located within the city, as well as on the outskirts, and there is a B&B to suit every budget. In fact, as you drive around Eureka Springs, you will surely notice that every other gingerbread house seems to have a B&B sign out front.

Are you looking for luxury lodging? Stay at the Queen Anne Eastlake Victorian home where you will be pampered with the perfect blend of old-world charm and genuine Southern hospitality.

If it is adventure that calls you, view the world from 30 feet up in one of the tree house cottages Eureka Springs has to offer located just a few minutes from downtown and situated on 30-plus acres of private Ozark forest. There are also many Beaver Lake cabins, which is just a stone's throw away from Eureka Springs.

If you love Victorian history, Eureka Springs hotels won't disappoint. For example, the 1886 Crescent Hotel and Spa, a member of the prestigious Historic Hotels of America, manages to provide 21st-century amenities while maintaining its genteel ambiance. Get a taste of what elegant lodging of yesteryear might have been like. After a day of shopping, experience what it is like to stay at the Crescent. Relax in the lap of luxury, try one of the several spa packages, have a romantic dinner at one of the many fabulous restaurants, and sleep in the most comfortable bed available anywhere.

Groups will find excellent accommodations at the different fine chain hotels in Eureka Springs, Arkansas. Some are noted for their award-winning gardens, while others can provide discounted tickets to all the tours, shows and other attractions in the area. Several provide FREE tour bus parking and handicap facilities.

Hotel Amenities

Adults Only: A	*Pet Friendly: PF*
Breakfast: B	*Pool: P*
Fireplace: F	*Restaurant: R*
Internet: I	*Some: S*

Jacuzzi/Hot Tub: J/HT	Weddings: W
Kitchen: K	

Hotels in Eureka Springs, AR with 3 Star Accommodations

1886 Crescent Hotel and Spa 75 Prospect Ave, Eureka Springs, AR 72632 (800) 678-8946 B, I, J, K, PF, P, R	New Orleans Hotel and Spa 63 Spring Street, Eureka Springs, AR 72632 (479) 253-8630 B, I, J(S)
Grand Central Hotel and Spa 7 N Main Street, Eureka Springs, AR 72632 (479) 253-6756 I, J, K, PF, R	Palace Hotel and Bath House 135 Spring Street, Eureka Springs, AR 72632 (479) 253-7474 I, J, R
Best Western Inn of the Ozarks 207 W Van Buren, Eureka Springs, AR 72632 (479) 253-9768 I, HT, PF, P, R	

Hotels in Eureka Springs, AR with 2 Star Accommodations

Apple Blossom Inn 3043 E Van Buren, Eureka Springs, AR 72632 (479) 253-5552 I, J	Land O Nod 109 Huntsville Road, Eureka Springs, AR 72632 (479) 253-6262 B, K, P, W
Alpine Lodge 2238 E Van Buren, Eureka Springs, AR 72632 (479) 253-7175 I, J	Mount Joy Lodge 216 E Van Buren, Eureka Springs, AR 72632 (479) 253 9568 P

Basin Park Magnuson Grand 12 Spring Street, Eureka Springs, AR 72632 (479) 253-7837 I, J/HT, PF, P, R	Motel 62 3169 E Van Buren, Eureka Springs, AR 72632 (479) 253-5600 I, J, PF, P
Best Western Eureka Inn 101 E Van Buren, Eureka Springs, AR 72632 (479) 253-9551 I, HT, PF, P, R	Pine Lodge 454 W Van Buren, Eureka Springs, AR 72632 (479) 253-8065 I, J(S), K(S), PF(S)
Brackenridge Lodge 352 W Van Buren, Eureka Springs, AR 72632 (479) 253 6803 I, J(S), K(S), P	Quality Inn 196 E Van Buren,Eureka Springs, AR 72632 (479) 253-5241 B, J(S)
Brydan Suites of Eureka Springs 139 Huntsville Road, Eureka Springs, AR 72632 (479) 253-7711 J(S)	Razorback Lodge 3109 E Van Buren, Eureka Springs, AR 72632 (479) 253-8952 I, J, P
Candlewick Inn and Suites 2094 E Van Buren, Eureka Springs, AR 72632 (479) 253-7111 I, J, P	Swiss Village Inn 183 E Van Buren, Eureka Springs, AR 72632 (479) 253-9541 I, J/HT, PF, P
Carolyn's Ozark Swiss Inn 3061 E Van Buren, Eureka Springs, AR 72632 (479) 253-6688 I,J, PF,	Stonegate Inn 2106 E Van Buren, Eureka Springs, AR 72632 (479) 253-8800 I, HT, PF, P
Express Inn 4042 E Van Buren, Eureka Springs, AR 72632 (479) 253-6665 I,HT, PF, P	The Regency Inn 4045 E Van Buren, Eureka Springs, AR 72632 (479) 253-5959 I,P

Colonial Inn 154 Huntsville Road, Eureka Springs, AR 72632 (479) 253-7300 I, J, K(S), P	The Trails Inn 2060 E Van Buren, Eureka Springs, AR 72632 (479) 253-9390 I, P
Days Inn Eureka Springs 120 Van Buren, Eureka Springs, AR 72632 (479) 253-8863 I, J, P	Thurman's Lodge 163 E Van Buren, Eureka Springs, AR 72632 (479) 253-8689 I, P
Edelweiss Inn 2066 E Van Buren, Eureka Springs, AR 72632 (479) 253-7316 I, HT	Travelodge Eureka Springs 110 Huntsville Road, Eureka Springs, AR 72632 (479) 253-8992 I, J, PF
Eureka Matterhorn Towers 130 W Van Buren, Eureka Springs, AR 72632 (479) 253-9602 J(S), PF, P	

Bed and Breakfast Amenities

Adults Only: A	*Jacuzzi/Hot Tub: J/HT*
Full Breakfast: FB	*Pet Friendly: PF*
Fireplace: F	*Some: S*
Internet: I	*Weddings: W*

Eureka Springs Bed and Breakfast

5 Ojo Inn Bed and Breakfast 5 Ojo Street, Eureka Springs, AR 72632 (479) 253-6734 A(S), F, FB, I, J, PF, W	**Harvest House Bed and Breakfast** 104 Wall Street, Eureka Springs, AR 72632 (479) 253-8401 J, HT, FP
11 Singleton House 11 Singleton Street, Eureka Springs, AR 72632 (479) 253-9111 FB, F(S), I, J/HT(S), W	**Heart of the Hills Inn** 5 Summit Street, Eureka Springs, AR 72632 (479) 253-7468 F(S), FB, I, J
66 Center Street Bed and Breakfast Center Street, Eureka Springs, AR 72632 (479) 981-0991 I, J(S), K	**Hidden Acres B&B** 23 Hillside Ave, Eureka Springs, AR 72632 (479) 253-8688 A, F, FB, HT, W
1884 Bridgeford House 263 Spring Street, Eureka Springs, AR 72632 (479) 253-7853 A(S), F, I, J, PF, W	**Inn at Rose Hall Bed and Breakfast** 56 Hillside Ave, Eureka Springs, AR 72632 (479) 253-8035 A,FB, F, I, J, W
A Wedding at Hidden Acres 7004 U.S. 62, Eureka Springs, AR 72632 (479) 253-7531 I, J, K, W	**Main Street Inn** 217 N Main Street, Eureka Springs, AR 72632 (479) 253-7765 F(S), FB, J(S), K, W
Angel at Rose Hall 46 Hillside Ave, Eureka Springs, AR 72632 (479) 253-5405 F, FB, I, J	**Mount Victoria Bed and Breakfast Inn** 28 Fairmont, Eureka Springs, AR 72632 (479) 253-7979 FB, I
Arsenic and Old Lace B&B 60 Hillside Ave, Eureka Springs, AR 72632 (479) 253-5454 A, F, FB, I, J, PF, W	**Peabody House Historic Inn** 7 Armstrong, Eureka Springs, AR 72632 (479) 253-5376 I, J(S), K

Briarwood Lodge 160 Spring Street, Eureka Springs 72632 (479) 253-2001 A(S),FB, I, J, W	Piedmont House 165 Spring Street, Eureka Springs, 72632 (479) 253-2001 A(S), F, FB, I, J/HT(S), W(S)
Carriage House and Main House 75 Lookout Lane, Eureka Springs, AR 72632 (479) 253-5259 K, PF	Red Bud Manor 7 Kings Hwy, Eureka Springs, AR 72632 (479) 253-9649 F, FB, I, J, PF, W
Cliff Cottage Inn - Luxury B&B Suites 42 Armstrong, Eureka Springs, AR 72632 (479) 253-7409 A,F, FB, I, J/HT, W	Ridgeway House B&B 28 Ridgeway Ave, Eureka Springs, AR 72632 (479) 253-6618 A(S), FB, F, I, J, W
Edgewood Manor 27 Paxos Street, Eureka Springs, AR 72632 (479) 363-6486 A,FB, I, J,W	Roadside Haven B&B 15638 U.S. 62, Eureka Springs, AR 72632 (479) 259-2644 F, FB, W
Elmwood House 1886 110 Spring Street, Eureka Springs, AR 727632 (479) 877-9674 A(S), FB, I, J, K, W	Rock Cottage Gardens B&B 10 Eugenia Street, Eureka Springs, AR 72632 (479) 253-8659 A, F, FB, I, J, PF(S), W
Enchanted Cottages 18 Nut Street, Eureka Springs, AR 72632 (479) 253-6790 J, FP	The Gilded Lily Bed and Breakfast 1 Kings Hwy, Eureka Springs, AR 72632 (479) 363-6470 F(S), FB, I, J(S)
Eureka Springs Hideaway 14 Angle Street, Eureka Springs, AR 72632 (479) 253-9582 A,FG, F, I, J, PF, W	TradeWinds Lodging and Bed and Breakfast 141 W Van Buren, Eureka Springs, AR 72632 (479) 363-6189 FB, I, J, PF

Evening Shade Inn B&B 3079 E Van Buren, Eureka Springs, AR 72632 (479) 253-6264 A, FB, F, I, J, W	

Cabins Amenities

Adults Only: A	*Lake/River: L/R*
Fireplace: F	*Pet Friendly: PF*
Internet: I	*Pool: P*
Jacuzzi/Hot Tub: J/HT	*Some: S*
Kitchen: K	*Weddings: W*

Eureka Springs Cabins

Arkansas White River Cabins 755 CR210, Eureka Springs, AR 72632 (479) 253-7117 A,K, L	Hidden Hollow Cabins 621 Hidden Hollow Road, Eureka , AR 72632 (479) 253-0323 J/HT, FP, I(S), K, PF(S), W
Beaver Lakefront Cabins 1234 CR 120, Eureka Springs, AR 72631 (888) 253-9210 A, J, F, I, K,L, W	Kettle Campground Cabins and RV Park 4119 E Van Buren, Eureka Springs, AR 72632 (479) 253-9100 I, P, W
Bear Mountain Log Cabins 15290 U.S. 62 West, Eureka Springs, AR 72632 (479) 253 6185 FP, J, K, PF, W	Lake Forest Luxury Log Cabins 351 Lake Forest Drive, Eureka Springs, AR 72631 (479) 363-9991 FP, I, K, J,W

Can-U-Canoe Riverview Cabins 161 CR 210, Eureka Springs, AR 72632 (479) 253-5966 FP, I, J/HT, K, PF, R,W	Lake Shore Cabins on Beaver Lake 2174 Mundell Road, Eureka Springs, AR 72631 (479) 253 7699 FP, I, J, K, L, W(S)
Cinnamon Valley 3134 E Van Buren, Eureka Springs, AR 72632 (479) 244-5942 A, FP, I, J, K, L, W	Livingston Junction Cabooses and Depot 1 Stonehaven Lane, Eureka Springs, AR 72631 (479) 253-7143 FP, J, PF, W
Domestic Tranquility Cabins 21031 U.S. 62,Eureka Springs, AR 72631 (479) 253-8223 FP, I, J,K, PF, W	Ozark Cabins and RV 423 CR 136, Eureka Springs, AR 72631 (479) 253-2018 FP(S), J(S), K(S), PF, W
Eagle's Nest Lodging 1058 CR 220, Eureka Springs, AR 72631 (479) 253-6180 FP, J/HT, K, PF, W	Pine Lodge 454 W Van Buren, Eureka Springs, AR 72632 (479) 253-8065 I, FP(S), J(S),K(S), PF(S), W
Eureka Springs Hideaway 14 Angle Street, Eureka Springs, AR 72632 (479) 253-9582 A,FB, I, J, W	Roadrunner Inn/Beaver Lake Log Cabins 3034 Mundell Road, Eureka Springs, AR 72631 (479) 253-8166 FP, I, J, K, L/R, W
Eureka Sunset Lodge and Cabins 10 Dogwood Ridge, Eureka Springs, AR 72632 (479) 253-9565 A(S), F, I, J, K,PF, W	Wisteria Lane Log Cabins 1093 CR 226, Eureka Springs, AR 72631 (479) 253-7544 J,FP, K, PF(S), W

Cottage and Treehouse Amenities

Adults Only: A	Lake/River: L/R

Fireplace: F	Pet Friendly: PF
Internet: I	Pool: P
Jacuzzi/Hot Tub	Some: S
Kitchen: K	Weddings: W

Eureka Springs Cottages and Treehouses

Beaver Dam Cottages and RV Park 8172 Arkansas 187, Eureka Springs, AR 72631 (479) 253-6196 F(S), K, PF, W	Rock Haus Lodge 85 CR 1190, Eureka Springs, AR 72632 (479) 244-5440 FP, I, J, K, W
Beaver Lake Cottages 2865 Mundell Road, Eureka Springs, AR 72632 (479) 253-8439 A(S), FP, I, K, L, PF(S), W	Rose of Sharon Cottage 11 Cliff Street, Eureka Springs, AR 72632 (479) 253-7851 FP, I, K PF
Crescent Cottages Lookout Manor Cottages 75 Prospect Ave, Eureka Springs, AR 72632 (479) 253-9766 FP, I,J,K, PF, W	Starry Night Cottage 180 Spring Street, Eureka Springs, AR 72632 (479) 253-8918 K, W
Daffodil Cottage 158 Spring Street, Eureka Springs, AR 72632 (479) 253-2001 FP(S), I, J, K(S), W	Tall Pines Inn 3 Pivot Rock Road, Eureka Springs, AR 72632 (479) 253-8096 F, I, J(S), P
Dogwood Cottages 3012 E Van Buren, Eureka Springs, AR 72632 (479) 253-5549 I, J, W	The Grand Tree House Resort 350 W Van Buren, Eureka Springs, AR 72632 (479) 253-8733 A, FP, I, J, W

Eureka Springs Tree Houses, Caves, Castles and Hobbits 526 W Van Buren, Eureka Springs, AR 72632 (479) 253-9493 A, FP, I,J, K, W	Tree House Cottages 165 W Van Buren, Eureka Springs, AR 72632 (479) 253-8667 A(S), FP, I, J, K, W
Heartstone Inn and Cottages 35 Kings Hwy, Eureka Springs, AR 72632 (479) 253-8916 FP(S), I, J, K(S), W	Turpentine Creek Wildlife Refuge Lodging 239 Turpentine Creek Lane, Eureka Springs, AR 72632 (479) 253-5841 A(S), FP(S), J/HT(S), K(S)
Historic Cottages of Lake Lucerne 48 CR 317, Eureka Springs, AR 72632 (479) 253-5376 FP, I(S), K(S), PF(S), W	Winterwood Lakeside Cottage Beaver Lake, Eureka Springs, AR 72632 (479) 253-2530 FP, I, J(S), K,
Oak Crest Cottages and Tree Houses 526 W Van Buren, Eureka Springs, AR 72632 (479) 253-9493 A,FP, I, J, K, W	

Resort Amenities

Adults Only: A	*Lake/River: L/R*
Fireplace: F	*Pet Friendly: PF*
Internet: I	*Pool: P*
Jacuzzi/Hot Tub: J/HT	*Some: S*
Kitchen: K	*Weddings: W*

Eureka Springs Resorts

Cabin Fever Resort 15695 Hwy 187, Eureka Springs, AR 72631 (479) 253-5635 FP, J, K, PF(S), R	Riverview Resort 17939 U.S. 62, Eureka Springs, AR 72632 (479) 253-8367 FP(S), J(S), K, R, W
Cherokee Mountain Log Cabin Resort 5307 U.S. 62, Eureka Springs, AR 72632 (479) 253-5353 FP, J, K, PF	Serenity Hilltop Retreat 5855 U.S. 62, Eureka Springs, AR 72632 (479) 363-6017 I, K
Dinner Bell Ranch and Resort 4462 CR 302, Eureka Springs, AR 72632 (479) 253-2900 FP,I, J, K, PF, W	Silver Ridge Resort 132 Silver Ridge Road, Eureka Springs, AR 72632 (479) 253-8719 FP, J, K, PF(S), W
Enchanted Forest Resort 1840 Arkansas 23, Eureka Springs, AR 72631 (800) 293-9586 FP, J/HT, I, K, PF(S), W	Spider Creek Resort 8179 Arkansas 187, Eureka Springs, AR 72631 (479) 253-9241 FP, I, J, K, L/R
Lazee Daze Log Cabin Resort 5432 Arkansas 23, Eureka Springs, AR 72632 (479) 253-7026 FP, I, J/HT, K, PF(S), W	Stone Meadow Resort 57 CR 242, Eureka Springs, AR 72631 (479) 253-6118 CB, HT, K, PF
Pond Mountain Lodge and Resort 1218 Arkansas 23, Eureka Springs, AR 72632 (800) 583-8043 A(S), FP, I, J, K(S), PF(S), P, W(S)	Sugar Ridge Resort 1216 Dam Site Road, Eureka Springs, AR 72631 (479) 253-554 FP, J, K, L, PF(S), W

Red Bud Valley Resort	The Retreat at Sky Ridge
369 CR340, Eureka Springs, AR 72632	637 CR 111, Eureka Springs, AR
(479) 253-9028	726321
A(S), FP, I, J, K, L, W	(479) 253-9465
	FP, I, J(SP, K, PF, W

RV Amenities

Tents: T	Pool/Lake/River: P/L/R
Electricity: E	Sewer: S
Water: W	Laundry: LA
Showers: SH	Open Year Round: O

Eureka Springs RV Parks

Eureka Springs KOA	Town of Beaver RV Park
15020 Arkansas 187, Eureka Springs, AR 72631	122 Parkway, Eureka Springs, AR 72632
(479) 253-8036	(479) 253-5469
T, E, W, P, SH, LA, S	T, E, W, L/R, S
Kettle Campgrounds Cabins and RV Park	Turpentine Creek RV Park
4119 E Van Buren, Eureka Springs, AR 72632	239 Turpentine Creek Lane,Eureka Springs, AR 72632
(479) 253-9100	(479) 253-5841
T, E, W, SH, P, S, LA, O	T, E, W, SH, S, O
Ozark Cabins and RV	Wanderlust RV Park
423 CR 136, Eureka Springs, AR 72631	468 Passion Play Road, Eureka Springs, AR 72632
(479) 253-2018	(479) 253-7385
T, E, W, SH, S, O	T, E, W, SH,LA,S, O

Eureka Springs Vacation Rentals

Vacation Rentals 2 Holiday Island Drive, Holiday Island, AR 72631 (479) 253-7700	The Island Motel and Resort #5 Woodsdale Drive, Holiday Island, AR 72631 (800) 874-1331
Island Rentals 35 WoodsdaleDrive, Holiday Island, AR 72631 (479) 253-7340	

THINGS TO DO AND SEE

The things to do in Eureka Springs, Arkansas are almost limitless. There are activities for every age group and there is something to suit everyone's idea of a memorable vacation. Whatever your pleasure, you will find it in Eureka Springs.

Picture yourself shopping in an alpine village of yesteryear. Tourists and local area residents alike flock to Eureka Springs to solicit the many unique and charming shops along the quaint downtown streets. From candy factories to a stringed-instrument shop to a delightful boutique devoted strictly to romance, it's a sure bet that you will find that special something you are looking for in one of Eureka Springs's unusual shops.

In Eureka Springs, you can wander in and out of shops and galleries, relax in a contemporary day spa, or indulge your sense of outdoor adventure as you horseback ride or fly through the air on an Ozark Mountain zip-line. If you are really daring, spend the night at the Turpentine Creek Wildlife Refuge and sleep with a tiger prowling just below your cabin.

Have the perfect wedding in the South's official "Wedding Capital," and end your special day with a romantic dinner at one of the restaurants featuring the recipes of awarding-winning chefs.

Visit the Christ of the Ozarks for FREE or take your family to see *The Great Passion Play*, America's #1 Outdoor Drama. Pine Mountain Theater is another wonderful family show, and the Thorncrown Chapel is a must-see.

Eureka Springs hosts a good number and variety of events every year. If you're a music lover, there are annual weekend celebrations for jazz, blues, classical and folk music, and in the summer, full operatic productions with orchestra are presented.

Additionally, there is a popular poetry festival held each year and there is, of course, a local theatre, the Eureka Springs City Auditorium, with numerous productions. Theatre is held downtown at the 1929 large stone auditorium, which was inaugurated with a concert by John Phillip Sousa.

Annual events include four annual *Diversity Weekends* for gays and lesbians, a UFO conference and several different auto shows including one each for

Corvettes, Mustangs and Volkswagens.

In May of each year, the city plays host to the May Fine Arts Festival. The celebration, which defines Eureka's creativity in the Arts, begins with what is called an Artrageous Parade. Additional events during the month-long festival include a Gallery Stroll where strollers tour the galleries and meet the artists. A PT Cruiser show is on the second Saturday.

Art in all its forms are celebrated in Eureka. It has been recognized as an art colony since the 1930s. There are more than 400 working artists and other creative people living in the area. Other top art destinations have nothing on Eureka. This alpine-like city in the Ozark Mountains of Arkansas consistently ranks as one of the top 25 art destinations ahead of Taos, NM, Laguna Beach and Carmel, CA.

Art
Galleries and Studios
83 Spring Street Gallery
83 Spring Street, Eureka Springs, AR 72632
(479) 253-8310

The main Studio Gallery for sculptor Mark Hopkins, 83 Spring Street Gallery has an impressive collection of his artwork including retired and sold-out pieces. The gallery also features Doug Hall, John Bundy, Don Goin, Kate Barger, Betsy Stafford, Allison Cantrell and other local artists.

Art Colony on North Main Street
185 N Main Street at Mill Hollow Road, Eureka Springs, AR 72632

Eureka Thyme
19 Spring Street, Eureka Springs, AR 72632
(479) 363-9600

Eureka Fine Art Gallery
2 Pine Street, Suite Y, Eureka Springs, AR 72632
(479) 363-6000

Eureka Springs School of the Arts
15751 U.S. 62 West, Eureka Springs, AR 72632
(479) 253-5384

Let noted and award-winning artists and crafts professionals guide you to learn new skills and art forms. Emerging professional artists can take advantage of regular workshops as they are offered throughout the year.

Fantasy and Stone
81 Spring Street, Eureka Springs, AR 72632
(479) 253-5891

Fire Om Earth Retreat Center
8872 Mill Hollow Road, Eureka Springs, AR 72632
(479) 363-9402
Tai chi, belly dance and yoga are offered in ongoing classes. Additionally, there are creative workshops, private and group retreats, and house concerts.

Fusion Squared
84 Spring Street, Eureka Springs, AR 72632
(479) 253-4999

JA Nelson Gallery
37 Spring Street, Eureka Springs, AR 72632
(479) 253-4314

Iris at Basin Park
8 Spring Street, Eureka Springs, AR 72632
(479) 253-9494

Keels Creek Winery and Art Gallery
3185 E Van Buren, Eureka Springs, AR 72632
(479) 253-9463

Mitchell's Folly Antiques and Fine Arts
130 Spring Street, Eureka Springs, AR 72632
(479) 253-7030

Paradise Pottery
320 CR 210, Eureka Springs, AR 72632
(479) 253-1547

Sweet Spring Studio
123 Spring Street, Eureka Springs, AR 72632
(479) 253-6652

Serendipity at the Crescent
75 Prospect Ave, Eureka Springs, AR 72635
(479) 253-2769

Studio 62
335 W Van Buren, Eureka Springs, AR 72632
(479) 363-9209

Quicksilver
73 Spring Street, Eureka Springs, AR 72632
(479) 253-7679
Two shopping levels feature the art of 120 artists. Many are local, but there are also works by regional and nationally known artists. You'll find wall tapestries, wildlife watercolors, photographs, jewelry, pottery and limited edition prints on display.

Zarks
67 Spring Street, Eureka Springs, AR 72632
(479) 253-2626

Performing Arts
Opera in the Ozarks at Inspiration Point
Opera in the Ozarks
16311 U.S. 62 West, Eureka Springs, AR 72632
(479) 253-8595

Following a month of study and practice by university students and graduates in Instrumental Music and related arts, three opera performances are put on each summer. Visit their website for the season schedule and tickets.

The New Great Passion Play
935 Passion Play Road, Eureka Springs, AR 72632
(479) 253-9200
Witness the greatest story ever told in America's #1 Attended Outdoor Drama theatre. The play is held in an outdoor amphitheater and has live animals and hundreds of cast members. Visitors come from all over the world to witness this one-of-a-kind outdoor drama.

Eureka Springs City Historic Auditorium
36 S Main Street, Eureka Springs, AR 72632
(479) 253-7788

Intrigue Theater
80 Mountain Street, Eureka Springs, AR 72632
(855) 446-8744

Ozark Mountain Hoe-Down
3140 E Van Buren, Eureka Springs, AR 72632
(800) 468-2113

Pine Mountain Theatre
2075 E Van Buren, Eureka Springs, AR 72632
(479) 253-9156

Museums

Eureka Springs Historical Museum
95 S Main Street, Eureka Springs, AR 72632
(479) 253-9417

Sacred Arts Museum
935 Passion Play Road, Eureka Springs, AR 72632
(800) 882-7529

Outdoors
Blue Spring Heritage Center
1537 CR 210, Eureka Springs, AR 72632
(479) 253-9244
The National Register of Historic Places includes this historic bluff shelter
and gardens that demonstrate crops, plants, flowers and healing herbs of the
Ozarks. The beautiful Blue Spring pours 38 million gallons of cold, clear water
each day into its trout-filled lagoon.

Ozark Mountain Ziplines
208 W Van Buren, Eureka Springs, AR 72632
(479) 363-6699

Pig Tail Kart N Golf
3173 E Van Buren, Eureka Springs, AR 72632
(479) 363-6642

Caves
Onyx Cave Park
338 Onyx Cave Lane, Eureka Springs, AR 72632
(479) 253-9321

Cosmic Cavern
6386 Hwy 21 North, Berryville, AR 72616
(870) 749-2298
Tour through one of the Ozarks' most beautiful caves and view two underground lakes billed as bottomless, one with trout, some of which are blind and colorless from being in the dark some 50 years.

Hiking
Lake Leatherwood City Park
1303 CR 204, Eureka Springs, AR 72632
(479) 253-7921
Open March through mid-November, Lake Leatherwood City Park offers visitors 1,600 acres of beautiful Ozark Mountain countryside, an 85-acre spring-fed lake, hiking, picnicking, walking trails, mountain bike trails, camping, fishing, cabins and a small marina for boating, canoes and paddleboats, which adds up to fun for the entire family!

Pivot Rock and Natural Bridge Rock Formations
1708 Pivot Rock Road, Eureka Springs, AR 72632
(479) 253-8860
This tranquil wooded park offers winding hiking paths through unique rock formations and the beautiful natural mountain scenery of the Ozarks.

Horseback Riding
Bear Mountain Riding Stables
15480 U.S. 62 West, Eureka Springs, AR 72632
(479) 253-6990

Hidden Valley Trail Rides
777 Hidden Valley Ranch Road, Eureka Springs, AR 72632
(479) 253-9777

Dinner Bell Ranch and Resort
4462 CR 302, Eureka Springs, AR 72632
(479) 253-2900

Lakes
Beaver Lake
A popular fishing and boating destination, Beaver Lake is 28,000 acres of beautiful, clear water. Beaver Lake allows swimming, water skiing, sailing, wind surfing, snorkeling, canoeing, house boating and party barge cruising. The Belle of the Ozarks offers sightseeing cruises along the scenic Beaver Lake shoreline.

Belle of the Ozarks
4024 Mundell Rd, Eureka Springs, AR 72631
(479) 253-6200

Beaver Lake Cruise

Table Rock Lake
North of Eureka Springs, Table Rock Lake covers 52,300 acres and offers over 800 miles of shoreline. The water is clean and clear and Table Rock is one of the top bass fishing lakes in the world. There is also plenty of walleye, crappie and catfish. Every water sport you can think of, including skiing, jet skis, swimming, paddleboats and scuba diving are available. Lakefront resorts and cabins are throughout the area.

Starkey Marina
4022 Mundell Road, Eureka Springs, AR 72631
(479) 253-8194

Fishing Guides
Big 1's Striper Fishing
402 N 9th Street, Rogers, AR 72756
(479) 633-0662

Mountain Biking
Lake Leatherwood City Park
1303 CR 204, Eureka Springs, AR 72632
(479) 253-7921
Lake Leatherwood offers many options for outdoor enthusiasts, but it is famous for its legendary and epic mountain trails. Mountain bikers and spectators from all over come to enjoy sporting events like the Fat Tire Festival and The Eurekan Multi-Sports Festival.

Rivers
Kings River
Kings River is wildly popular with canoe enthusiasts because along the rocky banks and bluffs, you are afforded a beautiful display of wild azaleas, ferns, umbrella magnolias and other plants. Oftentimes, visitors can also view a great many signs of wildlife.

Kings River - Riverside Canoe Service
3031 U.S.62 West, Berryville, AR 72616
(870) 423-3116

A float trip for everyone! Half day, full day or weekend float trips covering the entire Kings River are available. Riverside Canoe Service offers canoe rentals, shuttle service, guide service and canoe sales. You will find one of their float trips perfectly designed for you.

Kings River Outfitters
PO Box 483, Eureka Springs, AR 72632
(479) 253-8954

Fishing Guides
Kings River Adventure Fishing Guide
190 CR539, Eureka Springs, AR 72632
(870) 350-3690

White River
The White River tailwaters below Beaver Dam are great for canoeing and fly-fishing. These tailwaters are absolutely filled with rainbow and brown trout.

White River - Beaver Dam Store
8421 Arkansas 187, Eureka Springs, AR 72631
(479) 253-6154
The Beaver Dam Store is a popular and convenient shopping place covering all of your river adventure needs. Bait and tackle, lake maps, fishing instructions, information on fishing guides, fly tying and fly fishing instructions, canoe rentals and rafting on the White River are all available at the Beaver Dam Store.

Fishing Guides
Ryan's White River Guide Service
PO Box 141, Eureka Springs, AR 72632
(479) 244-6416

Custom Adventures Guide Service
1216 CR 113, Eureka Springs, AR 72631
(479) 363-9632

Shopping
Antique Shops
Castle Antiques at Inspiration Point
16498 U.S. 62, Eureka Springs, AR 72632
(479) 253-6150

Country Antiques
243 Stadium Road, Eureka Springs, AR 72632
(479) 253-8731

Crystal Gardens Antiques
190 Spring Street, Eureka Springs, AR 72632
(479) 253-9586

Curio Gallery
11 Ridgeway Ave,Eureka Springs, AR 72632
(479) 253-8742

Fleece 'n Flax
51 Spring Street, Eureka Springs, AR 72632

Gingerbread Antiques
185 E Van Buren, Eureka Springs, AR 72632
(479) 253-4284

Kathryn's
9 N Main Street, Eureka Springs, AR 72632
(479) 253-2767

Mike Cooper's Antiques and Collectibles
185 E Van Buren, Eureka Springs, AR 72632
(479) 253-4284

Silver Lining
184 N Main Street, Eureka Springs, AR 72632
(479) 363-4020

Sweet Springs Antiques
2 Pine Street, Eureka Springs, AR 72632
(479) 253-6644

The Old Sale Barn
65 Stadium Road, Eureka Springs, AR 72632
(479) 253-5388

Wonderland Antiques
6981 U.S. 62West, Eureka Springs, AR 72632
(479) 253-6900

Boutiques
Caroline's Collectibles ~ Eureka Springs working bunnies!
2045 E Van Buren, Eureka Springs, AR 72632
(479) 253-5537

Cottage Caboodle
11 N Main Street, Eureka Springs, AR 72632
(479) 363-6163

Lady Eureka Boutique
304 Village Circle, Eureka Springs, AR 72632
(479) 253-4000

Specialty Shops
Adventure Mountain Outfitters
151 Spring Street, Eureka Springs, AR 72632
(479) 253-0900

Bath Junkie
8 Spring Street, Eureka Springs, AR 72632
(479) 253-9696
Two hundred fragrances let you customize bath products including lotions, salts, scrubs, soaps and spa supplies.

Eureka Market - Organic Foods
121 E Van Buren Ste B, Eureka Springs, AR 72632
(479) 253-8136

Fain's Herbacy
61 N Main Street,Eureka Springs, AR 72632
(479) 253-5687
Fain's Herbacy is where the locals go to do their shopping for herbs and vitamins. The specialty shop was founded by Jim Fain, PhD with the ultimate goal of providing scientifically supported supplements to the community at the lowest prices.

Fresh Harvest
2075 E Van Buren, Eureka Springs, AR 72632
(479) 253-6247
Fresh Harvest offers shoppers premium extra virgin olive oils, spices, coffees, sauces and pasta, gift packs.

Kaleidokites
1C Spring Street, Eureka Springs, AR 72632
(479) 253-6596
Billing itself as a small store that offers a LARGE selection of kaleidoscopes and kites, Kaleidokites is a store that the kids will love and the parents will enjoy. It is one of the most unusual and adorable shopping experiences in all of NWA.

Kerusso Christian Outlet
105 Passion Play Road, Eureka Springs, AR 72632
(479) 253-2603

Magee Jewelry
80 Spring Street, Eureka Springs, AR 72632
(479) 253-9787

Pig Trail Harley-Davidson
2047 E Van Buren, Eureka Springs, AR 72632
(479) 363-6224

Razorback Gift Shop
579 W Van Buren, Eureka Springs, AR 72632
(479) 253-8294

Practical Magic Art Supply
34 N Main Street, Eureka Springs, AR 72632
(479) 363-6703

Regalia Handmade Clothing
16 White Street, Eureka Springs, AR, 72632
(479) 253-2202

The Amish Collection
3022 E Van Buren, Eureka Springs, AR 72632
(479) 253-2424

The Jewel Box
40 Spring Street, Eureka Springs, AR 72632
(479) 253-7828

Treasures from the Pacific
435 W Van Buren, Eureka Springs, AR 72632
(479) 981-0233

Two Dumb Dames Fudge Factory
33 S Main Street, Eureka Springs, AR 72632
(479) 253-7268
They make the fudge right on the premises and it really is the best fudge you can buy anywhere. They also have a full line of "Made in America" toys, games, wind chimes and t-shirts. Gift baskets are available for birthdays, weddings, anniversaries and any old day you can think of, and they'll ship their fudge to the lucky recipient!

Tummy Ticklers
51 1/2 S Main Street, Eureka Springs, AR 72632
(479) 253-6120
Located off the sidewalk, across from the courthouse, enter only if you love to eat! Tummy Ticklers Kitchen Store is a wonderful popular little kitchen store filled with unique and useful kitchen gadgets, utensils, fresh coffee beans, jams, Rada Cutlery and loose teas. If you enjoy shopping different kitchen stores, you'll love this tiny little store.

Velvet Otter
16514 U.S. 62, Eureka Springs, AR 72632
(479) 253-5155
Village Gifts
514 Village Circle, Eureka Springs, AR 72632
(479) 253-7047

Vintage Cargo
41 Kings Highway, Eureka Springs, AR 72632
(479) 253-5943

Spas
Carol Brown Massage Therapy
210 Stadium Road, Eureka Springs, AR 72632
(479) 253-5644

Eureka! Massage Therapy and Wellness Therapies
147 W Van Buren Street, Eureka Springs, AR 72632
(479) 253-9208

Flora Roja Community Acupuncture
119 Wall Street, Eureka Springs, AR 72632
(479) 253-4968

Grand Central Hotel and Spa
37 N Main Street, Eureka Springs, AR 72632
(479) 253-6756

Healthworks Massage Reflexology
75 Mountain Street, Eureka Springs, AR 72632
(479) 253-7977

Imago Massage
361 Beatrice Drive, Eureka Springs, AR 72632
(479) 244-5631

Laughing Hands Massage
121 E Van Buren, Eureka Springs, AR 72632
(479) 253-4909

New Moon Spa and Salon
75 Prospect Ave, Eureka Springs, AR 72632
(479) 253-2879

Palace Bath House
135 Spring Street, Eureka Springs, AR 72632
(479) 253-7474
For those who want to be pampered in unique accommodations, pay a visit to the Palace Hotel and Bath House. Originally built in 1901, it has been completely restored giving close attention to the original detail. It is listed on the National Historic Register and is really worth visiting.
All suites have the following: TV, wet bar, double size water-jet spa and a king size bed. A delicious continental breakfast is served every morning to each suite.

Ruby's Spa
3010 E Van Buren, Eureka Springs, AR 72632
(479) 253-5040
Serenity Spa
12 Spring Street, Eureka Springs, AR 72632
(479) 253-2796

Things to Do

Beaver Bridge
Hwy 187, Beaver, AR 72632
Bring your camera and snap away while you visit this famous one-lane bridge. It is called the Little Golden Gate and is well worth the ride from town. On the north side of the river, there is a short hiking trail.

Bible Museum
935 Passion Play Road, Eureka Springs, AR 72632
(800) 882-7529

Black Jack Adventure
404 Village Circle, Eureka Springs, AR 72632
(479) 253-6999

Castle Rogues Manor
Hwy 187, Beaver, AR 72631
(479) 253-4911

Christ of The Ozarks Statue
The New Great Passion Play
935 Passion Play Road, Eureka Springs, AR 72632
(479) 253-9200
Located on the grounds of the New Great Passion Play and free to view is the seven-story high Christ of the Ozarks statue. It was completed in 1966 and was sculpted by Emmet Sullivan, one of the artisans who sculpted Mount Rushmore. The statue's massive arm spread from fingertip to fingertip is 65 feet.

Cosmic Cavern "Silent Splendor"
6386 Hwy 21 North, Berryville, AR 72616
(870) 749-2298
Silent Splendor features one of the longest soda straw formations in the Ozarks and is one of Arkansas' most incredible underground jewels. Go gemstone panning and keep what you find. It's a terrific learning adventure for everyone in the family and it's open every day.

Culinary School - Cuisine Karen
PO Box 401, Eureka Springs, AR 72632
(479) 253-7461
Friday is demonstration and Saturday is hands-on at the Culinary School - Cuisine Karen. Take advantage of this French-style cooking class from 10 a.m. to 2 p.m.

Dinner Bell Ranch and Resort
4462 CR 302, Eureka Springs, AR 72632
(479) 253-2900

Eureka Springs and North Arkansas Railway
299 N Main Street, Eureka Springs, AR 72632
(479) 253-9623
Relive the locomotive transportation history of days-gone-by enjoying either the Excursion Train or the 1920s Eurekan Dining Car. Let clickety-clack take you back while you enjoy its sumptuous cuisine.

Fresh Harvest Tasting Room
2075 E Van Buren, Eureka Springs, AR 72632
(479) 253-6247
Premium extra virgin olive oils, spices, coffees, sauces, pasta and gift packs are available in this wonderful tasting room.

Judge Roy Bean's Old Time Photo and Weddings
29 S Main Street, Eureka Springs AR 72632
(479) 253-5848

Olden Days Carriage Services
Main Carriage Depot
156 N Main Street, Eureka Springs, AR 72632
(479) 981-1737
Experience historical romantic carriage rides throughout Eureka Springs from Olden Days Carriage Service. Carriage rides are great for weddings, and kids are always welcome.

The Palace Hotel and Bath House
135 Spring Street, Eureka Springs, AR 72632

(479) 253-8400

If you love to be pampered in unique accommodations, pay a visit to The Palace Hotel and Bath House. Originally built in 1901, it has been completely restored giving close attention to the original detail. It is listed on the National Historic Register and is really worth visiting.

All suites have the following: TV, wet bar, double size water-jet spa and a king size bed. A delicious continental breakfast is served every morning to each suite.

The only Victorian-era bathhouse that is still in operation is within the Hotel. The bathhouse offers visitors the opportunity to pamper themselves in the calming bliss of a whirlpool bath and massage therapy. Guests can soak in original claw foot tubs, or they can take themselves back in time to the turn of the century and indulge themselves with a eucalyptus steam treatment in the very same wooden barrels as travelers of yesteryear used to do.

Staff massage therapists are available for massage treatments. They use the Swedish technique, which emphasizes athletic massage. Typically, guests choose The Works, which consists of a whirlpool mineral bath, a revitalizing clay masque, a eucalyptus steam and a massage to top it off.

Thorncrown Chapel
12968 U.S. 62 West, Eureka Springs, AR 72632
(479) 253-7401
Thorncrown Chapel is available for visitation, retreats and weddings daily! Designed by renowned architect E. Fay Jones, Thorncrown Chapel is a stunning 6,000 square foot, 48-foot tall glass structure with 425 windows. Hidden deep within a wooded setting, the wood and glass creation has been described as the most beautiful chapel in the world.
Open for Sunday worship:
April to October, 9 a.m. and 11 a.m. in the Worship Center
June to October, 7:30 a.m. in the Chapel
November to December, 11:00 a.m. in the Chapel
Admission is FREE, but donations are gratefully accepted.

Turpentine Creek Wildlife Refuge
239 Turpentine Creek Lane, Eureka Springs, AR 72632
(479) 253-5841
For a wonderful experience for the entire family, visit this shelter for large cats such as lions, tigers and many other varieties. The shelter rescues these distressed animals from anywhere in the United States.

Writers Colony at Dairy Hollow
515 Spring Street, Eureka Springs, AR 72632
(479)253-7444
The Writers Colony at Dairy Hollow offers a unique residency program for writers, artists, composers, architects and chefs in the historic arts village of Eureka Springs.

Special Events/Festivals
2nd Saturday Gallery Stroll
From April to December on the second of every month and every Saturday in May, the galleries in Eureka Springs open their doors from 6 p.m. to 9 p.m. with special shows and artist receptions.

CICA International Summer Music Festival
The CICA International Summer Music Festival is a three-week celebration of classical music from June 18 to July 7, 2014.

Diversity Weekend
Celebrate diversity with the festive GLBT Pride and Cultural celebrations. April 4 through 6, August 1 through 3, and October 31 to November 2 are the weekends the celebrations will fall on in 2014.

Eureka Springs Blues Weekend
If you love the blues, you'll love the Eureka Springs Blues Weekend! This year, blues lovers will enjoy a weekend filled with great blues music from June 12 through June 15.

Eureka Springs Corvette Weekend
The first weekend of October, Corvette enthusiasts across the Midwest and beyond gather to enjoy the beautiful autumn scenery and weather, the unique charm of the Eureka Springs area, and just relax and have fun with hundreds of fellow Corvette fans.

May Festival of Arts
The May Festival of the Arts is Eureka Springs' month-long festival of, naturally the ARTS. It also naturally takes place in May!

Original Ozark Folk Festival
The Original Ozark Folk Festival is the longest continuously running annual folk festival in America. This year, enjoy folk music as you've never heard before from Oct. 7 to Oct. 11.

Tours
Crescent Hotel Ghost Tours
75 Prospect Ave, Eureka Springs AR 72632
(855) 725-5720
If you like ghost stories, then you simply must take the Crescent Hotel Ghost Tour. Many believe that the Crescent Hotel is the most haunted hotel in America. Take the Ghost Tour and see for yourself... if you dare!

Eureka Springs Downtown Network
Historic District Walking Tours
Eureka Springs Downtown
(877) 643-4972

Eureka Van Tours
2075 E Van Buren, Eureka Springs, AR 72632
(479) 253-8737

Joe Gunnels Tours
Historic District Tram Tours
5 Deer Run Lane, Eureka Springs, AR 72631
(479) 253-6852

Quigley's Castle
274 Quigley Castle Road, Eureka Springs, AR 72632
(479) 253-8311

Wedding
I Do Bridal Wear
132 Huntsville Road, Eureka Springs, AR 72632
(479) 244-5084

The Whispering Firefly
506 Village Circle, Eureka Springs, AR 72632
(832) 748-1484

Eureka Springs Wedding Guild
Various Locations, Eureka Springs, AR 72632

Wineries
Railway Winery and Vineyards
4937 Hwy 187, Eureka Springs, AR 72631
479-244-7798

Keels Creek Winery and Art Gallery
3185 E Van Buren, Eureka Springs, AR 72632
(479) 253-9463

RESTAURANTS

Eureka Springs has more fine restaurants per capita than any other city in NWA. Most are independently owned and operated and are known to cook from scratch.

Tourists drive to Eureka Springs from miles away just for the opportunity to eat one more time at the Local Flavor Café. The Stone House, Simply Scrumptious Tea Room and Emporium, Thai House Restaurant, Gaskins Cabin Steak house, Café Amore and Ermilio's Italian Home Cooking are all other very popular and unique Eureka Springs restaurants that also enjoy rave reviews.

Most boast fresh ingredients, friendly atmosphere and food to die for. What more could you ask for? Chefs from around the world looking to create wonderful recipes and live in an open, accepting lifestyle come to Eureka Springs to design award-winning culinary masterpieces.

Good food calls for good wine, and Eureka Spring's own Keels Creek Winery provides choice wine made from grapes grown in and around Eureka Springs.

Do yourself a favor; put one of Eureka's unusual dining establishments on your vacation itinerary. Your palate will be glad you did.

Restaurant Prices

$ - Budget	*$$$ - Upscale*
$$ - Mid-Range	

American

Anglers Grill	Pancake's Family Restaurant
14581 U.S. 62, Eureka Springs, AR 72632	2055 E Van Buren, Eureka Springs, AR 72632
(479) 253-4004	(479) 253-6015
$$	$$

Catfish Cabin 3085 E Van Buren, Eureka Springs, AR 72632 (479) 253-7933 $$	Rowdy Beaver Eureka Springs, AR 417 W Van Buren, Eureka Springs, AR 72632 (479) 253-8544 $$
Forest Hill Restaurant 3016 E Van Buren, Eureka Springs, AR 72632 (479) 253-2422 $	Simply Scrumptious Tea Room & Emporium 185 E Van Buren, Eureka Springs, AR 72632 (479) 253-2300 $
Garden Bistro 119 N Main Street, Eureka Springs, AR 72632 (479) 253-1281 $$	Smiling Brook Cafe 57 N Main Street, Eureka Springs, AR 72632 (479) 981-3582 $
Grandma's Beans and Cornbread 200 Village Circle Pine Mtn Village, Eureka Springs, AR 72632 (479) 253-6561 $$	Squid and Whale Pub and Grill 37 Spring Street, 10 Center Street, Eureka Springs, AR 72632 (479) 253-7147 $
Local Flavor Cafe 71 S Main Street, Eureka Springs, AR 72632 (479) 253-9522 $$	The Back Porch Restaurant 5 Woodsdale Drive, Holiday Island, AR 72631 (479) 253-8981 $$
Myrtie Mae's 207 W Van Buren, Eureka Springs, AR 72632 (479) 253-9768 $$	The Balcony Restaurant in the 1905 Basin Park Hotel 12 Spring Street, Eureka Springs, AR 72632 (479) 253-7837 $$
Mud Street 22 S Main Street, Eureka Springs, AR 72632 (479) 253-6732 $$	The Eureka Grill 71 Spring Street, Eureka Springs, AR 72632 (479) 253-6587 $

The New Delhi Cafe & Patio 2 N Main Street, Eureka Springs, AR 72632 (479) 253-2525 $$	Route 62 Diner 3029 E Van Buren, Eureka Springs, AR 72632 (479) 253-8776 $
Oscar's Cafe 17 White Street, Eureka Springs, AR 72632 (479) 981-1436 $	

Asian

Lucky Dragon Café 301 Eureka Ave, Berryville, AR 72616 (870) 423-6686 $$	Thai House 2059 E Van Buren, Eureka Springs, AR 72632 (479) 363-6632 $$
Nd's Pagoda Box 147 E Van Buren, Eureka Springs AR 72732 $$	

Bakeries

Cravings By Rochelle 2043 E Van Buren, Eureka Springs, AR 72632 (479) 363-6576	TLC Bakery 137 E Van Buren, Eureka Springs, AR 72632 (479) 253-2000
Eureka Sweets 53 Alamo Street, Eureka Springs, AR 72632 (479) 363-8129	

Bars/Music/Pubs

Chelsea's Corner Cafe 10 Mountain Street, Eureka Springs, AR 72632 (479) 253-6723	Island Grill & Sports Bar Forest Park Drive, Holiday Island, AR 72631 (479) 363-6140
Eureka Live Underground 35 1/2 N Main Street, Eureka Springs, AR 72632 (479) 253-7020	Henri's Just One More 19 Spring Street, Eureka Springs, AR 72632 (479) 253-5795
Eureka Springs Ale House and Distillery 426 W Van Buren, Eureka Springs, AR 72631 (479) 244-0304	The Blarney Stone Irish Pub 85 S Main Street, Eureka Springs, AR 72632 (479) 363-6633
Eureka Stonehouse 89 S Main Street, Eureka Springs, AR 72632 (479) 363-6411	Voulez-Vous Lounge 63 Spring Street, Eureka Springs, AR 72632 (479) 363-6595

Burgers

Pied Piper Pub/Cathouse Lounge 82 Armstrong Street, Eureka Springs, AR 72632 (479) 363-9976 $$	Sparky's Roadhouse Cafe 147 E Van Buren, Eureka Springs, AR 72632 (479) 253-6001 $

BBQ

Bubba's Barbecue 166 W Van Buren, Eureka Springs, AR 72632 (479) 253-7706 $$	The Rockin' Pig Saloon 2039 E Van Buren, Eureka Springs, AR 72632 (479) 363-6248 $$

Candies/Fudge

Martin Greer's Candies 22151 U.S. 62, Garfield, AR 72733 (479) 656-1440	Sweet's Fudge Kitchen 36 Spring Street, Eureka Springs, AR 72632 (479) 253-5810
Rocky Mountain Chocolate 5 Spring Street, Eureka Springs, AR 72632 (479) 253-6597	Two Dumb Dames 33 S Main Street, Eureka Springs, AR 72632 (479) 253-7268

Coffee

Eureka Daily Roast 27 Spring Street, Eureka Springs, AR 72632 (479) 253-2229 $	Nibbles Eatery 79 Spring Street, Eureka Springs, AR 72632 (479) 253-7722 $

Fast Food

Blimpie 102 Passion Play Road, Eureka Springs, AR 72632 (479) 253-6558 $	Sonic 411 W Trimble Ave, Berryville, AR 72616 (870) 423-3717 $
KFC- Kentucky Fried Chicken 918 W Trimble Ave, Berryville, AR 72616 (870) 423-2640 $	Subway 124 E Van Buren, Eureka Springs, AR 72632 (479) 253-511 $
McDonald's 148 E Van Buren, Eureka Springs, AR (479) 253-6106 $	Taco Bell 1000 W Trimble Ave, Berryville, AR 72616 (870) 423-5638 $

Pizza Hut 2048 E Van Buren, Eureka Springs, AR 72632 (479) 253-8258 $	

Fine Dining

Autumn Breeze Restaurant 190 Huntsville Road, Eureka Springs, AR 72632 (479) 253-7734 $$	Gaskins Cabin Steakhouse 2883 Arkansas 23, Eureka Springs, AR 72631 (479) 253-5466 $$
Cottage Inn Restaurant 450 W Van Buren, Eureka Springs, AR 72632 (479) 253-5282 $$	Grand Taverne Restaurant 37 N Main Street, Eureka Springs, AR 72632 (479) 253-6756 $$$
Eureka Springs & North Arkansas Railway 299 N Main Street, Eureka Springs, AR 72632 (479) 253-9623 $$	Horizon Lakeview Restaurant 304 Mundell Road, Eureka Springs, AR 72631 (479) 253-5525 $$
FRESH Farm to Table Fresh 179 N Main Street, Eureka Springs, AR 72632 (479) 253-9300 $$$	Tavern At Rogues Manor 124 Spring Street, Eureka Springs, AR 72632 (479) 253-4911 $$

German

Bavarian Inn Restaurant 325 W Van Buren, Eureka Springs, AR 72632 (479) 253-8128 $$	

Ice Cream

Big Dipper 2049 E Van Buren, Eureka Springs, AR 72632 (479) 253-5357 $	**Island Ice Cream Parlor** 4 Forest Park, Holiday Island 72631 (479) 363-6760 $
Pine Mountain Ice Cream 306 Village Circle, Eureka Springs, AR 72631 (832) 748-1484 $	

Italian

Cafe Amore 2070 E Van Buren, Eureka Springs, AR 72632 (479) 253-7192 $$	**DeVito's of Eureka Springs** 5 Center Street, Eureka Springs, AR 72632 (479) 253-6807 $$
Cafe Roulant USA 516 Village Cir, Eureka Springs, AR 72632 (479) 244-0207 $$	**Ermilio's Italian Home Cooking** 26 White Street, Eureka Springs, AR 72632 (479) 253-8806 $$
Cafe Luigi 91 S Main Street, Eureka Springs, AR 72632 (479) 253-6888 $$	

Mexican

Amigos Mexican Restaurant & Cantina 75 S Main Street, Eureka Springs, AR 72632 (479) 363-6574 $	La Cabana Mexican Restaurant 102 W Church, Berryville, AR 72616 (870) 423-4848 $
Casa Colina Mexican Grill & Cantina 173 S Main Street, Eureka Springs, AR 72632 (479) 363-6226 $$	Old Mexico 313 S Main Street, Berryville, AR 72616 (870) 423-3326 $
Caribe Restaurante& Cantina 309 W Van Buren, Eureka Springs, AR 72632 479-253-8102 $$	Taqueria Navidad 607 N Springfield Street, Berryville, AR 72616 (870) 423-1176 $
Dos Rios Mexican Cuisine 651 U.S. 62 Spur, Berryville, AR 72616 (870) 423-1181 $	The Oasis Original Ark-Mex 53 C Spring Street, Eureka , AR 72632 (479) 253-0886 $
La Familia 120 S Van Buren Street, Eureka Springs, AR 72632 (479) 253-2939 $	

Pizza

Chelsea's Corner Cafe 10 Mountain Street, Eureka Springs, AR 72632 (479) 253-6723 $$	Sky Bar Gourmet Pizza 75 1/2 Prospect Ave, Eureka Springs, AR 72632 (479) 253-9766 $$

Pizza Bar 13 N Main Street , Eureka Springs, AR 72632 (479) 253-7499 $$	

Sandwiches

Blimpie 102 Passion Play Road, Eureka Springs, AR 72632 (479) 253-6558 $	Subway 124 E Van Buren, Eureka Springs, AR 72632 (479) 253-5112 $
Simple Pleasures Smoothie & Sandwich Shoppe 79 Spring Street, Eureka Springs, AR 72632 (479) 253-5499 $	

Steaks

Crystal Dining Room Restaurant 75 Prospect Ave, Eureka Springs, AR 72632 (479) 253-9652 $$$	Port Orleans Restaurant Hwy 187, Eureka Springs, AR 72632 (479) 253-5258 $$$
Gaskins Cabin Steakhouse 2883 Arkansas 23, Eureka Springs, AR 72632 (479) 253-5466 $$$	

FAYETTEVILLE

Fayetteville Farmers Market

Visitors and residents love Fayetteville, and with good reason. Located at the edge of the Boston Mountains deep within the Ozarks, there are tons of things to do in and around the city. In fact, it can be argued that Fayetteville has it all; including jaw-dropping scenery, a vibrant and growing art and cultural scene, a thriving and expanding business community, world class culinary districts, and some of the most gorgeous country NWA has to offer. There is no shortage of things to do in this bustling city.

In addition, with a student enrollment of more than 20,000, the pride and joy of Fayetteville, NWA, and the entire state for that matter, is the University of Arkansas, or "U of A" as the locals call it. It's the U of A's main campus, naturally making it home to many cultural, community and sporting events.

During the fall and the spring, thousands of students come to the city to attend the university. This yearly influx of students greatly changes the complexion of this NWA city. During the school term when the University of Arkansas Razorbacks sports program is active, thousands of fans throng to the campus to support various university-supported athletic events. The Razorbacks are consistently top contenders in the SEC conference and are cheered on by many thousands of enthusiastic fans. In fact, it would be hard to find a louder or larger fan base anywhere. You show me an Arkansas native, and I'll show you a died-in-the-wool Arkansas Razorbacks fan.

Parade magazine listed Fayetteville as one of "America's Most Beautiful Cities" in 2012. CBSNews.com ranked it fourth in its list of the cheapest places to live in the U.S. USA Today named the city as having one of the "Top Libraries in America." Forbes ranked it seventh best college sports town and eighth best business and careers city. U.S News ranked it as one of the best places to retire. Perhaps most importantly, Forbes named the Fayetteville-Springdale-Rogers area as the second-best area in the U.S. for recovery from the current economic recession. That says a tremendous amount about this beautiful region, and it's no surprise why this area is still going strong.

Close to Bentonville, the home of Walmart, the city plays host in the Bud Walton Arena to the thousands of Walmart shareholders at their annual meeting. J. B. Hunt makes its headquarters in nearby Lowell, AR. Springdale, AR is the headquarters for the world-renowned Tyson Foods. These three mega-corporations, Walmart, J.B. Hunt and Tyson Foods, have been, and continue to be a huge driving force in the area.

History enthusiasts come to the city to explore its past. This is the perfect place to explore some of the most important Civil War sites, including The Battle of Fayetteville, Clinton House Museum, Ridge House, Headquarters House, Arkansas Air and Military Museum, the Country Doctor Museum, and the Fayetteville National Cemetery, which is one of 14 national cemeteries instituted by President Abraham Lincoln.

Each year, the city has more than 180 festivals, including the world-famous Bikes, Blues and BBQ, the Block Street Block Party, the Le Chocolate Feast and many others. Its lively entertainment districts, found downtown and on Dickson Street, are the places to find nightlife in the NWA region. Nightspots like George's Majestic Lounge, featuring an outdoor patio and live entertainment, has been wildly popular for years; Willy D's, a hot piano bar, keeps the heartbeat pumping for the city.

MAP OF FAYETTEVILLE

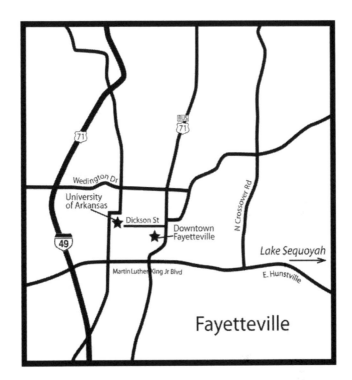

Neighborhoods

Neighborhoods

- There are six main areas of Fayetteville.
- The Fayetteville Square (downtown)
- The North Side (by the mall 71B)
- Dickson Street
- South Side (by MLK)
- West Side (out Weddington area)
- East Side (out Mission Crossover area)

What the Locals Say…

My favorite part of this guide! Let's decide what we're going to do in Fayetteville based on what Fayetteville locals recommend!

The locals list of must-things-to-do-and-see in Fayetteville includes:

- A visit to Dickson Street Bookshop
- Exploring Dickson Street as a whole because it's fun for all ages
- Visiting Fayetteville Downtown Square
- Touring the University of Arkansas campus
- Trekking the trails all around the city
- Attending First Thursdays on the Square
- Checking out Fayetteville›s Farmer›s Market
- Seeing all the Christmas lights
- Attending Pratt Place events
- Visiting the beautiful Botanical Garden of the Ozarks

Some eating must-dos include not missing the lot on N College Ave with fabulous air-stream food trailers. You must also enjoy a meal at Arsaga's Espresso Café for fabulous coffee and crepes; Theo's for an extensive menu and fun-filled happy hour outdoors; and Does' Steakhouse for the best steaks around.

Aside from those eating suggestions, other local favorite Fayetteville, AR restaurants include:

- Pesto Café
- Greenhouse Grill
- El Camino Real
- Hugo's
- Damgoode Pies
- A Taste of Thai
- Catfish Hole
- Rick's Bakery

The locals› favorite event is the Bikes, Blues and BBQ. Approximately 400,000 people converge upon the city to attend the yearly Bikes, Blues and BBQ held in September. This popular event includes free music, a huge BBQ contest and numerous motorcycle competitions. It is wild and wildly popular, so make certain you book your accommodations at one of the numerous Fayetteville, AR hotels early!

You don›t have to be a local to discover that the picturesque Ozark Mountains are the perfect place to enjoy fun outdoor activities like hiking, biking and camping. In fact, if you are the outdoors type, why book your stay at the hotels in Fayetteville, AR when you can camp in the glorious Ozark Mountains instead!

Fayetteville is also close to the Buffalo River, which is the perfect body of water for canoeing, kayaking and floating. This is a popular and fun way that Fayetteville locals relax and enjoy the beautiful NWA outdoors.

One of the most unique and favorite activity of Fayetteville residents is the official «Calling the Hogs.» What is that? Well, if you are fortunate enough to be in town for one of the University of Arkansas' famous Razorback football or basketball games, don't miss the faithful fans calling the hogs. It is an awesome experience that you won't soon forget.

Itineraries and Day Trips

Fayetteville Itinerary #1 —Fayetteville Downtown Square Boutique Hopping

Of course, you could spend many days exploring the wonderful boutiques and one-of-a-kind businesses in Fayetteville, and I hope that you do! But, since this special itinerary is meant to be accomplished in just a single day, here are a few of Fayetteville's unique shopping opportunities that are sure to satisfy your shopping fever.

Before you get started, make a quick stop at Fayetteville Visitor's Bureau, which you'll find at 21 S Block Ave. Pick up maps and get directions from the friendly people who are working hard to make your visit to their city a pleasant and memorable one.

If you are a book lover, begin your day by visiting the Dickson Street Bookshop, one of the very best independent bookshops in the country. In business for more than 30 years and located at the corner of Dickson Street and N School, Dickson Street Bookshop deals in used and out of print books. Time passes fast when you are perusing its dusty bookshelves, which are filled to overflowing with more than 100,000 hard-to-find books on every conceivable subject imaginable, but heavy in books of literature, poetry, Irish studies, and Americana poetry. The store is a maze of books; the shelves are from floor to ceiling; there are more than 50,000 books waiting in storage to be put on the shelves. If you visit once, you will be hooked for life!

Take a coffee break at Brick House Kitchen located at 1 E Center Street on the square. Brick House Kitchen serves great coffee and has been in Fayetteville for years.

Next, head over to Dark Star Visuals, which is at 106 N Block. This is primarily a women's clothing store, but customers say, "You can get just about any look you want in this specialty shop." Since 1991, it has been known as the home of design-your-own jewelry. It is the largest full-service bead store using high-quality gemstones, glass, silver and gold filled supplies. Go once, and you will make it a regular stop every visit.

After you're done making your own jewelry, head over to David Adams Jewelry, which is located at 100 W Center. David Adams offers unique custom jewelry created from platinum, gold and silver. David Adams, a fine jeweler, apprenticed under the famed Orlando Feriozzi where he learned hand fabrication. Visit this store for a thrilling opportunity to see, and shop, turn of the century jewelry making techniques.

Next, check out Cheap Thrills, located at 120 S East, which features a vast array of merchandise from multiple eras and great customer service. A terrific shop to find contemporary resale and vintage clothing and adult costumes. The owner has a real eye for style, and you will feel comfortable knowing not everyone and their cousin has the same outfit. If you have a special occasion on the horizon, you will likely find exactly what you need with the friendly help of Cheap Thrills' owner and staff.

Located at 108 N Block, Good Things Boutique features organic clothing, fair trade gifts, local artist jewelry and 100-percent pure skincare and cosmetics. The shop also offers a good selection of active wear. Whether you are just kicking it with friends, going to the gym, or hitting the trails, you will love the soft, breezy organic cotton active wear featured for the summer.

The Himalayan Mountain Shop is Located at 100 W Center and sells unique imported gifts. It also has a huge collection of leggings to go with simple cotton tops. The cotton dresses and outfits are nothing short of gorgeous. You will love this shop.

Town and Country Shop, located at 9 S Block, stocks upscale women's clothing, shoes and accessories. Town and Country Shop features unforgettable, statement-making style from designers like Ming Wang, Eileen Fisher, Mycra Pac, Elliott Lauren and many others. Brighton charms and charm holders are also available.

Time for lunch and here are three fantastic restaurants in downtown Fayetteville, AR to choose from:

- Hugos' at 33 N Block Street

- Little Bread Company at 116 N Block Ave

- Fresco Café & Pub at 112 W. Center Street #100

After some culinary delight, visit Luxe Beauty located at 339 N West. This specialized salon sells premium makeup and facial products. It sets the standard for beauty and fashion and has unparalleled service. This is the boutique to get the Vi Peel, which improves skin tone, texture and clarity; reduces or eliminates age spots, freckles, and hyper-pigmentation, including melasma; softens lines and wrinkles; clears acne and reduces or eliminates acne scars.

If you're visiting Fayetteville with your special someone, Romance Diamond Company, located at 248 W Dickson Street, specializes in bridal jewelry, watches and designer jewelry. As the jeweler says, "Welcome to Romance Diamond Company, where you'll find exclusive collections from the most exciting designers around the world, including some of our very own."

Block Street Records, located at 17 N Block, sells vintage vinyl records, CDs, music products, clothes, jewelry and tobacco products. If you enjoy music, you will love this store.

The Mustache Goods and Wears, located at 15 S Block, stocks clothing, shoes and gifts. This fun little shop specializes in unique T-shirts, Arkansas and Razorback clothing, and cool-looking hats.

I've mentioned only a few of the Fayetteville Downtown Square shops... just enough to whet your appetite for the truly unique shopping to be had in this charming downtown square. The square has everything you could imagine in the way of one-of-a-kind shopping, restaurants and historic buildings. I hope you've enjoyed the fabulous shopping I've suggested, and I hope you've seen many more retailers that increase your desire to return for a second shopping outing... and a third... and a fourth!

Fayetteville Itinerary #2 – NWA Dickson Street and Downtown Nightlife

Without a doubt, Fayetteville is the pulsating heartbeat of entertainment in Northwest Arkansas. If you ask a local where to go for good food, fun, music and nightlife, they will tell you to head on down to Dickson Street in Fayetteville.

The Downtown and Dickson Street areas are where it is happening for the entire Northwest Arkansas region. After the sun sets over the city, Fayetteville's entertainment district comes alive with a high-energy atmosphere that is the norm and enjoyed by all.

Hit the nightspots for a fun-filled evening. There is something for everyone, including tasty food, great music and dancing, pool shooting, boutique and gallery shopping, and even people watching. What is your pleasure? You will find it as you walk down Dickson Street and the Downtown area of Fayetteville.

There are many delectable restaurants and exciting bars and clubs that make the Downtown and Dickson Street area NWA's top entertainment district. If you only have a night or two, however, you can't beat the ones I've listed below.

The Common Grounds Gourmet Espresso Bar - Make it a point to visit this popular hot spot at 412 W Dickson Street. The coffee fever is alive and well in this popular Dickson Street restaurant, but coffee is not the only thing on the menu that is first-rate. Common Grounds escorts in the exciting Fayetteville nightlight with wonderful after dinner drinks. If you need a cup of Joe to give you the energy to dance the night away, the restaurant has a coffee menu that rivals the best in the region. And even though we are talking about nightlife, Common Grounds' world-class salads and sandwiches are worth trying when you're looking for a place to eat lunch the following day.

Farrell's Lounge Bar and Grill - Located at 311 W Dickson Street, Farrell's is a "GastroPub," which is British English for a pub with a chef-driven menu . Enjoy 10 large high-def screens, shoot a game or two of pool, and feast upon out-of-this-world food made from the freshest ingredients found in the northwest corner of the state. The wait staff is efficient, friendly and really cool, and the management knows how to create a festive party atmosphere. Cityscapes rated it the best sports bar in NWA in 2011.

George's Majestic Lounge - Better known as "George's" and located at 519 W Dickson Street, this lounge is "Where Live Music Lives." George's is the oldest and longest-running nightclub venue in the whole of Arkansas. It is best known for the many outstanding acts that have performed there over the years, including Little River Band, Pat Green, Sam Bush, Cate Brothers, Michael Burks, Chubby Carrier, and many others too numerous to mention.

Speakeasy Nightclub and Lounge - Located at 509 W Spring Street, Suite 250, Speakeasy Nightclub and Lounge is the perfect place to spend the latter part of your evening. Speakeasy features two distinctly different entertainment venues. One is an elegant and intimate vintage-style cigar and martini bar, and the other is a high-energy, state-of-the-art nightclub where you can dance until your feet fail you or just kick back, relax and have fun with your friends. The cigar and martini bar has an extensive cigar menu and over 100 different palate-pleasing martinis from which to choose.

Fayetteville Itinerary #3 – Antiquing in Fayetteville

Several antique stores are conveniently clustered in the downtown Fayetteville area. This gives you an opportunity to have a delightful breakfast at one of the many unique downtown eateries. Grabbing breakfast downtown will allow you to cover a lot of ground easily so you can shop 'til you drop, and take a much-needed coffee break during your shopping spree.

Arsaga's Depot - Start your morning off right at Arsaga's Depot located at 548 W Dickson Street. Arsaga's is a great choice for breakfast. Their crepes, a delicious specialty, consistently receive rave reviews from regulars, travelers and vacationers alike. You only live once, right? So, go ahead, blow your diet and try one of their sweet scrumptious crepes!

French Quarters Antiques - After breakfast, begin your tour of the Fayetteville antique shops with French Quarters Antiques. Located in the heart of the city at 11 N Block Street, this unique store has a plentiful collection of 18th and 19th century fine and affordable French and European antiques. Owners, Chris and Storm, personally select every inventory piece, not from catalogs, but from examining each piece firsthand as they travel abroad, including trips to the Paris markets and the French countryside.

French Metro Antiques - Located on Dickson Street in downtown Fayetteville, French Metro Antiques is 7,000 square feet of carefully selected French accessories and furniture, all handpicked. If you have a passion for French culture, you will love wandering through French Metro Antiques' showroom space, which is full of beautiful authentic pieces. You can opt for their dependable shipping service if you do not wish to carry your purchases home with you.

Long Ago Antiques - Located at 1934 E Huntsville Road, this premier antique shop specializes in all things beautiful, but they are primarily known for their authentic American antiques. Just like many of you, the owners started out as "collectors." Currently, a selection of oak dressers, chests, highboy chests, washstands, and nightstands and beds are on display. They also do antique and other wood furniture restoration.

Coffee Break Time - Big Mamma's Coffee and Espresso Bar at 609 W Dickson Street, Suite 104, is a fun place to have a delicious coffee and a snack if you are hungry. Another terrific coffee house is The Common Grounds Gourmet Espresso Bar at 412 W Dickson Street. They are famous in NWA for having truly amazing coffee and wonderful salads and sandwiches.

Gift House Antiques - Located at 525 N Mission Blvd, Gift House Antiques consistently gets high ratings for having the perfect large furniture items and complimentary accessories to fill the empty spaces in your new or restored home. The ladies in the front are both friendly and knowledgeable, and they are very good at giving you decorating ideas for things that go together. New items arrive regularly, so if you don't find what you are looking for the first time, come back to the store on your next NWA trip. Gift House Antiques does not offer delivery service, so plan to have your purchases shipped yourself.

Flying Dog Vintage Mall – This vintage mall is located in the Evelyn Hills Shopping Center at 1330 North College Avenue. If you've discovered Ozark Natural Foods on your trip, then you know where the Flying Dog Mall is. Year after year, the Flying Dog continues to be an amazing and eclectic antique mall. Expect to find vintage, retro and mid-century treasures at this popular and one-of-a-kind mall. From my own experience, it is easy to lose track of time as you peruse the items in all the Mall's spaces. Each space displays different types of merchandise, ensuring that you will most likely find exactly what you are looking for. Particularly known for its antique and vintage furniture, it is a favorite with the locals and visitors alike.

Fayetteville Day Trip #1 – Pig Trail Scenic Byway

Regardless of the season, the Pig Trail Scenic Byway makes for a beautiful drive by car or ride by motorcycle. You can expect a thrilling trip past lakes and creeks; tree tunnels during spring, summer and fall; and historic buildings and towns. In the spring, you'll see colorful wildflowers, and in the fall, your vista is unparalleled brilliant autumn foliage.

The geology of the Ozarks produces stunning miles of scenery and exciting serpentine highways that almost continually twist and turn, allowing travelers to experience the rugged terrain up close and personal. There are many 15-mph hairpins, switchbacks, curves, and hills. It takes more than a little bravery to ride this particular section of the deeply wooded Ozark Mountains, but it's worth it.

The Pig Trail is 19 miles of pure fun. It begins at Arkansas 23 on the South boundary of the Ozark National Forest and goes to its intersection with Arkansas 16 at Brashears. It is said to be a motorcycle rider's paradise, and attractions along the route include a float trip on the Mulberry River, whitewater rafting, kayaking, and fishing.

Stop at the Turner Bend Store for your patch designating you as a Pig Trail survivor, and rest at one of the Turner Bend campsites or cabins. Turner Bend Outfitters can fix you up with campsite rentals, any gear you'll need, and boat rentals. They also sell t-shirts, homemade sandwiches, groceries, picnic and automotive supplies, tobacco products, and a good selection of beer. If you prefer wine, they carry wines native to the area. Best of all, they are open seven days a week.

Fayetteville Day Trip #2 – Family Fun in Little Rock

Little Rock is about a three-hour drive from Fayetteville and it's a great place to take the family for a day of educational and exciting activities. Don't worry parents, the kids will be having so much fun, they won't realize that they're learning things!

Once you arrive in Little Rock, an important thing to note is the River Rail Streetcar, which provides enjoyable transportation service to the Clinton Presidential Center, Heifer International Headquarters, many of the city's major entertainment venues, museums, parks, restaurants, libraries, and neighborhoods located in the downtown areas of both Little Rock and North Little Rock. Create some life-long memories with your children as you ride the River Rail Streetcar instead of driving yourself.

The River Rail operates three electric replica vintage cars on a 3.4-mile route covering some of the most interesting and exciting destinations in both cities, including traveling across the Main Street Bridge over the Arkansas River. The rail car operators entertain riders with information about the various historical sites, community events and current news. All three cars are equipped with heating and air-conditioning to keep you comfortable no matter the season you visit NWA.

Clinton Presidential Center - President William J. Clinton's Library is located at 1200 President Clinton Avenue in view of the Arkansas River. According to information found on the museum's website, "The Clinton Presidential Library welcomes visitors of all ages for an entertaining, educational experience. Families can tour the museum, participate in special programming and learn more about the American presidency." One item on display that the kids will particularly enjoy is the Presidential State Car that Clinton used when he was in office.

Heifer International - Plan to tour the headquarters for Heifer International while in Little Rock. This nonprofit organization is deeply committed to educating of all us on how we can help end hunger, poverty, and save our environment worldwide. If you've never heard of sending a heifer to a needy family to help them survive, you must visit this nonprofit's headquarters to learn more about the unique aid it offers and see its 30,000-gallon rainwater collection tower.

Little Rock Zoo - One of the Natural State's greatest treasures is the Little Rock Zoo, located in the heart of Arkansas at War Memorial Park, 1 Zoo Avenue. Open from 9 a.m. to 5 p.m., the zoo has more than 725 animals representing

200 different species (some of which are on the endangered list) housed within its 33 acres. The zoo is focused toward inspiring visitors to become involved in conserving animals in the wild. The zoo also has a vintage carousel, which children especially love to ride for its jumps and bumps.

The Arkansas River Trail System - Did you bring your bike? If so, you can see some of the most spectacular views in all of Arkansas. Anyone who participates in fitness activities like cycling, hiking, jogging, skating and walking will enjoy this unique and award-winning trail system, which is an 88-mile loop that winds through Central Arkansas, including Little Rock, North Little Rock, Maumelle and Conway. There is also a much shorter loop, 15.6-miles long, from the Clinton Presidential Bridge via North Little Rock to the Big Dam Bridge, the nation's longest bicycle and pedestrian bridge spanning 4,226 linear feet across the Arkansas River, and back to the Clinton Bridge.

Lovingly called "The Rep" by the locals, theater buffs should check out The Arkansas Repertory, which is the only professional, nonprofit theater of its size in the region, and this includes Memphis, New Orleans and Nashville. Popular productions such as "Les Miserable" and "The Second City" are the types of shows you will see performed at The Rep. For you history buffs, there is the Quapaw Quarter, home some of the oldest estates and mansions in the South, some of them dating to the Civil War era.

ACCOMMODATIONS

When staying in Fayetteville, whether you choose a hotel, a historic inn or a quaint B&B, you are sure to find accommodations to suit your style and pocketbook. From The Inn at the Mill, which enjoys a 4.5 star rating, to the first-class Dickson Street Inn, located in the heart of the Dickson Street Entertainment District, to one of the budget hotels in Fayetteville, AR, there is lodging for everyone.

Hotel Amenities

Breakfast: B	*Meeting Rooms: MR*
Business Center: BC	*Pet Friendly: PF*
Fitness Center: FC	*Pool: P*
Internet: I	*Restaurant: R*

Hotels in Fayetteville, AR with 3 Star Accommodations

Chancellor Hotel 70 NE Ave, Fayetteville, AR 72701 (479) 442-5555 BC, FC, I, MR, PF, P, R	Homewood Fayetteville 1305 N Palak Drive, Fayetteville, AR 72704 (479) 442-3000 B, BC, FC, I, P
Magnuson Grand Hotel of Fayetteville 1255 S Shiloh Drive, Fayetteville, AR 72701 (479) 521-1166 B, BC, FC, I, P, R	Staybridge Suites 1577 W 15th Street, Fayetteville, AR 72701 (479) 695-2400 B, BC, FC, I, PF, P
Courtyard Fayetteville 600 Van Asche Drive, Fayetteville, AR 72703 (479) 571-4900 BC, FC, I, P, R	The Inn at Carnall Hall 465 Arkansas Ave, Fayetteville, AR 72701 (479) 582-0400 B, FC, I, R

Hampton Inn 915 Krupa Drive, Fayetteville, AR 72704 (479) 587-8300 B, BC, FC, I, P	

Hotels in Fayetteville, AR with 2 Star Accommodations

Best Western Windsor Suites 1122 S Futrall Drive, Fayetteville, AR 72701 (800) 780-7234 B, BC, FC, I, MR, P	Motel 6 Fayetteville 2980 N College Ave, Fayetteville, AR 72703 (479) 443-4351
Candlewood Suites 2270 Martin Luther King Jr. Blvd, Fayetteville, AR 72701 (479) 856-6262 B, BC, FC, I, MR	Quality Inn 735 S Shiloh Drive, Fayetteville, AR 72704 (479) 695-2121
Comfort Inn and Suites 1234 Steamboat Drive, Fayetteville, AR 72704 (479) 571-5177 B, BC, FC, I, MR, P	Regency 7 675 S Shiloh Drive, Fayetteville, AR 72704 (479) 575-0777 B, I
Days Inn 523 S Shiloh Drive, Fayetteville, AR 72704 (479) 444-9800 B, BC, FC, I, PF, P	Sleep Inn 728 Millsap Road, Fayetteville, AR 72703 (479) 587-8700 B, I, PF
Econo Lodge 1000 S Futrall Dr, Fayetteville, AR 72701 (479) 442-3041 B,I, PF, P	Super 8 Fayetteville 1075 S Shiloh Drive, Fayetteville, AR 72701 (800) 536-0519 B, BC, I, MR, PF

Fairfield Inn Fayetteville 720 Millsap Road, Fayetteville, AR 72703 (479) 587-8600 B, I, MR	Value Place 2638 W Old Farmington Road, Fayetteville, AR 72704 (479) 443-6800 I
Holiday Inn Express Hotel and Suites Fayetteville - University of AR Area 1251 N Shiloh Drive, Fayetteville, AR 72704 (479) 444-6006 I, BC	

Fayetteville, AR Bed and Breakfasts

Dickson Street Inn 301 W Dickson Street, Fayetteville, AR 72701 (479) 695-2100	Pratt Place Inn and Barn 2231 W Markham Road, Fayetteville, AR 72701 (479) 966-4441
North Forty 40 N Crossover Road, Fayetteville, AR 72701 (479) 521-3739	Stay Inn Style Bed and Breakfast 117 W Rock Street, Fayetteville, AR 72701 (479) 582-3590

Fayetteville, AR Cabins

Devil's Den State Park 11333 Hwy 74 West, West Fork, AR 72774 (479) 761-3325	Lake Wedington Cabins and Group Lodge 15689 Lake Wedington Entry, Fayetteville, AR 72704 (479) 442-3527

Cabins 60 miles outside of Fayetteville

Buffalo Outdoor Center PO Box 1, Ponca, AR 72670 (870) 861-5514	Buffalo River Cabins Hwy 268, Mull, AR 72670 (870) 404-4987

Buffalo River Outfitters 9664 Hwy 65, Street, Joe, AR 72675 (870) 439-2244	
For More Information: *Cabins and Lodging Upper Buffalo River Area*	

THINGS TO DO AND SEE

You could spend a week in and around Fayetteville and barely tap the things to do in Fayetteville, Arkansas. If you are a history buff, visit the Arkansas Air Museum at Drake Field on U. S 71 South to see a flight simulator and tour through the state's largest wooden hanger. Or you can tour the Headquarters House and Grounds where in 1853 both Union and Confederate troops called the home headquarters during the Civil War.

If your tastes lean more toward a cultural experience, see the Walton Art Center located right in the heart of Dickson Street. More than 150,000 people every year experience its Broadway musicals, dance performances and other theater productions.

Sports enthusiasts can learn to 'Woo Pig Sooie' and take in a game at the Donald W. Reynolds Razorback Stadium where the world-famous Razorback's play football.

After the game, head on down to Dickson Street, where you can eat delicious food at one of the delightful Fayetteville, AR restaurants and party the night away with other Razorback maniacs at one of the many one-of-a-kind bars and music venues.

Arts/Culture

A Pottery Studio
2002 S School, Fayetteville, AR 72701
(479) 521-3171

Classes and workshops conducted by some of the world's top artists and potters covering all areas of ceramics and pottery are offered. Enjoy and explore one of the oldest crafts in existence.

Fayetteville Downtown Square

Fayetteville Downtown Square is a wonderful place to visit and a huge part of Fayetteville culture! It is home to many restaurants, unusual shops, historic buildings and modern offices and is often the focal point of many local activities. You will be delighted by the well-tended square gardens with their dazzling array of colorful flowers.

Fayetteville Underground Art
101 W Mountain, Fayetteville, AR 72701
(479) 871-2722

Fayetteville Underground is a studio/gallery space in downtown Fayetteville. They offer studios to working artists as well as the opportunity to be selected as an artist member (without studio space). They host shows by residents as well as visiting artists.

Heartwood Gallery
428 S Government Ave, Fayetteville, AR 72701
(479) 444-0888

Matt Miller Studio
21 W Mountain Street, Ste 26, Fayetteville, AR 72701
(870) 919-8651

Terra Studios
12103 CR 47, Fayetteville, AR 72701
(479) 643-3185

What is the Bluebird of Happiness? Visit Terra Studios and you will not only find out, but also enjoy an opportunity to watch expert glassmakers craft it. Terra Studios is home to some of the finest glass and pottery artisans in NWA, and it is no wonder why. The studio is nestled within the beautiful Ozark Mountains, where there is ample inspiration to encourage any artist to design a magnificent work of art. Not only will you enjoy viewing the artists at work, and purchasing some of their glorious wares, you can also wander the wooden paths throughout the property and view some of the most breathtaking country NWA has to offer.

Performing Arts
Arts Live Theatre
818 N Sang Ave, Fayetteville, AR 72702
(479) 521-4932

Arts Live Theatre, through summer youth theater training programs, offers after-school theatre programs, MainStage productions and Youthfest productions.

Theatre Squared
P.O. Box 4188, Fayetteville, AR 72702
(479) 443-5600

Northwest Arkansas›s regional professional theatre.

Symphony of Northwest Arkansas
PO Box 1243, Fayetteville, AR 72702
(479) 521-4166

The Symphony of Northwest Arkansas (SoNA) is an outstanding 70-piece orchestra that has, for more than 50 years in fact, entertained and educated NWA audiences. SoNA, in partnership with Walton Art Center, takes music to new heights. With a desire to enrich the NWA area with world-class artistry, these musicians, currently under the musical direction of Paul Haas, enrich their audiences with musical performances that are frequently dubbed to be of "uncompromising quality." You don't need to travel to New York City or Los Angeles to experience the best classical music in the land. SoNA rivals any orchestra in the U.S.

Walton Arts Center
495 W Dickson Street, Fayetteville, AR 72701
(479) 443-5600

As you've noted throughout this section of the NWA Travel Guide, Dickson Street is home to most of Fayetteville's action. The Walton Arts Center is one reason why visitors and locals flock to Dickson Street for much of their entertainment. This performing arts facility is NWA's largest, and entertains 150,000-plus people each year. You'll find all theatre has to offer, including comedy, musicals, and dance productions at Walton Arts Center.

Museums
Arkansas Air Museum
4290 S School (next to Drake Field), Fayetteville, AR 72701
(479) 521-4947

If you are an aviation buff, your visit to NWA will not be complete without stopping by Fayetteville's Arkansas Air Museum. Aviation from the 1920s through the 1940s is far different from the aviation we see today. This wonderful and educational museum teaches visitors what it was like during the days of what aviation calls "barnstorming." As you wander through the museum, either by guide or simply by yourself, you'll see fighter planes from World War I and the "Mystery Ship." What is that? It's a sleek aircraft that won the 1929 National Air Race. Movie buffs might also recognize it from its appearances in two Hollywood flicks!

Arkansas Country Doctor Museum
109 N Starr Ave, Lincoln, AR 72744
(479) 824-4307

The wonderful museums in Fayetteville don't just include the history of aviation. The history of medicine is also represented at the Arkansas Country Doctor Museum. Throughout the 19th and early 20th centuries, country doctors played a huge role in the overall health of the people of the Ozarks. Dr. Harold Boyer opened the Arkansas Country Doctor Museum to honor and draw attention to the selfless Arkansas country doctors. You'll see medical equipment from the days of old, including an iron lung, and wander through the clinic, and home, of Arkansas country doctors who practiced medicine at the facility from 1936 until 1973. This testament to human compassion is open from 1 p.m. to 4 p.m., Wednesday through Saturday. Admission is FREE.

Clinton House Museum
930 W Clinton Drive, Fayetteville, AR 72701
(479) 444-0066

The Clinton House Museum presents recent American history. I'm quite certain you've figured out by the name that this is the English bungalow where our 42nd President of the United States, William Jefferson "Bill" Clinton, and former Secretary of State Hillary Clinton were married. The Clinton House Museum was also Clinton's first home. When visiting this museum, you'll get a photographic and memorabilia peek into the Clinton's life when they were proud residents of Fayetteville. You will also see some of the campaign materials President Clinton used during his run for office. If you would like to get married where the Clintons did, you can! You may also book the Clinton House Museum for your wedding reception, meetings, or for a public tour.

Confederate Cemetery - Fayetteville, Arkansas
500 E Rock (Rock and Willow Streets), Fayetteville, AR 72701
(479) 521-1710

One of the most tragic times in American history is the Civil War. The battles of Pea Ridge and Prairie Grove were fought in Northwest Arkansas and many soldiers were buried near where they fell. The Southern Memorial Association founded Fayetteville's Confederate Cemetery in 1872 for the purpose of interring 500 fallen Confederate soldiers. These soldiers came from many different southern states, including Arkansas, Louisiana, Missouri and Texas. Because of its significance, the Confederate Cemetery has been added to the National Register of Historic Places.

Evergreen Cemetery
University and Williams Street, Fayetteville, AR

Listed on the National Register of Historical Places, Evergreen Cemetery has over 3,000 interments and is also a final resting place for many Confederate Soldiers. It is the burial site of Arkansas soldier, Statesman and Governor Archibald Yell, as well as Senator J. William Fulbright, the educator Sophia Sawyer, and the industrialist Lafayette Gregg

Fayetteville National Cemetery
700 S Government, Fayetteville, AR 72701
(479) 444-5051

President Abraham Lincoln established 14 National Cemeteries throughout the U.S. and the Fayetteville National Cemetery is one of them. Another reminder of the Civil War tragedy that rocked our nation in the 19th century, the Fayetteville National Cemetery is the final resting place for 1,600 soldiers who lost their lives during our nation's split. The remains of numerous other veterans who served our country are interned at Fayetteville National Cemetery. In fact, this sacred ground is one of the South's oldest military burial sites.

Fayetteville Public Library
401 W Mountain Street, Fayetteville, AR 72702
(479) 571-2222

Fayetteville Public Library is a beautiful 88,000-square-foot building, which houses a comprehensive genealogical collection, the Fulbright Fireplace Room, and extensive programming for children and adults. It was chosen in 2005 as the destination library for the *Thomson Gale/Library Journal* "Library of the Year" award.

The library's many services include local newspapers, free Internet access for visitors, popular magazines, music, movie and audio books, fiction and non-fiction materials, and online databases. The Fayetteville Public Library also has a café on site.

Headquarters House
118 E Dickson Street, Fayetteville, AR 72701
(479) 521-2970

During the Civil War, this home was the headquarters for both the Confederate and Union armies. It was originally built by Judge Jonas Tebbets in 1853. Today, it is the headquarters for the Washington County Historical Society. To arrange a tour of the home, call the above number.

Ozark Military Museum
4360 S School Ave., Fayetteville, AR 72701
(479) 587-1941

Whether you are a World War II historian or fascinated with the military equipment of today, the Ozark Military Museum is home to a comprehensive collection of historical military vehicles and other memorabilia spanning decades of combat history. You'll find the Ozark Military Museum at the Fayetteville Airport, and you'll find on display in the museum:

- Military vehicles of all kinds, including the U.S. Army's Willys Jeep and a WC-54 Ambulance from World War II

- From the Korean War, a M37 3/4-ton Cargo Truck

- From Desert Storm, a 2 1/2-ton 6 x 6 Cargo Truck

- A Ferret Light Armored Scout Car used by the Brits

- From World War II, an Aeronca L-3 Observation Aircraft

- The "Canadian Queen," which is a Beech 3NM (Twin Beech) used by the Royal Canadian Air Force from 1952 to 1967

There are numerous other military air and land vehicles on display, some restored to their former glory, but the museum also presents military memorabilia of a different kind. While wandering through the Ozark Military Museum, you'll see the exact model of tent stoves many Civil War soldiers used. You'll also see numerous World War II items, such as the daggers of German soldiers, military helmets, and patches which identified the unit of which a soldier was a member.

Nightlife/Entertainment

Dickson Street
Downtown Fayetteville, AR 72701

People of all ages enjoy Dickson Street. It is the place to see and be seen in Fayetteville. The streets are filled with unusual and colorful shops, galleries, restaurants and clubs, and the atmosphere is typically quite lively. The college crowd loves Dickson Street as it is located close to the University of Arkansas, but people from all over NWA frequent the area for its music, terrific shops and unique Fayetteville, AR restaurants.

Live Music
George's Majestic Lounge
519 W Dickson, Fayetteville, AR 72701
(479) 527-6618

Hookah Java Cafe & Lounge
311 W Dickson St #104, Fayetteville, AR 72701
(479) 301-2200

Mojo›s Pints & Pies
1200 Garland Ave #7, Fayetteville, AR 72703
(479) 935-3459

Smoke & Barrel
324 W Dickson St, Fayetteville, AR 72701
(479) 521-6880

Bowling
Ozark Bowling Lanes
2300 N College Ave, Fayetteville, AR 72703
(479) 442-4275

Skating
Starlight Skatium
612 N. College, Fayetteville, AR 72701
(479) 444-7827

Starlight Skatium is family-fun destination for roller derby teams and skaters of all ages. It provides a 10,000 square-foot hardwood skating floor as well as a snack bar and plenty of seating.

Theatres
112 Drive-In
3352 Hwy 112 North, Fayetteville, AR 72707
(479) 442-4542

Yes, it's a real outdoor drive-in movie that features recent full-length movies. A real movie going adventure, the 112 Drive-In is one of the very few left in the entire country.

Razorback Theatre
3956 N Steele Ave, Fayetteville, AR 72703
(479) 442-4542

Razorback Theatre is a stadium seating movie theater with 16 screens showing current movies located near restaurants and shopping.

Regal Fiesta Square 16
3033 N College Ave, Fayetteville, AR 72703
(479) 575-0393
Regal Fiesta Square is another 16-screen theater showing current movies.

Sports

Donald Reynolds Razorback Stadium
Razorback Road, University of Arkansas Campus, Fayetteville, AR 72701
(479) 575-05255
Renovated in 2011, the University of Arkansas' football stadium has a seating capacity of 80,000, and features a 30-feet-high by 107-feet-wide LED video display. The display brings amazing graphics and replay to virtually every fan in the stadium.

Bud Walton Arena
Razorback Road and Leroy, University of Arkansas Campus, Fayetteville, AR 72701
(479) 575-8618

The roaring atmosphere of Bud Walton Arena is second to none. Why? Because designers packed the most seats in the least space than in any other sports facility in the world. Be prepared, because the yelling and stomping of the tightly packed fans is earsplitting. In fact, decibels have reached heights that have literally shaken the ground! The floor of Bud Walton Arena is a spring-mounted floor, and it will shake when the fans stomp and scream loud enough.

Noise isn't the only thing that makes this arena a must-visit for any rabid Razorback sports fan. From the Tommy Boyer Museum and numerous displays located in the concourse to the sound system and laser light show to the floor-side and luxury box seating, there is no sports facility that can match Bud Walton's total package.

Baum Stadium
15th Street and Razorback Road, Fayetteville, AR 72701
(479) 575-3655

Baseball America named Baum Stadium the country's number one college baseball facility in 1998. Baseball America's survey stated that the stadium features amenities that put it "in a class of its own." The state-of-the-art 3,300-

seat stadium stands as a tribute to the University of Arkansas' baseball program.

Randal Tyson Indoor Track Center
1380 S Beechwood, Fayetteville, AR 72701
(479) 575-5151

Randal Tyson Indoor Track Center is one of the finest sports arenas in the U.S. It consistently hosts such track championships as the NCAA National Indoor Championships, the SEC Championships, and the Tyson Invitational.

Golf
Blessings Golf Course
5826 Clear Creek, Fayetteville, AR 72704
(479) 444-6330

This golf course is a private, 18-hole course designed by Robert Trent Jones, Jr. It is also the home course for the Razorback Golf Teams.

Fayetteville Country Club
3335 Country Club, Fayetteville, AR 72701
(479) 442-5112

The private golf course at the Fayetteville Country Club is an oldie, but goodie! It opened in 1919. The greens feature 18 holes of challenging golf, covering 6,208 yards from the longest tees. Fayetteville Country Club golf course's slope rating is 132. The greens are Bermuda grass, and the course is rated overall at 69.6.

Paradise Valley Golf Course
3728 Old Missouri, Fayetteville, AR 72703
(479) 521-5841

The Paradise Valley Golf course is a private, 18-hole course and is open year-round. There is a golf pro on-site. The course also includes a driving range.

Razorback Park Golf Course
2514 W. Lori, Fayetteville, AR 72703
(479) 443-5862

This public 18-hole course is open year-round and includes a driving range.

Stonebridge Meadows Golf Course
3495 E Goff Farm Road, Fayetteville, AR 72701
(479) 571-3673

Stonebridge Meadows Golf Course is a beautiful 18-hole public course that is open year round. A golf pro is on site and there is a driving range. Metal spikes are not allowed.

Camping/Hiking/Outdoors

Fayetteville City Parks & Trails

Fayetteville City Trails features over 18 paved miles of trails. Trails include:

- Bayarri Park Trail (0.3 miles)
- Bryce Davis Park Trail (0.2 miles)
- Clabber Creek Trail (.65 miles)
- Clear Creek Trail (2.25 miles)
- Dale Clark Park Trail (0.6 miles)
- Dickson Street/U of A Loop (3.7 miles)
- Finger Park (0.6 miles)
- Frisco Trail (0.6 miles)
- Gordon Long Park (.06 miles)
- Gregory Park Trail (0.6 miles)
- Gulley Park Trail (1.5 miles)
- Hamestring Creek Trail (.06 miles)
- Joe Clark Trail at Lake Wilson (2.6 miles)
- King Fisher Trail at Lake Sequoyah (3.0 miles)
- Lake Fayetteville Trail (5.5 miles)
- Meadow Valley Trail (2.3 miles)
- Mount Kessler (8 miles)
- Mount Sequoyah/Historic District Trail (0.9 miles)
- Mud Creek Trail (2.35 miles)
- Oak Ridge Trail (0.5 miles)
- Raven Trail (0.26 miles)
- Red Oak Trail (0.2 miles)

- Scull Creek Trail (4.4 miles)
- Shiloh Trail (0.75 miles)
- St. Paul Trail (0.78 miles)
- Town Branch Creek Trail (0.4 miles)
- TSA LA GI Trail (0.2 miles)
- Walker Park (0.7 miles)
- Wilson Lake Park Trail (0.9 miles)

Buffalo River and Surrounding Area

There are numerous mountain bike trails and camping areas on the outskirts of Fayetteville. Canoeing the Buffalo River is always a local and tourist favorite.

Botanical Garden of the Ozarks
4703 Crossover Road, Fayetteville, AR 72764
(479) 750-2620

For a wonderfully relaxing afternoon, visit the Botanical Garden of the Ozarks. A local favorite, these beautiful and expertly maintained gardens are home to foliage representing the delicate and glorious ecosystem of the Ozarks. Alongside the breathtaking gardens, visitors can also enjoy the Totemeier Horticulture Center, a timber-framed education center ready to teach you all there is to know about the Ozarks plant life.

Mt. Sequoyah
Mount Sequoyah Retreat and Conference Center
150 NW Skyline Drive, Fayetteville, AR 72701
(479) 760-8126

Mt. Sequoyah is of interesting historical importance, as it is part of the Trail of Tears route taken by the Indians as they trudged west to find new Reservations in which to live. Mt. Sequoyah is named after one of the Cherokee's most important leaders. Sequoyah was a Cherokee silversmith who brought language to the tribe by creating the Cherokee alphabet. Sequoyah is also credited for translating the New Testament into Cherokee. Mt. Sequoyah is the highest point in Fayetteville, with an elevation of 1,700 feet.

Chotkowski Gardens
16142 Pin Oak Road, Fayetteville, AR 72704
(479) 587-8920

Lakes
Cedar Creek Ski Park
P.O. Box 240, Elkins, Arkansas 72727
(479) 643-4181

Cedar Creek Water Ski Park is a man made two lake park featuring water skiing – jump, slalom and tricks. Perfect for family fun as well as a host to national competitions and trials, open May – Sept.

Lake Wedington Recreation Area
15592 Lake Wedington Entry Road, Wedington Township, AR 72704
(479) 442-3527

The Lake Wedington Recreation Area is a 424-acre outdoor oasis. Included within this 424-acre recreation area is a 102-acre forest lake. Visitors drive a mere 15 miles west from Fayetteville to enjoy all the activities this recreational area has to offer. Enjoy a wonderful picnic, camp, fish, hike, boat and swim – you can do it all at the Lake Wedington Recreation Area.

Lake Fayetteville
511 E Lakeview Dr, Fayetteville, AR 72764
(479) 444-3471

Lake Fayetteville is a 194-acre lake on the northern edge of Fayetteville. The park itself is 640 acres, and offers many recreational opportunities including hiking, picnicking, softball and other sports, as well as boating and fishing.

Pig Trail Scenic Drive

Considered the most beautiful and scenic route in Northwest Arkansas, the Pig Trail is a curvy 110-mile round trip through some beautiful Ozark country. To traverse it, hop into your rental car and drive:

- Hwy 16 East leaving Fayetteville
- Go south on Hwy 23 to Ozark
- Return to Fayetteville by then taking I-40 West to Alma
- Take Hwy 71 North to Fayetteville, or...
- Continue heading west to Fort Smith and then take Hwy 49 North

Scenic Highway 71/U.S. 49

If you enjoyed your Pig Trail scenic drive, take another drive along the scenic Hwy 71/U.S. 49 route. You'll enjoy the beautiful Ozark valleys and hills on this drive, as well. The directions are:

- Hop on U.S. 49/I-49 from Fayetteville to Scenic Hwy 71
- Drive south to I-40
- Take I-40 West
- Hop on 49 North to head back to Fayetteville

Dog Parks
Gulley Park
1850 E Township St, Fayetteville, AR 72703

IAMS Dog Park
1595 N Dartmouth Avenue, Fayetteville, AR 72704

Lake Wilson Off Leash Area
S Lake Wilson Rd, Fayetteville, AR 72701
(479) 444-3456

State & National Parks
Devil's Den State Park
11333 Hwy 74 West, West Fork, AR 72774
(479) 761-3325

Outdoor enthusiasts get to explore wild backcountry in Devil's Den State Park and the surrounding Ozark National Forest. The area provides hiking, backpacking and mountain bike trails.

Prairie Grove Battlefield State Park
Prairie Grove, AR
(479) 846-2990

Nationally recognized Prairie Grove Battlefield State park is one of America's most intact Civil War battlefields. Visitors can drive the 6 1/2 mile tour or take the 1-mile Battlefield trail, which features wayside exhibits.

Shopping
Northwest Arkansas Mall
4201 N Shiloh Drive, Fayetteville, AR 72703
(479) 521-6151

Fayetteville's Northwest Arkansas Mall has a huge variety of specialty shops, national stores and dining venues. It is the largest shopping facility in NWA, so there is always plenty going on at Fayetteville's Northwest Arkansas Mall.

Antique/Vintage
410 Vintage
410 N College Ave, Fayetteville, AR 72701
(479) 521-2444

Fayetteville>s Funky Yardsale
693 W. North St. Ste. 1, Fayetteville, AR 72701
(479) 445-6545

In Retrospect - Vintage.Kitsch.Flea-tabulous
10 E Township, Fayetteville, AR 72701
(479) 521-2100

Sara Kathryn's
600 N. Mission, Fayetteville, AR 72701
(479) 444-9991

The Flying Dog ~ Vintage
427 N. College, Fayetteville, AR 72701
(479) 856-6600

The French Door
2932 E. Huntsville Road, Fayetteville, AR 72701
(479) 445-6112

Vintage Violet
118 W. South Street, Fayetteville, AR 72701
(479) 966-4241

Boutiques
Country Outfitter
1 W. Center, Fayetteville, AR 72701
(479) 935-4970
Boots, Bags and Accessories

Good Things Boutique
108 N Block Avenue, Fayetteville, AR 72701
(479) 442-3689

Masons
1350 E Joyce Blvd, Fayetteville, AR 72703
(479) 582-9129

Maude Boutique
704 N College Ave, Fayetteville, AR 72701
(479) 935-4700

Something Urban
643 W Dickson Street, Fayetteville, AR 72701
(479) 442-0140

Specialty Shops
Bath Junkie
641 W Dickson Street, Fayetteville, AR 72701
(479) 444-0211

Mix and match your favorite scents and colors into luxurious lotions, bubble baths and bath salts. Bath Junkie is truly a delightful experience for the senses.

Block Street Records
17 N. Block, Fayetteville, AR
(479) 966-0623

Dickson Street Bookshop
325 W Dickson Street, Fayetteville, AR 72701
(479) 442-8182

Those who love books will need to prepare themselves for a real treat! You can easily lose a few hours in this funky shop filled with treasured used and out of print books.

Fayettechill Ozark Mountain Outfitters
329 N. West Ave., Fayetteville, AR 72701
(479) 575-0609

Nightbird Books
205 W Dickson Street, Fayetteville, AR 72701
(479) 443-2080

Nightbird Books is a locally owned, independent bookstore featuring a wide variety of hand-selected new books for adults and children.

The Handmade Market
1504 N College Ave, Fayetteville, AR 72703
(479) 582-5731

Pack Rat Outdoor Center
209 West Sunbridge, Fayetteville, AR 72703
(479) 521-6340

PIGMINT
18 E Center Street, Fayetteville, AR 72701
(479) 444-0404

Shindig Paperie
100 W Center Street, Suite 5, Fayetteville, Arkansas 72701
(479) 521-1778

Southern Trend Clothing
614 W Sycamore, Fayetteville, AR 72703
(479) 287-4020

The Curious Book Shoppe on Block Street
204 N. Block, Fayetteville, AR 72704
(479) 283-2225
Small specialized bookshop

Cork & Keg (Wine Bar)
509 W Spring Street, Ste 230, Fayetteville, AR 72701
(479) 966-4383

Uncle Sam's Safari Outfitters
1494 N College Ave, Fayetteville, AR 72703
(479) 521-7779

Wild Heart Designs
2016 N Shiloh Drive, Fayetteville, AR 72704
(479) 442-3889

Bike Shops
Arkansas Good Bikes
3300 Martin Luther King, Fayetteville, AR 72704
(479) 935-3345

The Bike Route
3660 N. Front #3, Fayetteville, AR 72703
(479) 966-4050

Highroller Cyclery Fayetteville
322 W. Spring, Fayetteville, AR 72701
(479) 442-9311

Lewis and Clark Outfitters (U of A Campus)
640 Garland, Fayetteville, 72701
(479) 695-0202

Phat Tire Bike Shop
3761 North Mall, Fayetteville, AR 72703
(479) 966-4308

Tattoo shops
Brainstorm Tattoo
930 N College Ave, Fayetteville, AR 72701
(479) 442-4877

Independent Tattoo Company
2417 N College Ave, Fayetteville, AR 72764
(479) 251-8282

Ink and Glass Company
339 West Ave #101, Fayetteville, AR 72701
(479) 966-4820

Supernova Tattoo Studio and Gallery
30 N Block Ave, Fayetteville, AR 72701
(479) 935-4431

Spas
5th Elements Massage
28 S. College, Fayetteville, AR 72701
(479) 442-5470

The Bodhi Tree Salon & Spa
2520 E. Mission, Fayetteville, AR 72703
(479) 444-6464

Bodyworks Therapeutic Massage Center
125 E. Township, Fayetteville, AR 72703
(479) 521-9119

The Crown Beauty Bar
509 W. Spring, Fayetteville, AR 72701
(479) 935-4070

Glo Limited
577 E. Millsap, Fayetteville, AR 72703
(479) 571-4456

I.M. Spa
25 N. Block, Fayetteville, AR 72701
(479) 251-7422

Inspire Eco Salon & Spa
675 N. Lollar, Fayetteville, AR 72701
(479) 301-2800

La Vida Massage
745 E. Joyce, Fayetteville, AR 72703
(479) 521-3232

Massage Matters
1011 N. College, Fayetteville, AR 72701
(479) 466-8859

Massage Therapy Professionals
28 S. College, Fayetteville, AR 72701
(479) 571-3020

Pure Solace Body Boutique
345 N. St. Charles, Fayetteville, AR 72701
(479) 443-1729

Tramps Salon & Day Spa
716 W. Sycamore, Fayetteville, AR 72766
(479) 521-4450

Revive Medical Spa
1444 East Stearns, Fayetteville, AR 72703
(479) 287-4738

White Lotus Salon & Massage
4750 E. Mission, Fayetteville, AR 72703
(479) 582-4806

Special Events
Bikes, Blues & BBQ
P.O. Box 712 Fayetteville, AR 72702
(479) 527-9993
Wildly popular motorcycle rally held in September of each year with an approximate attendance of 400,000 bike enthusiasts.

Fayetteville Farmers Market
Fayetteville Downtown Square
101 W. Mountain St, Fayetteville, AR 72701
(479) 236-2910

Fayetteville Downtown Square is the place to go on Tuesday, Thursday and Saturday mornings from April through October. Select from the best of locally grown produce, plants, flowers, honey and native crafts. Meet the growers and the artisans in person and have some hot coffee and donuts from vendors on the square and nearby Fayetteville, AR restaurants.

Sat: 7am-2pm (April – Nov)

Tues and Thur: 7am-1pm (April – Oct)

Jefferson Center Playground

Sun: 9am-1pm (May – Oct)

Fayetteville Farmers Market at the Botanical Garden of the Ozarks

4703 Crossover Road, Fayetteville AR 72764

Sat: 7am -12 (April-Nov)

Wed: 4pm-7pm (April – Nov)

Northwest Arkansas Farmers Market

Mae Farms, 4782 N. College, Fayetteville, AR 72703

(479) 225-5124

Wed: 3-7pm (March – Nov)

Sat-Sun: 7am-2pm (March, April, Oct and Nov)

Sat-Sun: 7am-7pm (May – Sept)

First Thursday Fayetteville

Fayetteville celebrates on the first Thursday of each month (April to October) at the city's historic downtown square. This event features live music, street performers, visual artists, food, and drink.

Washington County Fair is held from mid-to-late August every year. The Fairs are a true fall tradition and are enjoyed for their livestock shows, fair foods, special events and rides.

Lights of the Ozarks

The spirit of the holidays comes alive each year as millions of lights cover the Fayetteville town square. Families and visitors alike flock to the area to enjoy a celebration of the holiday spectacle beginning the day before Thanksgiving through New Year's Day.

Additional Festivals:

JANUARY

Le Chocolate Feast

FEBRUARY

Dig In Festival

Mardi Gras

MARCH

St. Patick's Day on the Hill

APRIL

Amazon Music Festival

Blues in the Natural State Music Festival

Springfest

MAY

Block Street Block Party

Fayetteville Foam Fest

AUGUST

Fayetteville Roots Festival

Washington County Fair

DECEMBER

Last Night Fayetteville

RESTAURANTS

If you don't live in Northwest Arkansas, you may be surprised to learn that the restaurants in Fayetteville are plenteous with many of them being unique to this NW corner of the state. Visitors from nearby towns, across the state, and from neighboring states come to Fayetteville on a regular basis just to sample the truly different cuisine found only in the area.

There are five distinct restaurant areas in Fayetteville:

1. The Downtown/Dickson Street area represents the downtown area, as well as the area that surrounds the U of A.

2. The area around College Avenue otherwise known as 71B.

3. Tasty eating joints in and around the Northwest Arkansas Mall.

4. Restaurants around the I-49 corridor.

5. Last, but not least, the Mission/Crossover area in the east part of Fayetteville.

Restaurant Prices

$ - Budget	*$$$ - Upscale*
$$ - Mid-Range	

American

Applebee's Neighborhood Grill 4078 N College Ave, Fayetteville, AR 72703 (479) 442-8841 $$	Logan's Roadhouse 3611 Shiloh Drive, Fayetteville, AR 72703 (479) 251-7775 $
AQ Chicken House 1925 N College Ave, Fayetteville, AR 72703 (479) 443-7555 $$	Mayflower (Coming Soon)

Denny's 2589 W 6th Street, Fayetteville, AR 72704 (479) 571-1433 $	Ricks Iron Skillet 1131 S School Ave, Fayetteville, AR 72701 (479) 442-2200 $
East Side Grill 1838 N Crossover Rd, Fayetteville, AR 72701 479) 966-4823 $$	Ruby Tuesday 1031 Krupa Drive, Fayetteville, AR 72704 (479) 442-7933 $
Frickin' Chicken 509 W Spring Street, Ste 210, Fayetteville, AR 72701 (479) 966-4667 $	Slim Chickens 2120 N College Ave, Fayetteville, AR (479) 443-7546 $
Golden Corral 4507 N College Ave, Fayetteville, AR 72703 (479) 443-0433 $	Slim Chickens 2403 Main Dr #1 Fayetteville, AR (479) 935-4444 $
Greenhouse Grille 481 S School Ave, Fayetteville, AR 72701 (479) 444-8909 $$	The Farmer's Table Café 1079 S School Ave, Fayetteville, AR 72701 (479) 966-4125 $
Hammontree's Grilled Cheese 326 NW Ave #8, Fayetteville, AR 72701 (479) 521-1669 $$	Village Inn 3364 N College Ave, Fayetteville, AR 72703 (479) 521-1880
IHOP Restaurant 3153 W Wedington Dr, Fayetteville, AR 72704 (479) 442-0770 $	Waffle House 2311 W 6th Street, Fayetteville, AR 72701 (479) 443-7549 $

Asian

Asian 1818 N Crossover Road, Fayetteville, AR 72701 (479) 251-1818 $$	Mong Dynasty 3101 N College Ave, Fayetteville, AR 72703 (479) 443-7666 $$
A Taste of Thai 31 E Center St, Ste 100, Fayetteville, AR 72701 (479) 251-1800 $$	P.F. Chang's 2203 Promenade Blvd, Fayetteville, AR 72703 (479) 621-0491 $
China Cafe 2630 E Citizens Dr #16, Fayetteville, AR 72703 (479) 442-3998 $	Salathai 701 S School Ave, Fayetteville, AR 72701 (479) 575-9311 $$
J D China Chinese Restaurant 1740 Martin Luther King Jr. Blvd, Fayetteville, AR 72701 (479) 442-5875 $$	Shogun Steak, Seafood, and Sushi of Japan 4096 N Steele Blvd, Fayetteville, AR 72703 (479) 442-9999 $$
Formosa Chinese Restaurant 1998 N College Ave, Fayetteville, AR 72703 (479) 571-8886 $$	Taiwan Chinese Restaurant 2227 Martin Luther King Jr. Blvd, Fayetteville, AR 72701 (479) 521-5210 $
Ginger Rice and Noodle Bar 1163 Martin Luther King Jr Blvd, Fayetteville, AR 72701 (479) 856-6965 $	Thai Diner 514 N College Ave, Fayetteville, AR 72701 (479) 582-1804 $

Hunan Manor Chinese Restaurant 1147 N Tahoe Place, Fayetteville, AR 72704 (479) 521-3883 $$	Thai E-San 2334 N College Ave , Fayetteville, AR 72703 (479) 587-8177 $
Kj Sushi and Korean BBQ 3223 N College Ave, Fayetteville, AR 72703 (479) 301-2008 $$	Thep Thai Restaurant 1525 S School Ave, Fayetteville, AR 72701 (479) 443-0029 $$
Kobe Hibachi Grill and Sushi 643 Van Asche Drive, Fayetteville, AR 72704 (479) 443-5622 $$	Tokyo Sushi and Bar 522 W Dickson Street, Fayetteville, AR 72701 (479) 444-8122 $$
Meiji Japanese Cuisine 3878 N Crossover Road #8, Fayetteville, AR 72703 (479) 521-5919 $$	Wasabi 313 W Dickson Street, Fayetteville, AR 72701 (479) 527-0268 $$

Bakeries

Bliss Cupcake Cafe 14 South Block Ave, Fayetteville, AR 72701 (479) 575-0575	Golden Kolache Bakery LLC 2212 Main Drive, Fayetteville, AR 72704 (479) 439-0835
Briar Rose Bakery and Deli 28 E Main Street, Farmington, AR 72730 (479) 300-6027	Little Bread Company 116 N Block Ave, Fayetteville, AR 72701 (479) 527-0622
Bouchee 1 E Center Street, Fayetteville, AR 72701 (479) 409-0509	Panera Bread 3638 N Front Street, Fayetteville, AR 72703 (479) 587-1188

Chuck's Cake Shoppe 407 N College Ave, Fayetteville, AR 72701 (479) 442-2253	Rick's Bakery 1220 N College Ave, Fayetteville, AR 72703 (479) 442-2166
Einstein Bros Bagels 1500 N College Ave, Fayetteville, AR 72703 (479) 587-8950	Shipley Do-nuts 1640 N College Ave, Fayetteville, AR 73703 (479) 442-1794
Fayetteville Pastry Shop 6315 Wedington Dr Unit #1, Fayetteville, AR 72704 (479) 530-3349	Stonemill Bread Co 2600 N Gregg Ave, Fayetteville, AR 72703 (479) 571-2295

BBQ

Boars Nest BBQ 1189 Steamboat Drive, Fayetteville, AR 72704 (479) 443-4152 $$	Penguin Ed's West 6347 W Wedington Dr, Fayetteville, AR 72704 (479) 251-7429 $$
Penguin Ed's B&B 230 S East Ave, Fayetteville, AR 72701 (479) 521-3663 $$	Sassy's Red House 708 N College Ave, Fayetteville, AR 72701 (479) 856-6366 $$
Ed's Penguin Cafe 2769 Mission Blvd, Fayetteville, AR 72701 (479) 587-8646 $$	The Bar-B-Q Place 3542 E Huntsville Rd, Fayetteville, AR 72701 (479) 301-2500 $
Herman's Ribhouse 2901 N College Ave, Fayetteville, AR 72703 (479) 442-9671 $$$	Wes's Barbeque 14 South University Av, Fayetteville, AR 72701 (479) 521-5901 $

Lucky Luke's BBQ 1220 Garland Ave, Fayetteville, AR 72703 (479) 521-7550 $$	Whole Hog Cafe 3009 N College Ave, Fayetteville, AR 72703 (479) 442-0100 $

Breweries/Pubs

21st Amendment 406 W Dickson Street, Fayetteville, AR 72701 (479) 856-6686 $$	Hog Haus Brewing Co 430 W Dickson Street, Fayetteville, AR 72701 (479) 521-2739 $$
Apple Blossom Brewing Company 1550 E Zion Road #1, Fayetteville, AR 72703 (479) 287-4344 $$	Hutch's Sports Bar 45 Colt Square Drive, Fayetteville, AR 72703 (479) 521-7129 $
Brewski's Draft Emporium 408 W Dickson Street, Fayetteville, AR 72701 (479) 973-6969 $$	Maxine's Tap Room 107 N Block Ave, Fayetteville, AR 72701 (479) 442-9601 $$
Buffalo Wild Wings 32 W Joyce Blvd, Fayetteville, AR 72703 (479) 251-9464 $	Mickey Finn's Irish Pub 644 W Dickson Street, Fayetteville, AR 72701 (479) 527-9333 $$
Dickson Street Pub 303 W. Dickson Street, Fayetteville, AR 72701 (479) 935-3579 $	Ryleigh's 313 W Dickson St #105, Fayetteville, AR 72701 (479) 444-7324 $$

Electric Cowboy 2127 Martin Luther King Jr. Blvd, Fayetteville, AR 72701 (479) 571-8100 $$	Speakeasy Nightclub and Lounge 509 W Spring St #250, Fayetteville, AR 72701 (479) 443-3279 $
Farrells Lounge Bar & Grill 311 W Dickson St #101, Fayetteville, AR 72701 (479) 301-2220 $$	Tanglewood Branch Beer Co 1431 South School Avenue, Fayetteville, AR , 72701 (479) 856-6500 $$
Foghorn's 1815 Green Acres, Fayetteville, AR 72703 (479) 527-9464 $	Tilted Kilt Pub and Eatery 3619 N Mall Ave, Fayetteville, AR 72703 (479) 442-0800 $$
Fossil Cove Brewing Co. 1946 N. Birch Avenue, Fayetteville, AR 72703 (479) 445-6050 $$	West Mountain Brewing Co 21 West Mountain Street, Fayetteville, AR (479) 442-9090 $$
Grub's Bar and Grille 220 NW Ave, Fayetteville, AR 72701 (479) 973-4782 $$	

Bistro

Table Mesa Bistro in Fayetteville 401 W Watson #203, Fayetteville, AR 72701 (479) 668-4019 $$	

Brunch

Cafe Rue Orleans (Sunday Brunch) 1150 N College Ave, Fayetteville, AR 72703 (479) 443-2777 $$	Greenhouse Grille (Sunday Brunch) 481 S School Ave, Fayetteville, AR 72701 (479) 444-8909 $$
Emelia's Kitchen (Sunday Brunch) 309 W Dickson Street, Fayetteville, AR 72701 (479) 527-9800 $$	

Burgers

Art's Place 2530 N College Ave, Fayetteville, AR 72703 (479) 443-7113 $	Mr. Burger 1139 N Lindell Ave, Fayetteville, AR 72703 (479) 521-2680 $
Bear's Place 504 E 15th Street, Fayetteville, AR 72701 (479) 521-2327 $	Red Robin Gourmet Burgers 695 Van Asche Drive, Fayetteville, AR 72703 (479) 521-3524 $$
Curt's Place 2135 Main Drive, Fayetteville, AR 72704 (479) 571-3490 $	ROTC and the Grill 3582 N Hwy 112, Fayetteville, AR 72704 (479) 521-2674 $
Deluxe Burger 550 W Dickson St, Ste 2, Fayetteville, AR 72701 (479) 445-6086 $$	Schoolhouse Cafe and Market 177 East Bowen Blvd, Fayetteville, AR 72703 (479) 444-6500 $

Feltner Brothers 2768 N College Ave, Fayetteville, AR 72703 (479) 935-4545 $	**Steak 'n Shake** 4074 N Mall Ave, Fayetteville, AR 72703 (479) 444-6343 $
Grub's Uptown 3467 N Shiloh Drive, Fayetteville, AR 72704 (479) 582-4782 $$	**The Burger Patti** 3327 W Wedington Dr, Fayetteville, AR 72704 (479) 301-2343 $$
Hugo's 25 1/2 N Block Ave, Fayetteville, AR 72701 (479) 521-7585 $$	**The Garage (Coming Soon)** 100 E Joyce Boulevard, Fayetteville, AR 72703
JJ's Grill of Fayetteville 1271 N Steamboat Dr, Fayetteville, AR 72704 (479) 443-0700 $$	**Whataburger (Coming Soon)** 1920 W Martin Luther King Jr. Blvd, Fayetteville, AR 72701
The Boardwalk Bar and Grill 3878 N Crossover Road, Fayetteville, AR 72703 (479) 287-4151 $$	

Catering

Jason's Deli 745 E Joyce Blvd #114, Fayetteville, AR 72701 (479) 442-5500	**The Garden Room** N Church Ave, Fayetteville, AR 72701 (479) 966-7132
Trav's Rib Shack Competition BBQ & Catering 1643 E Mission Blvd, Fayetteville, AR 72703 (479) 841-2690	

Coffee

Arsaga's Espresso Cafe 548 W Dickson Street, Fayetteville, AR 72701 (479) 443-9900 $	Mama Carmen's Espresso Cafe 2850 N College Ave, Fayetteville, AR 72703 (479) 521-6262 $
Baba Boudan's Espresso 701 N College Ave, Fayetteville, AR 72701 (479) 582-9540 $	Onyx Coffee Lab 2418 N Gregg Ave, Fayetteville, AR 72703 (479) 444-6557 $
Big Momma's Coffee and Espresso 609 W Dickson St #104, Fayetteville, AR 72701 (479) 444-6780 $	Starbucks 1021 W Dickson Street, Fayetteville, AR 72701 (479) 575-4120 $
Brick House Kitchen 1 E Center St, Ste 160, Fayetteville, AR 72701 (479) 587-9500 $	Starbucks 3901 N Shiloh Drive, Fayetteville, AR 72703 (479) 444-3380 $
Coffee Creations 56 Yukon Way, Farmington, AR 72730 (479) 267-5300 $	Starbucks 111 Ozark Ave, Fayetteville, AR 72701 (479) 444-3380 $
Hookah Java Cafe and Lounge 311 W Dickson St #104, Fayetteville, AR 72701 (479) 301-2200 $	Starbucks 2117 W Martin Luther King Jr. Blvd, Fayetteville, AR 72701 (479) 575-0654 $
Jammin' Java 21 W Mountain St #228, Fayetteville, AR 72701 (479) 443-2233 $	The Common Grounds 412 W Dickson Street, Fayetteville, AR 72701 (479) 442-3515 $

Jammin' Java 4201 N Shiloh Drive, Fayetteville, AR 72701 (479) 582-2739 $	The Perk II 3980 W Wedington Dr, Fayetteville, AR 72704 (479) 856-6382 $
Latte Da 3232 N North Hills Blvd, Fayetteville, AR 72703 (479) 695-1334 $	The Red Kite Coffee Company 1852 N Crossover Road, Fayetteville, AR 72701 (479) 527-0690 $

Fast Food

Arby's 1263 W 6th Street, Fayetteville, AR 72701 (479) 571-2056 $	McDonald's 3080 W Wedington Dr, Fayetteville, AR 72704 (479) 442-7774 $
Arby's 220 East Joyce Blvd, Fayetteville, AR 72703 (479) 582-2336 $	Popeye's Louisiana Kitchen 2100 W 6th Street, Fayetteville, AR 72701 (479) 935-4665 $
Burger King 2345 N College Ave, Fayetteville, AR 72703 (479) 442-4335 $	Sonic 1144 N Colorado Drive, Fayetteville, AR 72704 (479) 444-9404 $
Chick-fil-A 1369 Martin Luther King Jr. Blvd, Fayetteville, AR 72701 (479) 444-6570 $	Sonic 1321 W 6th Street, Fayetteville, AR 72701 (479) 444-7858 $

Chick-fil-A 4180 N College Ave, Fayetteville, AR 72703 (479) 443-0343 $	Subway 121 W Township St #19, Fayetteville, AR 72701 (479) 443-7827 $
Chick-fil-A 435 Garland Ave #209, Fayetteville, AR 72701 (479) 575-5043 $	Subway 2000 N Crossover Road, Fayetteville, AR 72703 (479) 442-0003 $
Kentucky Fried 2992 N College Ave, Fayetteville, AR 72703 (479) 444-6641 $	Subway 3245 W Wedington Dr, Fayetteville, AR 72701 (479) 442-8363 $
Kentucky Fried 1882 Martin Luther King Jr. Blvd, Fayetteville, AR 72701 (479) 443-7040 $	Taco Bell 2055 Martin Luther King Jr. Blvd, Fayetteville, AR 72701 (479) 521-2538 $
McDonald's 1641 N College Ave, Fayetteville, AR 72701 (479) 521-1767 $	Wendy's 1473 W 6th Street, Fayetteville, AR 72701 (479) 443-2501 $
McDonald's 1963 Martin Luther King Jr. Blvd, Fayetteville, AR 72701 (479) 443-4777 $	Wendy's 2050 N College Ave, Fayetteville, AR 72703 (479) 571-1274 $

Fine Dining

Ella's Restaurant	Theo's
465 Arkansas Ave, Fayetteville, AR 72701	318 N Campbell Ave, Fayetteville, AR 72701
(479) 582-1400	(479) 527-0086
$$$$	$$$
Vetro 1925 Ristorante	
17 E Center Street, Fayetteville, AR 72701	
(479) 966-4649	
$$$	

Food Trucks

Shulertown Food Truck Court (Coming Soon)

Dickson Street, Fayetteville, AR

Owner Zac Wooden, who also owns Roger's Rec and 21st Amendment, has seven food truck owners leasing space inside the up and coming Shulertown Food Truck Court. They are:

- Greenhouse Grille
- Feltner Brothers
- Baller Foodtruck
- Shakedown StrEAT Grill
- Burton's Comfort Creamery
- Great Dang Pies and Tamales.

Other area food trucks include:

Best Frickin Chicken In Town	Kind Kitchen
Colorado's Chili	Kona Coast
Go Go's Energy Cafe	Nomad's Natural Plate
Hammontree's Grillenium	The Hopper Food Truck
Hawaiian Brian's	The Naan Stop
Holy Smokin' Fajoli	Zuppa Zuppa Soup Kitchen

Jack Frosting Cupcakes and Coffee	2 Fish 5 Loaves
Just a Smoker – Boilin Pot	
For More Information: Yacht Club on College	

Event Venue

324 Ballroom 324 W Dickson St, Fayetteville, AR 72701 (479) 527-6865	The Garden Room 215 West Dickson St. Fayetteville, AR 72701 (479) 966-7132
Teatro Scarpino 329 NW Ave, Fayetteville, AR 72701 (479) 966-7363	The North Forty 40 N Crossover Rd, Fayetteville, AR 72701 (479) 521-3739

Ice Cream ~ Frozen Yogurt

Andy's Frozen Custard 1513 Martin Luther King Jr. Blvd, Fayetteville, AR 72701 (479) 582-9404 $	Phoebe's Treats 2117 W Martin Luther King Jr. Blvd, Fayetteville, AR 72701 (479) 444-8939 $
Bobo's Ribbon Ice 1155 N Tahoe Place, Fayetteville, AR (479) 442-2333 $	Shake's Frozen Custard 2797 N College Ave, Fayetteville, AR 72703 (479) 444-9777 $
Braum's Ice Cream and Dairy Store 1894 W 6th Street, Fayetteville, AR 72701 (479) 444-6207 $	Shave the Planet (Shaved Ice) 3600 N College Ave, Fayetteville, AR 72703 (479) 871-1948 $

Cold Stone Creamery 160 E Joyce Blvd #109, Fayetteville, AR 72703 (479) 582-9050 $	Steak 'n Shake 4074 Mall Ave, Fayetteville, AR 72703 (479) 444-6343 $
Dippin' Dots 4201 N Shiloh Drive, Fayetteville, AR 72703 (479) 521-6881 $	TCBY - The Garland Shops 640 Garland Ave, Fayetteville, AR 72701 (479) 301-2719 $
Maggie Moo's 3155 N College Ave, Fayetteville, AR 72703 (479) 521-8898 $	Three Crazy Berries 1826 N Crossover Road #1, Fayetteville, AR 72701 (479) 287-4489 $
Orange Leaf Self Serve Frozen Yogurt 609 W Dickson St #201, Fayetteville, AR 72701 (479) 582-2200 $	

Italian

Bordinos Restaurant 310 W Dickson Street, Fayetteville, AR 72701 (479) 527-6795 $$	Olive Garden 3616 Mall Ave, Fayetteville, AR 72703 (479) 443-4438 $
Fresco Cafe and Pub 112 W Center St #100, Fayetteville, AR 72701 (479) 455-5555 $$	Pesto Cafe 1830 N College Ave, Fayetteville, AR 72703 (479) 582-3330 $$

Geraldi's 20 S University Ave, Fayetteville, AR 72701 (479) 575-0556 $$	Vetro 1925 Ristorante 17 E Center St, Fayetteville, AR 72701 (479) 966-4649 $$$
Noodles Italian Kitchen 3748 Mall Ave, Fayetteville, AR 72703 (479) 443-7100 $$	

Mediterranean

Coco's Lebanese Cafe 120 N. Block Ave., Fayetteville, AR 72701 (479) 799-0322 $$	Petra Cafe 31 E Center Street, Fayetteville, AR 72701 (479) 443-3090 $
Emelia's Kitchen (Sunday Brunch) 309 W Dickson Street, Fayetteville, AR 72701 (479) 527-9800 $$	Tangiers Mediterranean Food and Cafe 2800 N College Ave, Fayetteville, AR 72703 (479) 301-2211 $
Kosmos Greekafe 2136 N College Ave, Fayetteville, AR 72703 (479) 521-7482 $	Taziki's Mediterranean Cafe 95, E Joyce Blvd, Fayetteville, AR 72703 (479) 521-8291 $$
Nomad's Natural Plate (Food Truck) 205 W Dickson St, Fayetteville, AR 72701 (479) 435-5312 $	

Mexican

Acambaro Mexican Restaurant 2605 N College Ave, Fayetteville, AR 72703 (479) 442-3454 $$	La Hacienda 2901 E Zion Road #20, Fayetteville, AR 72703 (479) 444-0821 $$
Ay! Caramba 1120 N Lindell Ave, Fayetteville, AR 72703 (479) 444-1977 $$	La Hacienda Mexican Restaurant 1545 W 15th Street, Fayetteville, AR 72701 (479) 251-1555 $$
Burrito Loco 2155 W 6th Street, Fayetteville, AR 72701 (479) 527-9577 $	La Huerta Mexican Restaurant 2356 N College Ave, Fayetteville, AR 72703 (479) 521-7990 $$
Chipotle Mexican Grill 550 W Dickson St, Fayetteville, AR 72701 (479) 444-1466 $	Mangos Gourmet Taco Shop 2050 Martin Luther King Jr. Blvd, Fayetteville, AR 72701 (479) 301-2793 $
Chili's 772 Millsap Road, Fayetteville, AR 72703 (479) 521-9921 $	Mariachi's Grill and Cantina 4201 N Shiloh Dr, Fayetteville, AR 72703 (479) 718-0002 $$
El Camino Real 815 S School Ave, Fayetteville, AR 72701 (479) 521-6268 $	Mojito's Mexican Grill 100 E Joyce Blvd, Fayetteville, AR 72703 (479) 527-9200 $
El Matador Mexican Grill and Bar 1290 Steamboat Drive, Fayetteville, AR 72704 (479) 856-6950 $	Mexico Viejo 3901 N Shiloh Drive, Fayetteville, AR 72703 (479) 587-8181 $$

El Paso Mexican Grille Cantina 3980 W Wedington Dr, Unit 3, Fayetteville, AR 72704 (479) 287-4484 $$	Qdoba Mexican Grill 603 W Dickson Street, Fayetteville, AR 72701 (479) 444-7470 $
El Sol Mexican Restaurant 2630 E Citizens Drive, Fayetteville, AR 72703 (479) 443-0606 $$	The Flying Burrito Co 509 W Spring St #220, Fayetteville, AR 72701 (479) 521-3000 $
Jose's Mexican Restaurant 324 W Dickson Street, Fayetteville, AR 72701 (479) 521-0194 $$	

Pizza

Cable Car Pizza 2630 E Citizens Drive, Fayetteville, AR 72703 (479) 444-7600 $$	Mojo's Pints and Pies 1200 Garland Ave #7, Fayetteville, AR 72703 (479) 935-3459 $
CiCi's Pizza 637 E Joyce Blvd #101, Fayetteville, AR 72703 (479) 582-9292 $	Mojo's Pints and Pies 1200 Garland Ave #7, Fayetteville, AR 72703 (479) 935-3459 $
City Pizzeria and Salad Company 1641 W 15th St, Ste 1, Fayetteville, AR 72701 (479) 301-2100 $$	Papa John's Pizza 503 N College Ave, Fayetteville, AR 72701 (479) 444-1999 $$

Damgoode Pies 31 E Center Street, Fayetteville, AR 72701 (479) 444-7437 $$	Papa John's 1021 W Dickson Street, Fayetteville, AR 72701 (479) 575-8704 $$
Domino's Pizza 1065 Garland Ave, Fayetteville, AR 72701 (479) 442-3600 $	Pizza Hut 1754 N College Ave, Fayetteville, AR 72703 (479) 521-2992 $
Domino's Pizza 1814 N Crossover Road #1, Fayetteville, AR 72704 (479) 445-6555 $$	Tiny Tim's Pizza 21 W Mountain Street, Fayetteville, AR 72701 (479) 521-5551 $$
Eureka Pizza 826 N Leverett Ave, Fayetteville, AR 72701 (479) 443-7777 $	Tim's Pizza 1813 E Mission Blvd, Fayetteville, AR 72703 (479) 521-5056 $
Gusano's Chicago Style Pizzeria 1267 Steamboat Dr #2, Fayetteville, AR 72701 (479) 287-4000 $$	U S Pizza Co 202 W Dickson Street, Fayetteville, AR 72701 (479) 582-4808 $
Jim's Razorback Pizza 2020 W 6th Street, Fayetteville, AR 72701 (479) 443-2265 $	Wood Stone Craft Pizza 557 S School Ave, Fayetteville, AR 72701 (479) 444-8909 $
Marley's Chicago Style Pizzeria 609 W. Dickson Street #103, (Inside the Dickson) Fayetteville, AR 72701 (918) 551-7744	Ye Olde King Pizza 3162 Martin Luther King Jr. Blvd, Fayetteville, AR 72704 (479) 442-5464 $

Mellow Mushroom	Zs Brick Oven Pizza
1460 E Augustine Lane, Fayetteville, AR 72703 (479) 521-1001 $$	2730 N College Ave, Fayetteville, AR 72703 (479) 935-4299 $

Music

Georges Majestic Lounge	J R's Pizzeria and Lightbulb Club
519 W Dickson Street, Fayetteville, AR 72701 (479) 442-4226	21 N Block Ave, Fayetteville, AR 72701 (479) 444-6100

Sandwiches

Atlanta Bread Co	Panera Bread
3196 N College Ave, Fayetteville, AR 72703 (479) 442-2900 $$	3638 N Front Street, Fayetteville, AR 72703 (479) 587-1188 $
Firehouse Subs	Quiznos
2612 Martin Luther King Jr. Blvd, Fayetteville, AR 72701 (479) 251-1122 $	1021 W Dickson Street, Fayetteville, AR 72701 (479) 575-2954 $
Firehouse Subs	The Green Submarine Espresso Cafe & Sub Shop
1364 E Augustine Lane, Fayetteville, AR 72703 (479) 251-0044 $	3315 W Wedington Dr, Fayetteville, AR 72704 (479) 287-4588 $
Jason's Deli	Tropical Smoothie Cafe
745 E Joyce Blvd #114, Fayetteville, AR 72701 (479) 442-5500 $$	3878 N Crossover Road, Fayetteville, AR 72703 (479) 582-4444 $$

Jimmy John's Gourmet Sandwiches 518 W Dickson, Fayetteville, AR 72701 (479) 571-0600 $	Tropical Smoothie Cafe 2350 N College Ave, Fayetteville, AR (479) 966-4660 $$
Lenny's Sub Shop 160 E Joyce Blvd, Fayetteville, AR 72701 (479) 521-1731 $	Schlotzsky's 2548 N College Ave, Fayetteville, AR 72703 (479) 443-5000 $
Loafin Joe's 201 W Mountain Street, Fayetteville, AR 72701 (479) 443-9944 $	Subway 121 W Township St #19, Fayetteville, AR 72701 (479) 443-7827 $
Little Bread Company 116 N Block Ave, Fayetteville, AR 72701 (479) 527-0622 $	Subway 2000 N Crossover Rd, Fayetteville, AR 72703 (479) 442-0003 $
McAlister's Deli 4055 N Steele Blvd, Fayetteville, AR 72703 (479) 521-7900 $	Subway 3245 W Wedington Dr, Fayetteville, AR 72701 (479) 442-8363 $
Natural State Sandwiches 3251 N College Ave, Fayetteville, AR 72701 (479) 935-4575 $	Zaxby's 1670 Martin Luther King Jr. Blvd, Fayetteville, AR 72701 (479) 575-9171 $
Packard on Block (Coming Soon)	Zaxby's 3251 N College Ave, Fayetteville, AR 72703 (479) 935-4575 $

Seafood

Cafe Rue Orleans 1150 N College Ave, Fayetteville, AR 72703 (479) 443-2777 $$	Mermaids 2217 N College Ave, Fayetteville, AR 72703 (479) 443-3737 $$
Catfish Hole 4127 W Wedington Dr, Fayetteville, AR 72704 (479) 521-7008 $$	Powerhouse Seafood and Grill 112 N University Ave, Fayetteville, AR 72701 (479) 442-8300 $$
Juicy Tails 745 E Joyce Blvd, Ste 218, Fayetteville, AR 72704 (479) 935-4100 $$	Red Lobster 3885 N Shiloh Drive, Fayetteville, AR 72703 (479) 442-2317 $$

Steaks

Colton's Steak House and Grill 642 Millsap Road, Fayetteville, AR 72703 (479) 973-0876 $$	Doe's Eat Place 316 W Dickson Street, Fayetteville, AR 72701 (479) 443-3637 *$$$*

LOWELL

Lowell, AR nicknamed "Mudtown," is a city in Benton County, AR, and is part of the Fayetteville-Springdale-Rogers metropolitan statistical area.

J. B. Hunt is headquartered in this thriving municipality situated between Rogers and Fayetteville. This Arkansas based trucking company was incorporated in August of 1961, and has seen enormous growth since its modest beginnings. Starting off with five trucks and six refrigerated trailers, J.B. Hunt now operates over 12,000 trucks and 47,000 trailers. Aside from being one of the largest employers in the area, the company hires people from across the company to maintain its huge transportation business. Currently, the company employs around 16,000 people worldwide.

Visitors to Lowell may easily access the accommodations, recreational opportunities and amenities found in the nearby cities of Rogers, Fayetteville and Bentonville. Indeed, it is hard to know where one city ends and the other one begins.

The city is growing at a breakneck speed, however, and has much to offer in its own right. It is located in the center of booming NWA and the gorgeous Ozark Mountains. Restaurants are plentiful, recreation of every kind is within minutes, and hotel accommodations are on par with the best in the country.

ACCOMMODATIONS

There are many, many quality hotels along with other types of accommodations within a 6-mile radius of Lowell. Please check the Bentonville, Rogers and Fayetteville sections for additional accommodations. In Lowell, however, you'll find the:

Hotel Amenities

Breakfast: B	*Meeting Rooms: MR*
Business Center: BC	*Pet Friendly: PF*
Fitness Center: FC	*Pool: P*
Internet: I	*Restaurant: R*

Super 8 Motel I-540 Exit 78 Hwy 264 509 Hospitality Ave, Lowell, AR 72745 B, BC, FC, I, MR, P,	

THINGS TO DO AND SEE

Fast Lane Entertainment provides some of the best family fun in NWA. It has the largest arcade in NWA, first-class bowling, GoKarts, Laser Tag and the largest pizzas anywhere to satisfy any appetite.

If you are a history buff, you should visit the FREE Lowell Historical Museum downtown while you are staying in the area. It features antiques, photos and other memorabilia from Lowell's interesting and colorful past.

BMX racing enthusiasts can challenge themselves at the Mudtown BMX track at Ward Nail Park. The park also offers a pond where you can sit and relax the afternoon away, a 3.4-mile walking trail, covered outdoor stage area, picnic tables, basketball courts and playgrounds.

Another Lowell, AR park is McClure Park. This beautiful park offers visitors a covered picnic pavilion, a softball field and a playground.

Just down the road, you'll find Lowell Park where the Lowell Basketball Gym is made available to players with reservations. There is also a covered pavilion, a playground and an outdoor basketball court.

History buffs will enjoy Lowell's Heritage Park. It has a retired 1975 American La France Fire Engine truck on display.

Fast Lane Entertainment
1117 N Dixieland Street, Lowell, AR 72745
(479) 659-0999

Golf
Golf Mountain
115 Dixieland Road, Lowell, AR 72745
(479) 659-0001

Golf Mountain is NWA's premier mini-golf course with 36 holes and numerous dips, bumps, inclines, water hazards and advanced mini-golf multi-textured surfaces.

The Links at Lowell
105-A N Dixieland Street, Lowell, AR 72745
(479) 770-2100
9 hole public golf course

Museum
<u>*Lowell Historical Museum*</u>
304 Jackson Place, Lowell, AR 72745
(479) 770-0191

Parks
Ward Nail Park
801 McClure Ave, Lowell, AR 72745

McClure Park
121 McClure Ave, Lowell, AR 72745

Lowell Park
110 McClure Ave, Lowell, AR 72745

Heritage Park
218 Jackson Street, Lowell, AR 72745

RESTAURANTS

Both American and ethnic restaurants prosper in Lowell. You'll find eateries featuring everything you can think of from down-home American fare to Indian cuisine to the Palm Noodle Bar, where the noodles are freshly made on the premises. Lowell is also home to Dickey's Barbeque Pit and the top-rated Genuine Chicago Pizza. You will find most restaurants on Bloomington Street in Lowell, but the exact addresses are in the table below.

Restaurant Prices

$ - Budget	*$$$ - Upscale*
$ - Mid-Range	

American

Arby's 111 S Dixieland Street, Lowell, AR 72745 (479) 770-0092 $	My Cafe 320 N Bloomington Street, Lowell, AR 72745 (479) 659-0500 $
Dairy Queen 119 S Bloomington Street, Lowell, AR 72745 (479) 770-0808 $	Ron's Hamburgers and Chili 109 N Bloomington Street, Lowell, AR 72745 (479) 770-4420 $
KFC - Lowell 207 S Bloomington Street, Lowell, AR 72745 (479) 770-0781 $	Sonic Drive-In 115 S Bloomington Street, Lowell, AR 72745 (479) 770-0656 $
McDonald's 503 W Monroe Ave, Lowell, AR 72745 (479) 770-3300 $	Taco Bell 106 S Bloomington Street, Lowell, AR 72745 (479) 770-0948 $

Asian

Palm Noodle Bar	Thai Ginger
200 S Bloomington St Lowell, AR 72745	903 North Bloomington St Lowell, AR 72745
(479) 770-0011	(479) 202-5005
$	$

BBQ

Dickey's Barbecue Pit	
105 S Dixieland Road, Lowell, AR 72745	
(479) 770-0123	
$	

Mexican

Acambaro Mexican Restaurant	
406 N Bloomington Street, Lowell, AR 72745	
(479) 659-8919	
$	

Pizza

Jim's Razorback Pizza	Pizza Hut
326-B N Bloomington Street, Lowell, AR 72745	903 N Bloomington Street, Lowell, AR 72745
(479) 878-2525	(479) 659-5062
$	$

Sandwiches

Quiznos	SUBWAY Restaurants
225 N Bloomington Street, Lowell, AR 72745	200 S Bloomington Street, Lowell, AR 72745
(479) 419-9959	(479) 770-0057
$	$

ROGERS

Pinnacle Hills Promenade

Rogers is a booming, lively community, with a terrific new shopping district featuring both independent and national stores. The Promenade shopping area, along with Village on the Creeks, takes a backseat to no one. Simply stated, if you want something, this shopping hub will have it.

If you enjoy music, you will love the Walmart Arkansas Music Pavilion (Walmart AMP) This 10,000 seat outdoor music venue attracts top musical acts from multiple genres and is considered one of the top 100 amphitheaters in the nation.

Like the outdoors? Then you are going to really enjoy Beaver Lake. This manmade pristine lake covers 28,000 acres, includes 650 campsites and offers all kinds of fishing, water sports, boating and hiking. Beaver Lake is host to the Walmart FLW Tour Beaver Lake Bass tournament which draws professional fishermen from all over the country.

Rogers is also home to the Pinnacle Country Club, a world-class venue for championship golf.

Restaurants in Rogers, AR include locally owned as well as multiple chain eateries that offer delicious menus with a large variety of cuisines. Many Rogers restaurants are located along the I-49 corridor, which the locals call "restaurant row."

MAP OF ROGERS

Neighborhoods

Rogers, AR is made up of three wonderfully unique, yet interwoven neighborhoods. A local and tourist favorite is the Rogers downtown area. Here, you will find charming cobblestone streets leading you to many eclectic shops and eateries. Downtown Rogers is also home to exciting events and festivals.

The I-49 corridor runs through Rogers, and the area along this major thoroughfare is considered the second neighborhood section in the city. Naturally, you'll find plenty of necessities in this neighborhood, including food and shopping establishments and places to rest your head just off I-49.

The Promenade shopping area makes up Rogers third neighborhood, and, of course, you'll find a ton of shopping opportunities in this part of the city. There are also numerous restaurants in the Promenade shopping area. I'll discuss the shopping and eating in more detail in each section of this guide.

What the Locals Say...

As with the other sections in this travel guide, I took the time to listen to what the Rogers locals had to say about their fun and exciting city, and the first thing the locals raved about was the historical downtown Rogers area.

According to its residents, the historic district of Rogers offers something for everyone. Whether you are looking to do some serious shopping or eating, downtown Rogers has every kind of shop and restaurant imaginable and available to you daily. As I mentioned before, the downtown area is also the portion of Rogers that plays host to various weekly and monthly events.

Some of the downtown weekly events that the locals mentioned include Pickin' in the Park and the super-fun Farmer's Market. The third Friday of each month offers the Twilight Walk.

Annual events in downtown Rogers that are local faves include the Frisco Festival, the Goblin Parade, Christmas in the District and the Main Street Rogers Golf Tournament.

Rogers locals love to eat out, and they had plenty to say about their favorite and outstanding restaurants in the city. When visiting, the locals say the notable restaurants in Rogers, AR include:

- Shogun
- The Rail
- Mellow Mushroom
- The Egg and I
- Damgoode Pies – pizza pies, that is!
- Bonefish Grill
- Catfish John's
- Crabby's
- Mister B's
- Wesner's
- Basil's
- Carrabba's
- Iron Horse

Speaking of eateries, Rogers locals absolutely love Suzie Q, an old-fashioned, order at the window, and wait in your car while listening to rock and roll music until your number is called drive-in! Suzie Q has been around forever, and according to the locals, it makes the best Cherry Limeade, homemade milk shakes and curly fries.

Speaking of drinks, the WXYZ bar at the Aloft Rogers, AR hotel is hopping even on Monday nights. And what do the locals have to say about Alicia, the bartender? She's "great"!

Of course, while in Rogers, AR you simply must shop The Promenade. The locals love shopping in the many terrific shops and high-end national stores located in the mall.

I've mentioned it before, and I'll mention it again because it bears repeating: Rogers, AR is home to some wonderful food. You're going to eat a ton while visiting Rogers. Who says you can't keep fit while you're in the area even though you're enjoying all the fabulous Rogers, AR restaurants? The locals love the five World Gyms in their area. The gyms feature pools, tennis, spin classes, TRX classes, RIPPED, Zumba, tanning and traditional workout equipment. In addition, kids fit classes and childcare are provided.

If you can find a way to book a tee time, the locals say you must golf the Champions Golf Course. This premier golf course is manicured to perfection. As if it were visiting a Rogers spa, it receives a very high level of service and pampering... and so do the golfers who tackle the course! As such, it is no wonder that it is the location of an annual LPGA event. Champions Golf Course is members only, but if you are a guest at John Q. Hammons hotel, you can play as long as you pay.

Beautiful Beaver Lake has more than 28,000 surface acres of water, with more than 650 campsites. The lake is huge and a local favorite. Why? Because it offers all kinds of fishing, water sports, boating, camping and hiking. It also has many picnic areas and smaller hiking trails for your family to enjoy on a Sunday afternoon.

The locals also rave about the Rogers-area parks available for their use daily and yours, too, while you're visiting! Hobbs State Park is a mentionable must-visit located along the southern shore of Beaver Lake. Hobbs is Arkansas's largest state park and covers a natural area in excess of 12,000 acres. You'll see the typical, beautiful Ozark Mountain countryside the locals have come to know and love. The area is also great for camping, hiking and fishing.

Itineraries and Day Trips

Rogers-Lowell Itinerary #1 – Outdoor Lovers

The stunningly beautiful countryside and abundant lakes around the Rogers-Lowell area are filled with terrific opportunities for everyone to have fun, regardless of his or her age. Located in the spectacular Ozark Mountains, it's an ideal place to get up close and personal to nature.

Whether you just want to kick back and relax around a crackling campfire, angle for some of the biggest bass in the region, or go water skiing, you can find it all and so much more in the Rogers area on and around Beaver Lake.

Beautiful Beaver Lake, only a few short minutes from Rogers, with its 28,200 surface acres of water is renowned for its varied fishing opportunities. You can find Blue, Channel and Flathead Catfish; Bluegill; Bream; Redear Sunfish; Largemouth, Smallmouth, Spotted, Striped, Hybrid and White Bass; Warmouth; and Trout. If you are a competitive fisherman or fisherwoman, the lake is also home to several different amateur and professional fishing tournaments. Guides are available, such as E & C Striper Guide at (479) 631-3858 / StriperGuides.net. Cabela's at 2300 Promenade Blvd in Rogers can fix you up with any equipment you need. Yes, this NWA area does have its own Cabela's and the number is (479) 616-1925.

In addition to fishing, the lake's sparkling blue water is an ideal place to enjoy boating, water skiing, scuba diving, swimming, kayaking, sailing, and wakeboarding. There are many boat launch ramps around the lake and many of the marinas are open year-round.

The U. S Army Corps of Engineers is a good place to find a spectacular Beaver Lake campsite. It manages 11 parks and operates 650 campsites with electrical hookups around the 450 miles of gorgeous lake shoreline. Booking a camping site is easy, contact the Corps of Engineers at (479) 636-1210, or go online to Recreation.gov to check for campsite availability.

There are also several private campgrounds in the area, which can be contacted by calling the Rogers-Lowell Area Chamber of Commerce at (479) 636-1240 or by going online at RogersLowell.com to check for private campsite availability.

Other outdoor activities include hiking and biking trails. In the planning stages is the Trails Master Plan, which, when finished, will be 60 miles of greenway trails looping through Rogers and eventually stretching from corner-to-corner of the city. In the meantime, hikers can try the Pigeon Roost Trail, an 8.5-mile trek located within 12,056-acre Hobbs State Park.

For a shorter, less strenuous trail, try the Shaddox Hollow Trail, a 1.5-mile jaunt overlooking Beaver Lake and going through narrow hollows, up along ridges, and through stands of hardwoods, pines and typical Ozark vegetation. In winter, you may be lucky enough to see one of the many Bald Eagles that make the Beaver Lake area home. For a shorter handicapped accessible trail, take the Van Winkle Hollow trail.

Before using any of the trails, make a visit to the Hobbs State Park Conservation Area Visitor's Center located just off Hwy 12. At the center, you can view an introductory film and play with interactive kiosks that explain the park's history, geology, caves and wildlife. Call (479) 789-5000 or go online to the Hobbs State Park Conservation Area Visitors Center website.

If spelunking is the outdoor activity that excites you, head on over to War Eagle Cavern off scenic Hwy 12 and take the 60-minute guided tour. You can access the cave via car, boat or R.V. Storytelling guides take you straight into the mountain through its large natural entrance. The cave features wide walkways with no tight places or stairs. Call (479) 789-2909 for detailed directions and information.

Traveling with children? Rogers has many city parks offering a variety of outdoor activities. Of particular note are the new Rogers Skate Park and the Rogers Aquatics Center located at 1707 S 26th Street in Rogers. Call (479) 631-3350 or feel free to email the Parks Department at parks@rogersarkansas.com for more detailed information. Generally speaking, however, children 3 and under can splash away in smaller pools, and older children can enjoy swimming, the racing slides, bowl slide, lazy river and rock climbing. Passes are available for both residents and non-residents. The resident rate is less expensive, and if you buy your pass online, there is no way to check for residency.

Rogers-Lowell Itinerary #2 – Let's Go Shopping!

Shopping opportunities in the Rogers area rival top shopping scenes in much larger cities. Divided into five distinct districts, each of Rogers shopping districts offers a unique type of shopping experience depending upon what you are looking for.

Dixieland District – The Frisco Station Mall at Walnut Street and Dixieland Road in Rogers is near everything and has over 30 prime stores and restaurants that are unique to the Rogers area. Located on the west side of the mall, craft's people will enjoy shopping the largest Hobby Lobby in NWA. This 242,535-square-foot, one-level mall is great for walking. For more information, call (479) 631-0006, or visit the mall's website at FriscoStationMall.com.

Downtown District – Located just a few minutes from I-49 and the John Q. Hammons Convention Center, Rogers vibrant downtown district with its brick-paved streets and historic architecture is a delightful mixture of bustling businesses, trendy eateries, commerce, art, shopping, professional services, theater and history. Shop unique antique and craft shops and boutiques of every description, then get some lunch at one of the downtown Rogers, AR restaurants where the service is terrific and the food is simply scrumptious.

Pinnacle Hills District–Located at 2203 Promenade Blvd in Rogers, the Pinnacle Hills Promenade Mall features elegant shops, lush landscaping, and the one and only Cabela's, the world's foremost outfitter of hunting, fishing and outdoor gear. The store is located next to the Pinnacle Hills Promenade Mall.

Shoppes at Pinnacle Hills, located within the Pinnacle Hills District at Pinnacle Hills Pkwy and Market Street, compare favorably to the best urban shopping in the nation. Shoppes features trendy, moneyed shopping and upscale restaurants serving the best food in NWA. You can choose from eateries like the Bonefish Grill, Carrabba's Italian Grill, Grub's Bar and Grill, and Theo's Steak.

Village on the Creeks at Horsebarn Road and I-49 is also part of the Pinnacle Hills District. It features a scenic, relaxed park-like atmosphere with a 12-acre lake, a walking trail, beautiful landscaped garden areas, fountains, sculptures, and the Osage and Turtle Creeks. Shop 'til you drop, and then have a lovely patio meal in this relaxing setting.

Scottsdale District – The Scottsdale District is located from Walnut Street and 46th Street to Walnut Street and Promenade Blvd. Scottsdale District is home to many large and small national retail chains, like Marshalls and Shoe Carnival, and an array of wonderful restaurants collectively known as "restaurant row." The Malco Theater is also located here.

Kingston Centre at 4404 W Walnut Street within the Scottsdale District has plenty of shopping and dining options. The new Bob Evans Farms is in this shopping center.

Pleasant Crossing District – The Pleasant Crossing Shopping Center located at Pleasant Grove and I-49 in Rogers is the place to go if you are in the market for furniture. Hanks, More Fine Furniture and Ashley's Furniture are all in this district. There is also a Walmart Supercenter and several chain restaurants in this shopping district.

Tuscany Square Shopping Center within the Pleasant Crossing District is located at Pleasant Grove and I-49 in Rogers. It is right across the street from the Walmart Supercenter. A terrific mix of national, regional and local stores, you'll find everything from a sporting goods store to a day spa, and there are plenty of restaurants and even a Starbucks to help you enjoy your shopping day.

Not in any particular district, but a truly unique store, is the A. G. Russell Knives store, the oldest mail-order knife company in America. If you are looking for something different in a knife, the A. G. Russell Knives store at 2900 S 26th Street in Rogers is the store for you. They make every kind of knife imaginable and many of them are still handmade. A recent special A. G. was running was on a neck knife, the Hunter's Scalpel. It features a 2 1/4-inch blade and has an overall length of 4 3/4-inches. Available in either hunter orange or black, it is the exact right size to wear on a lanyard around your neck.

Rogers-Lowell Itinerary #3 – Exploring Rogers

There are many things to see and do in the Rogers area. The Daisy Airgun Museum, located in Downtown Rogers at 2nd and Walnut, houses the world's largest collection of antique airguns, BB guns and commemorative rifles. The collection includes more than 150 air rifles and toys, including Napoleon-era guns, original Daisy advertising, movie memorabilia, Red Ryder collectibles and vintage Daisy products.

Daisy Rifles are not the only thing going on downtown. You'll also find the perfect mixture of aromas, cultures, tastes, sounds and textures. Downtown Rogers is a harmonious blend of art, music, shopping, theater, commerce and professional services. You could spend the day walking the inviting brick streets leading to perfectly restored buildings and trendy boutiques.

If you get an early start, go by the charming Farmer's Market held at the corner of Arkansas and Elm Streets every Wednesday and Saturday from 7 a.m. to 1 p.m. The Rogers Farmer's Market is a market where growers, farmers, artists, crafters, and other Rogers businesses sell self-produced products to the public. The Market closes in November for the season, re-opening in the spring.

Many think that Walmart store #1 is in Bentonville, but this is not true. Walmart's first store, opened in 1962, was located at 719 W Walnut Street in Rogers. The original building has a plaque commemorating the historic designation. Walmart store #1 is now located at 2110 W Walnut Street in... Rogers!

War Eagle Mill is located Hwy 12 a mere 13 miles east of Rogers and is a fully functioning water-powered gristmill. See how stone-ground whole grains were made before modernization did away with the need for these beautiful old water-powered mills. Wander the grounds and see historic home sites and the War Eagle Bridge. Visit the gift shop where you can see and buy Arkansas products, including jams and jellies, just milled whole-grain meals and mixes, crafts and baskets. Watch the friendly, knowledgeable miller at work, and then have breakfast or lunch at the Bean Palace Restaurant. Also, if you are visiting during the spring or fall months, you may be fortunate enough to attend one of the regionally renowned crafts fairs. War Eagle Mill is open daily March through January 1, 8:30 a.m. to 5 p.m. For more information, call (866) 492-7324.

House of Webster has been open since 1934 and is located at 1013 N 2nd in Rogers. House of Webster is a log-cabin store filled with every imaginable kind of Southern delicacy, including fruit preserves packed in Mason jars with hand-written labels, green tomato relish, chow chow, watermelon pickles and scuppernong jelly, and country-cured and hickory-smoked bacon. Products from the House of Webster are shipped all over the country. For more information, call (479) 636-4640.

Visit Rogers Historical Museum at 1895 Hawkins House and the Frisco Caboose. The Historical Museum, accredited by the American Alliance of Museums, and Hawkins House tell the interesting story of Rogers. There are both permanent and traveling exhibits and programs. The Hawkins House uses its six period rooms to present an accurate flashback of how a middle-class family at the turn of the 20th century lived. Admission is FREE. For more information, call (479) 621-1154.

After the sun sets for the day, explore a different side of downtown Rogers. There are exciting, enticing nightspots and tantalizing eateries. It's the perfect place to enjoy delicious food, smooth drinks and trendy music with your friends. Downtown Rogers, a nostalgic city, will keep you coming back for more.

ROGERS DAY TRIPS

Altus, AR – for Wine Lovers Only

If you are a wine connoisseur or one who just loves to enjoy a glass of really good wine, you will definitely have a wonderful day in Altus, AR. Just an hour-and-a-half's drive from Rogers, take I-49 to I-40, then take Exit 41, and drive south on Highway 186 for 2.3 miles to Altus.

Located in the foothills of the Ozark Mountains, Altus is the heart of the wine industry for the entire state of Arkansas. In 1880, two European families settled in the Arkansas River Valley, and, led by Jacob Post and Johann Wiederkehr, the wine heritage and viticulture in Arkansas began.

Today, there are four primary wineries in the Altus area: Chateau Aux Arc, Wiederkehr Wine Cellars, Post Winery and Mount Bethel Winery.

Each winery offers free tours and operates a tasting room, and some offer other amenities like a restaurant, gift shop, bed and breakfast inn, and RV park. In addition to these four wineries, you can drive a short distance to Paris, AR to visit Cowie Wine Cellars and the Arkansas Historic Wine Museum. The museum preserves the history of Arkansas winemaking with biographical histories of Arkansas winemakers and with winemaking artifacts.

Chateau Aux Arc Vineyards and Winery – The Chateau Aux Arc Vineyards and Winery is the first vineyard and winery you will see when you arrive in Altus. The winery is on Hwy 186 and is an eco-friendly winery that has the largest Chardonnay vineyard outside of California. It is also the largest Zinfandel planter in Arkansas, and the world's largest planter of Cynthiana grapes. Located on the top of beautiful St Mary's Mountain, the tasting room is open daily from 10 a.m. to 5 p.m. Featuring scenic views of the vineyards and landscaped grounds, the tasting room is a beautiful place to spend a sunny afternoon with friends or that special someone. In addition to the incredible wines, samples of gourmet food are offered daily. The gift shop is stocked with art and crafts, food and wine-related items, and gourmet food. R.V.'s are welcome in the large parking lot. For more information and to arrange a wedding or other special event call (800) 558-WINE.

Wiederkehr Wine Cellars - Located in Altus on Hwy 186 South about four miles from Exit 41 (you will see the signs) is Wiederkehr Wine Cellars, the oldest and largest winery in mid-America. It boasts more than 130 years of Swiss winemaking history. Plan to enjoy touring the cellars of Wiederkehr Winery, have fun in Wiederkehr Village, and dine at the famous Weinkeller Restaurant. Have your wedding at the beautiful scenic winery and spend time exploring the award winning wines. Tours of the winery and cellars are every 45 minutes from 9 a.m. to 4:30 p.m. daily except Sunday, when tours start at 12 noon. There are no tours on major holidays.

If possible, plan your visit to coincide with the Annual Wiederkehr Village Weinfest held in October. During the Weinfest, you will enjoy concessions with International cuisine, FREE wine tasting tours, carriage and tram rides through the vineyards, dining at the Weinkeller Restaurant, arts and crafts displays, a Championship Grape Stomp, conga line dancing through the wine cellars, contests and door prizes, live entertainment, and sing-along's in German and English. For more information, call (800) 622-WINE or (479) 468-WINE.

Post Familie Vineyards – Established in 1880 and located near downtown Altus, Post Winery is a family-owned and operated winery offering tours of wine production, a wine store and gift shop, and a newly remodeled kitchen with fresh food, gourmet food, soda drinks and coffee. The Post family winegrowing tradition of excellence continues through the current fifth generation, who are today producing Gold Medal winners. You are welcome to taste the Post tradition. Come "Toast with Post." There is plenty of parking and restrooms are available. For more information, call (800)275-84223 or (479)468-2741.

Mount Bethel Winery – Located on 5014 Mount Bethel Drive just off Highway 64, approximately 1/4 mile east of Altus, Arkansas (just follow the signs), Mount Bethel Winery is operated by Eugene Post and eight of his children. The winery has a tasting room and store, which are open Monday through Saturday from 8:30 a.m. to 6 p.m., and on Sun noon to 5 p.m. Mount Bethel produces a wide variety of wines native to America, like Cynthiana (sometimes known as Norton), Muscat, Niagara, Muscadine and Concord. They also produce a full range of fruit wines and, if you enjoy Port, some of the finest Port wine made anywhere. For a semi-sweet crisp flavor that is both light and delicious, they highly recommend their new Harvest Moon Vignoles. For more information, call (479) 468-2444.

Cowie Wine Cellars and Vineyards: If you have a bit of time left, drive the short distance, about 22 miles on Hwy 64, then on Hwy 309 to Paris, AR, and visit the Cowie Wine Cellars and Vineyards, which are operated by Robert G. J. Cowie and family. A small winery located in the Arkansas River Valley between the Ozark and Ouachita Mountains, it produces a limited amount of the finest wine available in Arkansas. Stay at the B&B, take the tour, and have a taste of their fine wine. See how wine is actually made and enjoy the down-home atmosphere. Also, take time to see the only wine museum in the United States dedicated to preserving the wine history of a complete state. For more information, call (479) 963-3990.

Visiting these five wineries will give you a good idea of what winemaking in Arkansas is like, and it will also provide you with a full, exciting day of activities you are sure to enjoy.

ACCOMMODATIONS

Rogers has 21 hotels at publication date and the hotels in Rogers, AR range from the Razorback Inn at $39/night up to the MainStay Suites, which is a five star hotel that enjoys rave reviews from both business travelers and carefree tourists looking for a memorable vacation. Another notable mention is the Aloft Rogers, AR hotel, an accommodation that consistently receives rave reviews. Whatever your budget, you will be able to book just the right accommodations for yourself and your family.

Hotel Amenities

Breakfast: B	**Meeting Rooms: MR**
Business Center: BC	**Pet Friendly: PF**
Fitness Center: FC	**Pool: P**
Internet: I	**Restaurant: R**

Hotels in Rogers, AR with 3 Star Accommodations

Aloft Rogers, AR 1103 S 52nd Street, Rogers, AR 72758 (479) 268-6799 BC, FC, I, MR, P, R	Hyatt Place 4610 W Walnut Street, Rogers, AR 72756 (479) 633-8555 B, I, BC, FC, I, MR, P, R
Embassy Suites Northwest Arkansas - Hotel, Spa and Convention Center 3303 S Pinnacle Hills Pkwy, Rogers, AR 72758 (479) 254-8400 BC, FC,I, MR, P,PF, R	Residence Inn by Marriott 4611 W Locust Street, Rogers, AR 72756 (479) 636-5900 B, BC,I, MR, PF

Holiday Inn Hotel and Suites Rogers - Pinnacle Hills 1803 S 52nd Street, Rogers, AR 72758 (479) 845-1300 BC,FC,I, MR, P, R	Staybridge Suites 1801 S 52nd Street, Rogers, AR 72758 (479) 845-5701 BC, FC, I, MR
Homewood Suites 4302 W Walnut Street, Rogers, AR 72756 (479) 636-5656 B, BC, FC, I, MR, P	

Hotels in Rogers, AR with 2 Star Accommodations

Candlewood Suites 4601 Rozell Street, Rogers, AR 72756 (479) 636-2783 BC, FC, I, MR, P	Hampton Inn 4501 W Walnut Street, Rogers, AR 72756 (479) 986-0500 B, BC, FC, I, MR, P
Country Inn and Suites Rogers, AR 4304 W Walnut Street, Rogers, AR 72756 (479) 633-0055 B, BC, FC,I, MR, P	Razorback Inn 2931 W Walnut Street, Rogers, AR 72756 (479) 631-6000 PF, I
Fairfield Inn and Suites 4611 Rozell Street, Rogers, AR 72756 (479) 936-5900 B, BC, FC, I, P	

Hotels in Rogers, AR offering Extended Stay Accommodations

Mainstay Suites 301 South 45th Street, Rogers, AR, 72758 (479) 636-3232 B, BC, FC, MC, I, P	Microtel Inn and Suites 909 S 8th Street, Rogers, AR 72756 (479) 636-5551 B, BC, I

THINGS TO DO AND SEE

Rogers is home to a wide range of unusual attractions and things to do, and I've already touched on many of them briefly, but they deserve repeating. For example, even if you've never owned or held a BB gun, you will enjoy the Daisy Airgun Museum located in downtown Rogers. The museum is run by a nonprofit organization dedicated to the preservation and collection of Daisy vintage products.

Pinnacle Hills in Rogers offers many unique shopping opportunities. Pinnacle Hills Promenade and Village on the Creeks are located right off I-49 in Rogers between Bentonville and Fayetteville. Between the two, you will find first-rate chain stores, unique and fashionable shops, and superior restaurants like the Bone Fish Grill and Ruth Chris Rogers represented. In fact, the Promenade Mall in Rogers is said to have the best rated shopping and dining in all of Arkansas.

Don't miss a historic site, one that is listed on the National Register, in fact! See Poor Richard's Gift and Confectionery Shop. It began as a drug store with a soda fountain back in 1907. It has been restored using original fixtures. Today, it is best known for local and regional art, which includes pottery, paintings, baskets, wood and textiles, photography, stained glass and jewelry. Looking at public reviews, all who visited Poor Richard's gave it a positive review.

Another shopping location is the Frisco Station Mall with its modern chain stores, such as Bath and Body Works, Tuesday Morning, Hobby Lobby and Hibbett Sporting Goods.

Close to Rogers in the unincorporated community of War Eagle, Arkansas is War Eagle Bridge, also listed on the National Register of Historic Places. The original mill on War Eagle Creek was torn down and rebuilt twice, but today is an operating mill that produces whole grain flours along with 25 other products. The Bean Palace Restaurant, located on the mill premises, serves breakfast and lunch. Its shop has gifts, crafts and gadgets for the kitchen. The annual arts and crafts fair, hosted by the mill, is the largest crafts fair in the state.

Do you like to fish? Beaver Lake is home to a variety of fish including Crappie, Largemouth Bass, Smallmouth Bass, Striped Bass, Trout, White Bass, Striped and Hybrid Striper, and several varieties of pan fish and Catfish. Kick back, relax and fish 28,200 beautiful acres of sparkling blue waters.

Although Beaver Lake is known the world over as a fishing haven, there is also sailing, hiking, camping and bird watching for those not inclined to drop a hook. The 450 miles of beautiful shoreline around Beaver Lake is home to caves, wildlife and breathtaking limestone bluffs. The U. S. Army Corps of Engineers maintains 650 campsites, all with electrical hookups, in 11 parks around the lake.

To satisfy your spirit of adventure, check out AdrenaLINE at Zipline Tours, hike the Ozark Mountains, or maybe spend a day Spelunking at War Eagle Cavern.

If your idea of fun is shopping, art museums, or a visit to a full-service pamper spa, you will find all that and more to help you luxuriate your day away.

The Club Frisco in Rogers offers a laid-back atmosphere and $3 beer. Grab a sandwich from the Iron Horse, take a load off, and have a cold one with a bunch of friends.

Arts/Culture
Art Galleries
Poor Richard's Art
101 W Walnut, Rogers, AR 72756
(479) 636-0417
Poor Richard's Art offers original art and fine crafts in a variety of media created from local artists in and around Northwest Arkansas.

White River Gallery
115 S Second Street, Rogers, AR 72756
(479) 936-5851
White River Gallery features artwork by artist Ed Cooley.

Museums
Rogers Daisy Airgun Museum
202 W Walnut Street, Rogers, AR 72756
(479) 986-6873

The Rogers Daisy Airgun Museum is home to the Daisy Air Rifle and the Daisy BB Gun. People of all ages enjoy this amazing collection. Older visitors can enjoy Daisy models they used when they were young, and youths get to see the latest in fascinating air guns, ammo and accessories.

The gift shop has limited edition items that can only be purchased from the museum gift shop.

Pea Ridge National Military Park
U.S. 62 North, Pea Ridge, AR 72751

Pea Ridge National Military Park is located northeast of Rogers and is situated on 4,300 acres. The Pea Ridge Civil War battle honors some 26,000 soldiers who saw action there on March 7 and 8, 1862. It was fought to secure the upper reaches of the Mississippi and Missouri rivers and to keep the state of Missouri under federal control.

At the Visitor's Center, there is a video, a museum and a gift shop. There is also a self-guided auto tour that features markers and audio descriptions of the battlefield. Additionally, there is a horse and hiking trail.

Rogers Historical Museum
322 S 2nd Street, Rogers, AR 72756
(479) 621-1154

A great way to experience local history through permanent and changing exhibits, educational programs and special events. Fun for the entire family including:

- The Attic - Experience the past in a museum within the museum designed for hands-on fun for all ages.
- The 1895 Hawkins House - Step into the early 1900s with a guided tour.
- First Street - A fun-filled re-creation of a downtown of yesteryear. Youngsters will especially enjoy the "please touch" shelf.

FREE admission!

Performing Arts
Arkansas Music Pavilion
5079 W Northgate Road, Rogers, AR 72758
(479) 443–5600

This large outdoor space within Washington County Fairgrounds hosts a range of concerts suiting all musical tastes!

Rogers Little Theater
116 S 2nd Street, Rogers, AR 72756
(479) 631-8988

Throughout the year in the beautifully restored Victory Theater in downtown Rogers, the Rogers Little Theater presents a variety of dinner theater and other regular performances.

Outdoors
Beaver Lake
2260 N 2nd Street, Rogers, AR 72756
(479) 636-1210

Beaver Lake, with 487 miles of shoreline, is located high in the Ozark Mountains. Completed in 1966 by the U. S. Corps of Engineers, the 28,370-acre lake offers many recreational opportunities, including 2,008 acres of campgrounds and 650 individual campsites.

Cabins, resorts, marinas, outfitters and spectacular fishing opportunities surround the lake. Other facilities that are available include swimming beaches, sailing, water skiing, hiking trails, sanitary dump stations, group picnic shelters and amphitheaters.

Smallmouth Bass, Largemouth Bass and Striper Bass fishing is excellent on the lake, but there are also ample opportunities to catch Bream, Crappie, Channel and Spoonbill Catfish and White Bass. Beaver Lake is a fishing paradise.

Camping and Hiking
Beaver Lake Dam Site
Hwy 187, Beaver Lake, AR
(479) 253-5828

Description: 95 Campsites, electrical hookups, boat dock and ramp, water, restrooms, trail and marine dump stations, swimming, showers and playground. Located 9 miles west of Eureka Springs on U.S. 62, then 2 1/2 miles south on paved access road Hwy 187.

Devil's Den State Park
11333 West Hwy 74 West Fork, AR 72774
(479) 761-3325

Description: 16 Rustic Cabins, 150 camping sites. Many have electrical, water and sewer hook ups.

Hickory Creek
Hwy 264, Beaver Lake, AR
(479) 750-2943

Description: 61 campsites, electrical hookups, boat dock and ramp, water, restrooms, trailer and marine dump stations, swimming, showers and playground. Located 4 miles north of Springdale on U.S. 71, then 7 miles east on Hwy 264.

Horseshoe Bend
Beaver Lake, AR
(479) 925-2561

Description: East 160 campsites, west 125 campsites, electrical hookups, boat dock and ramp, water, restrooms, swimming, showers, dump station and playground. Located 8 miles east of Rogers on Hwy 94.

Lost Bridge
12861 Marina Rd, Garfield, AR 72732
(479) 359-3222

Description: North 48 campsites, south 36 campsites, electrical hookups, boat dock and ramp, water, restrooms, swimming, youth group camp area and playground. Located 5 miles southeast of Garfield on Hwy 127.

Monte Ne RV Park Campgrounds and Cabins
Hwy 94, Rogers, AR
(479) 925-1265
Description: 80 campsites, 30/50 AMP service, city water/sewer.

Indian Creek
Beaver Lake, AR
(479) 656-3145

Description: 33 Campsites, boat ramp, water, restrooms and swimming. Located 1 1/2 miles east of Gateway on U.S. 62, then south 5 miles on a gravel access road.

Prairie Creek
Beaver Lake, AR
(479) 925-3957

Description: 108 campsites, electrical hookups, boat dock and ramp, water, restrooms, trailer and marine dump stations, swimming, showers and playground. Located 3 1/2 miles east of Rogers on Hwy 12, then 1 mile on an access road.

Rocky Branch
Beaver Lake, AR
(479) 925-2526

Description: 50 campsites, electrical hookups, boat dock and ramp, water, restrooms, swimming, trailer and marine dump stations, and playground. Located 11 miles east of Rogers on Hwy 12, and then 4 1/2 miles NE to the paved road on Hwy 303.

Rocky Branch Resort
20510 Park Road, Rogers, AR 72756
(800) 925-1688

War Eagle
Beaver Lake, AR
(479) 750-4722

Description: 26 campsites, electrical hookups, boat dock and ramp, dump station, water, restrooms and swimming. Located 10 miles east of Springdale on Hwy 68, then 3 miles north on a paved access road.

War Eagle Cavern on Beaver Lake
Hwy 12, War Eagle, AR 72756
(479) 789-2909

See fossils, waterfalls, soda straws and domes as you walk through a stunning natural entrance straight into the mountainside. Hear strange and fascinating stories of draft dodgers, outlaws, Indians and moonshiners. See a bat up close and personal, visit the gift shop, and eat at the mouth-watering Smoke Signal Cafe. Pan for treasure at the War Eagle Mining Company or lose yourself in the Lost in the Woods maze. Fun for the entire family. Truly, an attraction you don't want to miss.

War Eagle Mill
1045 War Eagle Road, Rogers, AR 72756
(479) 789-5343

See an authentic working undershot water-powered gristmill that is still producing all natural organic grains, flours and mixes right before your eyes. American families that live in the Arkansas Ozarks hand-pack the grains.

Eat in the Bean Palace Restaurant or shop in the old-fashioned mercantile for unique handcrafted items and packed grains.

U.S. Army Corps of Engineers
Beaver Project Office, Beaver Lake, AR
(877) 444-6777

Description: Reservations at various sites on Beaver Lake run by the U.S. Army Corps of Engineers. Available May 17 to September 15. They have instituted a Recreation Day User Fee Program. Annual Passes are available.

Dog Parks
Murphy Memorial Dog Park
E Nursery Rd & S 5th St, Rogers, AR 72756

Fishing
FISHING LICENSES

Prices for non-resident permits start at$11 for three days, and go up to $40 for one year, while Arkansas resident permits start at $5. Trout fishing licenses are purchased in addition to general fishing licenses.

Purchase your license online at agfc.com, or in sporting goods stores, hunting and fishing supply stores and other locations including Walmart.

Visit the Arkansas Game and Fish Commission website at agfc.com or call 501-223-6300.

Buddy Bass Tournament

In early May each year, anglers from across the region compete on Beaver Lake. The Buddy Bass Tournament is one of the largest and oldest tournaments in NWA. Prior to the event, anglers can obtain a registration form by calling (800) 364-1240 or (479) 636-1240.

FLW Bass Tournament
Prairie Creek Park
9300 N Park Road, Rogers AR 72756
(479) 636 -1210

Every year in the spring, the FLW Tour® stops at Rogers and Beaver Lake for the Walmart FLW Bass Tournament. The tournament is the Tour's only annual stop and it attracts the media, hundreds of anglers both professional and amateur, and their families and friends to the area.

Bait and Tackle
Cabela's
2300 Promenade Blvd, Rogers, AR 72758
(479) 616-1925

Hickory Creek Marina
12737 Hickory Creek Road, Lowell, AR 72745
(479) 751-7366

Hook Line and Sinker
98 E Locust Street, Rogers, AR 72756
(479) 631-8118

Prairie Creek Marina
1 Prairie Creek Marina Drive, Rogers, AR 72756
(479) 925-1623

Fishing Guides
Andreasen's Striper Guide Service
Beaver Lake, Rogers, AR 72756
(479) 359-2322

Bailey's Beaver Lake Guide Service
8369 Campground Circle, Rogers, AR 72756
(479) 366-8664

Big 1's Striper Fishing on Beaver Lake
402 N 9th Street, Rogers, AR 72756
(479) 633-0662

Big Dog's Guide Service
13821 Toepfer Road, Garfield, AR 72732
(479) 359-2601

E&C Striper Guide (Ed Chapko)
451 Valley West Drive, Rogers, AR 72756
(479) 631-3858

J.T. Crappie Guide Services
(479) 595-2483

Joe Farkas Striper Guide Service
PO Box 179, Gateway, AR 72733
(479) 640-2386

Golf
Big Sugar Golf Club
1101 Sugar Creek Road 4, Pea Ridge, AR 72751
(479) 451-9550

Public Course

Lost Springs Golf and Athletic Club
3024 N 22nd Street, Rogers, AR 72756
(479) 631-9988
Public Course

Pinnacle Country Club
3 Clubhouse Drive, Rogers, AR 72758
(479) 273-0500

The Pinnacle Country Club plays host to the LPGA® Northwest Arkansas
Championship. This stunning 530-acre private golf course promises to take
its place among the nation's best. The gorgeous course offers golfers of all
abilities an enjoyable experience.

Private Course

Prairie Creek Country Club
1585 Rountree Drive, Rogers, AR 72756
(479) 925-2414

Public Course

Shadow Valley NWA
7001 Shadow Valley Road, Rogers, AR 72758
(479) 203-0000

Private Course

The Creeks
1499 S Main Street, Cave Springs, AR 72718
(479) 248-1000

Public Course

The Greens on Blossom Way Golf and Country Club
2808 S 28th Place, Rogers, AR 72758
(479) 631-1811

Public Course

Mountain Biking
Hobbs State Park-Conservation Area
20201 Hwy 12, Rogers, AR 72756
(479) 789-5000

Hobbs State Park is the largest in land area of the 51 state parks in Arkansas. Hobbs State Park is still in its initial development phase at this time. It currently offers many wonderful recreational opportunities for the people of Arkansas, including the Historic Van Winkle Trail, the Pigeon Roost Trail and the Shaddox Hollow Trail. The last two trails are 1.5-mile environmental education loops that explore a variety of Ozark microclimates. In addition, the Park offers interpretive programs, undeveloped access to Beaver Lake, regulated season hunting and an all-weather public firing range.

RV Parks
Beaver Dam Cottages and RV Park
8172 Hwy 187, Eureka Springs, AR 72631
(479) 253-6196

Beaver Lake Hide-A-Way
8369 Campground Circle, Rogers, AR, 71756
(479) 925-1335
Description: 140 campsites. Off Hwy 303 in the Rocky Branch area.

Highway 12
15479 E Hwy 12, Rogers, AR 72756

This RV park caters to long-term and fulltime RVers. It has full hookups, including 70-plus channels of cable TV. There are no public restrooms or showers, but there is a laundry room available for residents. The park is about 5 miles from downtown Rogers and just a couple of miles from Beaver Lake.

Rogers/Pea Ridge Garden RV
Beaver Lake, AR 72732
(479) 451-8566
Description: 50 campsites. On U.S. 62 east of Rogers.

The Creeks RV Resort and Golf Course
1499 S Main Street, Cave Springs, AR 72718
(479) 248-1000

Description: 60 fully paved deluxe sites, 30/50 AMP service, city water/ sewer, Cable TV, Wi-Fi, 18 hole golf course and clubhouse.

Gyms
Planet Fitness
100 Dixieland Mall, Rogers, AR 72756
(479) 636-1111

Shopping
Antique Shops
Abundant Treasure Flea Market
1140 W Walnut Street, Rogers, AR, 72756
(479) 936-7200

Figgy Pudding
719 W Walnut St, Rogers, AR, 72756
(417) 529-0163

Homestead Antique Mall
3223 W Hudson Road, Rogers, AR 72756
(479) 631-9003

Miss Judi's Wisteria Lane
103 W Walnut St Rogers, Arkansas 72756
(479) 790-4711

Not too Shabby
810 Lester Lane, Rogers, AR 72756

Rock Paper Scissors
121 W Elm, Rogers, AR 72756
(479) 372-4002

Red Door Vintage
322 S. 1st Street, Rogers, AR 72758
(479) 721-8033

Rose Antique Mall and Flea Market
2875 W Walnut Street, Rogers, AR 72756
(479) 631-8940

Somewhere In Time Antique Mall
719 W Walnut Street, Rogers, AR 72756
(479) 636-0474

The Cottage at The Barn
121 E Poplar, Rogers, AR 72756
(479) 621-0333

Trader J's Furniture and More
210 W New Hope Road, Rogers, AR 72758
(479) 685-9850

The Rusty Chair
109 W Walnut Street, Rogers, AR 72756
(479) 202-5588

Vintage Antiques
120 W Walnut Street, Rogers, AR72756
(479) 636-3900

Boutiques
3 Monkeys
3301 S Market Street, Rogers, AR 72758
(479) 271-0701
Children's Boutique

Belle Boutique
2603 Pleasant Crossing Blvd, Rogers, AR 72712
(479) 899-6434

Haute Pink Boutique
4204 Green Acres Road, Rogers, AR 72758
(479) 636-7930

Lola Boutique
3201 Market Street, Rogers, AR, 72758
(479) 464-9433

Ropa Boutique
3201 Market Street, Ste 103, Rogers, AR 72758
(479) 273-0022

She Said Yes Bridal
265 N 46th Street, Rogers, AR 72756

(479) 631-2006

The Haley Boutique
2011 Promenade Ave, Ste 410, Rogers, AR 72758
(479) 936-7000

The White Dress Boutique
211 W Walnut Street, Rogers, AR 72756
(479) 287-2148

Specialty Shops
AG Russell Knives
2900 S 26th Street, Rogers, AR 72758
(479) 631-0130
This is the granddaddy of all knife stores that was established in 1964 by A.G. Russell, an Arkansas native. You'll see every kind of knife you can imagine in the store, and they all come with a concrete guarantee: "We guarantee total satisfaction. You, the customer, decide what satisfaction is. You decide how long you are entitled to be satisfied." Guarantees don't get much better than that!

Alternique
226-B S 1st Street, Rogers, AR 72756
(479) 899-6896
Arts and Crafts Supply Store

Dilly Dally's
3301 S Market Street, Rogers, AR 72758
(479) 273-5557
Toy Store

Gearhead Outfitters
2203 S Promenade Blvd, Rogers, AR, 72758
(479) 877-2541

Lewis and Clark Outfitters
2530 Pinnacle Hills Pkwy, Rogers, AR 72758
(479) 845-1344

Moser Corporation
601 N 13th Street, Rogers, AR 72756
(479) 636-3481
Office and Teacher Supplies

Party Place
4202 W Green Acres Road, Rogers, AR 72758
(479) 230-9494

Pepper Palace
2203 S Promenade Blvd, Rogers, AR 72758
(479) 899-6990
One stop shop for hot sauce, BBQ sauce, salsa, pickled items, jellies and jams, beef jerky and more!

Perfect Party Depot
5204 Village Pkwy #5, Rogers, AR 72758
(479) 268-6808
Party Supplies

Rush Running Store
226 S. 1st Street, Rogers, AR 72756
(479) 202-5918

Signed, Sealed and Delivered
3301 S Market Street #105, Rogers, AR 72758
(479) 899-6699

Shirley's Flowers & Gifts
128th N. 13th, Rogers, AR
(479) 636 -0118

Bike Shops
Highroller Cyclery Rogers
402 S Metro Pkwy, Rogers, AR 72758
(479) 254-9800

Ozark Bicycle Service
W New Hope Rd, Rogers, AR 72758
(479) 715-1496

Motorcycle Fun
Heritage Indian Motorcycle of NWA
1711 West Hudson Road, Rogers, AR 72712
(479) 222-1907

Pig Trail Harley-Davidson / Buell
2409 W Hudson Rd, Rogers, AR
(479) 636-9797

Tattoo Shops
Daddy O's Tattoo
2505 N 17th St # 403, Rogers, AR 72756
(479) 631-9600

Jimmy Romance Tattoos and Body Piercing
2505 N 17th St, Rogers, AR 72756
(479) 631-9600

Shopping Centers
Frisco Station Mall
100 N Dixieland Road, Rogers, AR 72756
(479) 631-0006

Hobby Lobby anchors this one-level mall, which is also home to 25 additional unusual stores and eating establishments. Frisco Station Mall is a 242,535 square foot shopping center, and since it is all on one level, it attracts many walkers to take advantage of the controlled temperature and the flat surface.

Historic Downtown Rogers

I-49 Exit 85 – between 8th and 1st Streets centered around Walnut Street, Rogers, AR 72756

Historic Downtown Rogers is a wonderful blend of sounds, aromas, tastes, sights, textures, cultures and generations where there is always something for every member of the family to do and enjoy. It's a lively community of thriving businesses, eateries, shopping opportunities, art, music, history, theater and professional services.

Pinnacle Hills Promenade
2203 Promenade Blvd, Ste 3200, Rogers, AR 72758
(479) 936-2160

The Pinnacle Hills Promenade is considered by many to be the best shopping experience in all of NWA. Dillard's and J.C. Penney are the anchor stores, but there are plenty of other top-quality specialty stores to choose from, too. Hungry? The Promenade experience also includes several premium restaurants. Looking for entertainment? Check out the Malco 12-screen theatre.

Scottsdale Center

I-49 Exit 85 – corner of 46th Street and Walnut Street, Rogers 72756
Several traditional stores such as the Gap, Barnes and Noble, and Kohl's occupy the Scottsdale Center located facing I-49 in Rogers. There are also numerous dining options in the Scottsdale Center.

Restaurants such as Copeland's of New Orleans, Johnny Carino's, Applebee's, On the Border, Chili's, Famous Dave's, as well as several others also occupy the Center and for entertainment, there is the Rogers Towne Cinema 12-screen movie theatre.

Village on the Creeks

Rogers Pinnacle Hills
5308 Village Pkwy #2 (Exit 83 off I-49), Rogers, AR 72758
(479) 464-4292

Enjoy a lakeside picnic, visit unique shops, or eat a patio meal. Village on the Creeks is the perfect place to kick back, relax and let the challenges of the day fade away amid their beautifully landscaped public areas, which include streams, gardens, sculptures and fountains.

Spas

Belle Journee Spa
5311 Village Pkwy, Rogers, AR 72758
(479) 616-1690

Body Restore
3201 S Market Street, Rogers, AR 72712
(479) 715-6772

Brieshi
2203 Promenade Blvd, Rogers, AR 72758
(479) 246-0502

Hull Aesthetics
599 S Horsebarn Road, Rogers, AR 72758
(479) 254-9662

Massage Envy
2603 W Pleasant Grove Road, Rogers, AR 72758
(479) 633-8340

Paradise Cosmetic MedSpa
#11 Halsted Circle, Ste D, Rogers, AR 72756
(479) 586-6162

Red Carpet Salon and Spa
615 W Walnut, Rogers, AR 72756
(479) 372-7440

Spa Botanica
3303 Pinnacle Hills Pkwy, Rogers, AR 72758
(479) 845-3293

Special Events/Festivals
Arts and Crafts Events

Festivals and arts and crafts are a big deal in NWA. Various events are held in May and October annually, and they attract more than 250,000 crafts enthusiasts from all over the country.

Festivals include:

- Long's Old Orchard and Farm Arts and Crafts Festival
- Ozark Regional Arts and Crafts Show
- Rogers Antique Show and Sale
- Rogers Expo Center
- Sharp's Show of War Eagle
- Spanker Creek Farm Arts and Crafts
- War Eagle Fair
- War Eagle Mill Antique and Crafts Show
- Bella Vista Arts and Crafts
- Craft Fair Around the Square
- Frisco Station Mall Arts and Crafts
- Hillbilly Corner
- Jones Center Arts and Crafts

Daisy National BB Gun Championship Match

This national championship match is the granddaddy of them all. Both boys and girls ages 8 to 15, having worked their way up through the state competition, may participate. Rogers, the home of Daisy Outdoor Products and the Daisy Airgun Museum, plays host to this annual contest, which judges safety and marksmanship.

Farmer's Market

Located in Historic Downtown Rogers
At the corner of Arkansas and Elm, Rogers, AR
Rogers Farmer's Market is a seasonal open-air market that offers fresh produce and local crafts. A fun way to spend the morning!
Open May through October

Frisco Festival ~ Downtown Rogers

The readers of *Celebrate Arkansas Magazine* voted this festival the "Very Best 2013." This fun-filled annual festival is an opportunity for the entire family to enjoy themselves. The first festival was held more than 20 years ago, and it has since grown to be the biggest street party around. Live entertainment, carnival rides, scrumptious food, a beer and wine garden, arts and crafts and much, much more. For more information, call (479) 936-5487.

NWA International Festival ~ Downtown Rogers

Another fun, family-friendly festival typically held in the early summer features all kinds of traditional ethnic foods, international dance and music performances, free children's activities, cultural exhibits and more, including an international fashion show. More than 50 different countries participate in sharing their country's traditional culture. The event aims to encourage interaction with the different languages and traditions of the many cultures represented in NWA.

Rogers Art show in October
Art on the Creeks at Village on the Creeks in Rogers, AR
Saturday, October 4th.

Third Friday in Downtown Rogers

Various events the Third Friday in Downtown Rogers. Everything from shrimp boils to Twilight walks, Live music, food and fun.

Walmart NW Arkansas Championship Presented by P&G

Attracted by a sizeable purse of $2 million, an international field of the LPGA's best players converge upon the gorgeous course at the Pinnacle Country Club in Rogers annually. Presented by P&G, the tournament is accompanied by a variety of community activities. For more information or to inquire about tickets, call (479) 715-6100.

Explore

Wild Wilderness Drive-Through Safari
20923 Safari Road, Gentry, AR 72734
(479) 736-8383

Bring your family and spend a wonderful afternoon or an entire day on a 4-mile drive-through seeing wild and exotic animals along the way. The Wilderness drive-through safari is in Gentry, AR and is situated on 400 beautiful acres complete with several ponds.

Within the park, there are walk-through areas and petting parks for easy and safe interaction with the animals. You may be lucky enough to pet a tiger cub or a snake the day you are there. Every member of your family will enjoy seeing, petting and learning about the animals.

Bring a picnic lunch or enjoy the snack bar. Open every day at 9 a.m., including holidays.

RESTAURANTS

Rogers, AR restaurants offer some of the most diverse and mouth-watering food anywhere. If you want more information concerning a specific restaurant, simply click on the name of the restaurant to find out "what the locals say."

Restaurants in Rogers are located throughout the city; however, like most cities, when you locate one, there are usually several more close by. In fact, as I mentioned in the Neighborhoods section of this guide, there are three major areas that comprise Rogers. It is these areas where the majority of the eating establishments are located. Specifically:

1. The downtown area is home to several interesting independent cafes, coffee shops and restaurants.

2. The I-49 corridor is location to many chain and fine-dining eating establishments.

3. The Promenade shopping area also offers a wide variety of chain and fine-dining restaurants.

The restaurants in Rogers offer an almost endless array of delicious food. One of the many benefits of being in a booming area is the increase in the number and quality of gourmet restaurants specializing in exceptional cuisine.

Restaurant Prices

$ - Budget	*$$$ - Upscale*
$$ - Mid-Range	

American

Bob Evans Restaurant 4200 W Walnut Street, Rogers, AR 72756 (479) 636-1603 $$	IHOP International House of Pancakes 4604 E Walton Blvd, Rogers, AR 72756 (479) 631-2467 $

Cedar Creek Bistro 3303 Pinnacle Hills Pkwy, Rogers, AR 72758 (479) 254-8400 $	Monte Ne Inn Chicken Restaurant 13843 Hwy 94, Rogers, AR 72758 (479) 636-5511 $$
Corona Restaurant 14340 East Hwy 12, Rogers, AR 72756 (479) 925-3158 $	Mimi's Cafe 2105 Promenade Blvd, Rogers, AR 72758 (479) 936-7983 $$
Don and Ada's Restaurant 921 S 8th St, Rogers, AR 72756 (479) 636-2529 $	The Dixie Cafe 4600 Rozell St, Rogers, AR 72756 (479) 631-8700 $$
Green Bean 5208 Village Pkwy, Rogers, AR 72758 (479) 464-8355 $	The Egg & I 5206 Village Pkwy, Rogers, AR 72758 (479) 657-6630 $
Heirloom Food and Wine 113 S 2nd Street, Rogers, AR 72756 (479) 936-8083 $$	Wesner's Grill 117 W Chestnut St, Rogers, AR 72756 (479) 636-9723 $$
Houlihan's Restaurant 2203 S Promenade Blvd, Rogers, AR 72758 (479) 246-0296 $	Williams Soul Food Express 915 1/2 S. 8th St, Rogers, AR 72756 (479) 372-4835 $

Asian

Asian and Sushi 2603 W Pleasant Grove Rd, Rogers, AR 72758 (479) 633-0000 $	P.F. Chang's China Bistro 2203 S Promenade Blvd, Rogers, AR 72703 (479) 621-0491 $$

Genghis Grill 440 Promenade Blvd, Rogers, AR 72758 (479) 717-2695 $$	Silk Road Thai Restaurant 1023 S 8th Street, Rogers, AR 72756 (479) 621-9099 $
Hunan Chinese Restaurant 509 S 8th Street, Rogers, AR 72756 (479) 621-5300 $$	Thailand 104 N 12th Street, Rogers, AR 72756 (479) 636-2250 $$
Panda Express 2004 S Promenade Blvd, Rogers, AR 72758 (479) 936-8449 $	Wasabi 609 S 8th Street, Rogers, AR 72756 (479) 636-6363 $$

Bakeries

Atlanta Bread Company 4602 W Walnut Street, Rogers, AR 72756 (479) 936-5800 $	Great American Cookies 2203 Promenade Blvd, Rogers, AR 72758 (479) 986-0700 $
Auntie Anne's Pretzels 2203 S Promenade Blvd, Rogers, AR 72758 (479) 899-6600 $	Kirby's Kupcakes 128 S 2nd Street, Rogers, AR 72756 (479) 633-8400 $$
Bigwag Dog Bakery 2301 W Walnut Street, Rogers, AR 72756 (479) 631-2924 $	Panaderia Cuscatleca Arkansas 2515 N 17th Street, Rogers, AR 72756 (479) 899-6164 $
B's Cakes 1707 Henry Drive Rogers, AR 72756 (479) 644-5681 $	Panaderia Vega 115 N Dixieland Road, Rogers, AR 72756 (479) 636-4059 $

Bread N Buttery Bakery 113 W Walnut Street, Rogers, AR 72756 (479) 246-0100 $	**Savoy Tea Company** 2203 Promenade Blvd, Rogers, AR 72758 (479) 372-4995 $
Einstein Bros Bagels 1728 S 46th Street, Rogers, AR 72758 (479) 631-6200 $	**Panaderia Gaby** 1803 S 8th Street, Rogers, AR 72756 (479) 621-0063 $
For the Love of Brownies 2111 Perry Road, Rogers, AR 72758 (479) 619-7799 $	

Bars/Clubs/Pubs

Brick Street Brews 208 W Walnut Street, Rogers, AR 72756 (479) 633-8483 $	**Houlihans** 2203 Promenade Blvd., Ste 15100, Rogers, AR 72758 (479) 246-0296 $$
Boar's Nest 4404 W Walnut Street, Rogers, AR 72756 (479) 899-6282 $	**JJ's Grill** 4500 W Walnut, Ste 3, Rogers, AR 72756 (479) 372-4460 $$
Club Frisco 105 W Poplar Street, Rogers, AR 72756 (479) 633-0141 $	**Ozark Beer Company (Brewery)** 1700 S 1st St, Rogers, AR 72758 (479) 636-2337
Crabby's Seafood Bar and Grill 1800 S 52nd Street, Rogers, AR 72758 (479) 273-0222 $$	**Rockin' Pig Saloon Concert Venue** 2407 W Hudson Road, Rogers, AR 72756 (479) 633-8111 $

Grub's Rogers	WXYZ Bar at Aloft Hotel
3001 Market Street, Rogers, AR 72758	1103 S 52nd Street, Rogers, AR 72758
(479) 268-4810	(479) 268-6799
$$	$$
Heirloom Food and Wine	
113 S 2nd Street, Rogers, AR 72756	
(479) 936-8083	
$$	

Buffets

Hibachi Grill Buffet	Golden Corral
102 S 21st Street, Rogers, AR 72758	2605 Pleasant Crossing Dr, Rogers, AR
(479) 636-8888	72758
$$	(479) 986-9201
	$$
Panda Buffet	
2701 W Walnut Street, Rogers, AR	
72756	
(479) 621-6668	
$	

Burgers

Back Yard Burger's	Red Robin Gourmet Burgers
4301 Pleasant Crossing Blvd, Rogers,	4300 W Walnut Street, Rogers, AR
AR 72758	72756
(479) 621-0990	(479) 936-9797
$	$$
Chili's Grill and Bar	Sam's OldeTyme Hamburgers
420 N 46th Street, Rogers, AR 72756	223 E Locust, Rogers, AR 72756
(479) 936-9990	(479)-986-9191
$	$

Five Guys Burgers and Fries	Susie Q Malt Shop
2007 S Promenade Blvd, Rogers, AR 72758	612 N 2nd Street, Rogers, AR 72756
(479) 621-5600	(479) 631-6258
$	$

BBQ

Dickey's Barbecue Pit	Pit Master's BBQ
4204 W Green Acres Road, Rogers, AR 72758	100 N Dixieland Road, Rogers, AR 72756
(479) 631-9999	(479) 202-5344
$$	$$
Famous Dave's	Smokin' Joe's Ribhouse
609 N 46th Street, Rogers, AR 72756	803 W Poplar Street, Rogers, AR 72756
(479) 631-1172	(479) 621-0181
$$	$$
G & D's Barbecue	
2405 N 2nd Street, Rogers, AR 72756	
(479) 619-5841	
$$	

Candies

Candy Craze	Rocky Mountain Chocolate Factory
2203 Promenade Blvd, Rogers, AR 72758	2203 Promenade Blvd, Rogers, AR 72758
(479) 936-7302	(479) 899-6700
Martin Greer's Candies	
22151 U.S. 62, Garfield, AR 72732	
(479) 656-1440	

Catering

Copeland's of New Orleans 463 N 46th Street, Rogers, AR 72756 (479) 246-9455 $$	K-Mac Catering 2605 Pleasant Crossing Dr, Rogers, AR 72758 (479) 966-0353 $$
Back Yard Burger's 4301 Pleasant Crossing Blvd, Rogers, AR 72758 (479) 621-0990 $	Monte Ne Inn Chicken Restaurant 13843 Hwy 94, Rogers, AR 72758 (479) 636-5511 $$
Damgoode Pies 3604 W Walnut Street, Rogers, AR 72756 (479) 636-7437 $$	On the Border Mexican Grill and Cantina 577 N 46th Street, Rogers, AR 72756 (479) 616-1991 $$
Famous Dave's 609 N 46th Street, Rogers, AR 72756 (479) 631-1172 $$	Penguin Ed's Catering 700 W Walnut Street, Rogers, AR 72756 (479) 251-7429 $

Coffee

Bliss Cupcake Cafe 4204 W Green Acres Road, Rogers, AR 72758 (479) 903-7030 $	Starbucks 4520 W Walnut, Rogers, AR 72756 (479) 936-8250 $
Fill My Cup Coffee Lounge 100 N Dixieland Rd, Ste D9, Rogers, AR 72756 $	Starbucks 2003 Promenade Blvd, Rogers, AR 72758 (479) 636-0386 $

Latte'Da 808 S 52nd Street, Rogers, AR 72758 (479) 878-1828 $	Starbucks 2404 Promenade Blvd, Rogers, AR 72758 (479) 986-1100 $
Savoy Tea Company 2203 Promenade Blvd, Rogers, AR 72758 (479) 372-4995 $	The Iron Horse 220 S 1st Street, Rogers, AR 72756 (479) 631-9977 $
Starbucks Coffee Company 2605 W Pleasant Grove Rd, Rogers, AR 72758 (479) 986-8875 $	

Fast Food

Arby's 3929 W Walnut Street, Rogers, AR 72756 (479) 633-0092 $	Quiznos 4505 W Walnut Street, Rogers, AR 72756 (479) 936-7849 $
Arby's 501 S 8th Street, Rogers, AR 72756 (479) 631-2304 $	Sonic 923 W Walnut Street, Rogers, AR 72756 (479) 636-1122 $
Back Yard Burger's 4301 Pleasant Crossing Blvd, Rogers, AR 72758 (479) 621-0990 $	Sonic 303 W Hudson Road, Rogers, AR 72756 (479) 636-8507 $
Braum's 1102 W Walnut Street, Rogers, AR 72756 (479) 631-8977 $	Sonic 200 E New Hope Road, Rogers, AR 72758 (479) 936-8727 $

Burger King 500 S 8th Street, Rogers, AR 72756 (479) 636-8584 $	Subway 405 S 8th Street, Rogers, AR 72756 (479) 633-8834 $
Chick-fil-A 2601 W Pleasant Grove Rd, Rogers, AR 72758 (479) 246-0003 $	Subway 2301 W Walnut Street, Rogers, AR 72756 (479) 636-6699 $
Chick-fil-A 4001 W Walnut Street, Rogers, AR 72756 (479) 636-4664 $	Subway 2511 N 2nd Street, Rogers, AR 72756 (479) 621-8330 $
Freddy's Frozen Custard and Steakburgers 4507 W Walnut, Rogers, AR 72756 (479) 903-7197 $	Steak 'n Shake 1715 S 46th Street, Rogers, AR 72758 (479) 936-8865 $
KFC 507 S 8th Street, Rogers, AR 72756 (479) 636-9531 $	Susie Q Malt Shop 612 N 2nd Street, Rogers, AR 72756 (479) 631-6258 $
McDonald's 903 W Walnut Street, Rogers, AR 72756 (479) 636-1729 $	Taco Bell 604 S 8th Street, Rogers, AR 72756 (479) 631-7484 $
McDonald's 203 W Hudson Road, Rogers, AR 72756 (479) 631-7363 $	Taco Bueno 4303 Pleasant Crossing Blvd, Rogers, AR 72758 (479) 636-3501 $

McDonald's 100 N 46th Street, Rogers, AR 72756 (479) 636-7818 $	Wendy's 2200 W Walnut Street, Rogers, AR 72756 (479) 621-6757 $
Panda Express 2004 S Promenade Blvd, Rogers, AR 72758 (479) 936-8449 $	

Fine Dining

Bonefish Grill 3201 Market Street, Rogers, AR 72758 (479) 273-0916 $$	Ruth's Chris Steak House 3529 S Pinnacle Hills Pkwy, Rogers, AR 72758 (479) 633-8331 $$$
Mister B's Steakhouse 1043 W Walnut Street, Rogers, AR 72756 (479) 636-3122 $$	Theo's Steak 3300 Market Street, Rogers, AR 72758 (479) 657-6720 $$$

Food Trucks

Rockin' Pig Saloon 2407 W Hudson Road, Rogers, AR 72756 (479) 633-8111 $	

French

Copeland's of New Orleans 463 N 46th Street, Rogers, AR 72756 (479) 246-9455 $$	Mimi's Cafe 2105 Promenade Blvd, Rogers, AR 72758 (479) 936-7983 $$

Ice Cream

Andy's Frozen Custard's 2205 W Walnut Street, Rogers, AR 72756 (479) 636-2639 $	Freddy's Frozen Custard and Steakburgers 4507 W Walnut, Rogers, AR 72756 (479) 903-7197 $
Braum's 1102 W Walnut Street, Rogers, AR 72756 (479) 631-8977 $	Northwest Arkansas TCBY 2005 Promenade Blvd, Rogers, AR 72758 (479) 636-8229 $
Cold Stone Creamery 3301 Market Street, Rogers, AR 72758 (479) 271-8530 $	Steak 'n Shake 1715 S 46th Street, Rogers, AR 72758 (479) 936-8865 $
Dairy Queen 119 S Bloomington Street, Lowell, AR 72745 (479) 770-0808 $	Yum Yo's Frozen Yogurt 2203 Promenade Blvd, Rogers, AR 72758 (479) 202-5311 $

Indian

Chennai Cafe 2850 W Walnut St, Rogers, AR 72756 (479) 899-6215 $	

Italian

Carrabba's Italian Grill 3300 S Pinnacle Hills Pkwy, Rogers, AR 72758 (479) 273-2962 $	Olive Garden Italian Restaurants 1716 S 46th Street, Rogers, AR 72758 (479) 631-8480 $$
Johnny Carino's 535 N 46th Street, Rogers, AR 72756 (479) 633-0544 $$	Tony C's Italian Gardens 14528 Hwy 12, Rogers, AR 72756 (479) 925-3401 $
Napoli's Italian Restaurant 4408 W Walnut Street, Rogers, AR 72756 (479) 270-5320 $$	

Kosher

Chabad of Northwest Arkansas 5402 W. Redbud Street, Rogers, AR 72758 (479) 464-7999	

Mexican

Abuelo's 4005 W Walnut Street, Rogers, AR 72756 (479) 621-0428 $$	Qdoba Mexican Grill 2005 SPromenade Blvd, Rogers, AR 72758 (479) 621-6111 $
Acambaro Mexican Restaurant 215 S 8th Street, Rogers, AR 72756 (479) 986-9901 $$	Metapan Restaurant 208 S 8th Street, Rogers, AR 72756 (479) 621-0900 $

Chili's Grill and Bar 420 N 46th Street, Rogers, AR 72756 (479) 936-9990 $	On the Border Mexican Grill and Cantina 577 N 46th Street, Rogers, AR 72756 (479) 616-1991 $$
Corona Restaurant 14340 Hwy 12, Rogers, AR 72756 (479) 925-3158 $	Rolando's 224 S 2nd Street, Rogers, AR 72756 (479) 621-1002 $$
King Burrito 903 S 8th Street, Rogers, AR 72756 (479) 631-0063 $	Taco Bell 604 S 8th Street, Rogers, AR 72756 (479) 631-7484 $
Las Palmas 200 W Poplar Street, Rogers, AR 72756 (479) 986-9622 $	Taco Bueno 4303 Pleasant Crossing Blvd, Rogers, AR 72758 (479) 636-3501 $
Maria's Mexican Restaurant 2813 W Walnut Street, Rogers, AR 72756 (479) 986-9276 $	Taqueria Vega 1553 W Hudson Road, Rogers, AR 72756 (479) 936-8801 $
Mojitos Modern Mexican Grill 2003 S Promenade Blvd, Rogers, AR 72758 (479) 903-7076 $$	

Pizza

Bariola's Pizzeria 1728 S 46th Street, Rogers, AR 72758 (479) 636-0088 $$	Mellow Mushroom Pizza Bakers 5204 W Village Pkwy, Rogers, AR 72703 (479) 464-8008 $$

Chuck E. Cheese's 2006 Promenade Blvd, Rogers, AR 72758 (479) 986-9852 $$	**Papa John's Pizza** 2810 W Walnut Street, Rogers, AR 72756 (479) 636-4700 $$
Damgoode Pies 3604 W Walnut Street, Rogers, AR 72756 (479) 636-7437 $$	**Papa Murphy's** 2006 W Walnut Street, Rogers, AR 72756 (479) 633-9393 $
Domino's Pizza 2100 W Hudson Road, Rogers, AR 72756 (479) 631-2000 $	**Pizza Hut** 1900 W Walnut Street, Rogers, AR 72756 (479) 631-2393 $
Eureka Pizza 2119 W Walnut Street, Rogers, AR 72756 (479) 621-9999 $	**Pizza Hut** 1717 W Walnut Street, Rogers, AR 72756 (479) 246-0009 $
Jim's Razorback Pizza 1710 W Hudson Road, Rogers, AR 72756 (479) 631-3838 $	**Pizza Hut** 814 W Cypress Street, Rogers, AR 72756 (479) 631-2316 $
Log Cabin Family Restaurant, LLC. 14550 Hwy 12, Rogers, AR 72756 (479) 925-7222 $	**Sbarro** 2203 S Promenade Blvd, Rogers, AR 72758 (479) 986-9332 $
Mad Pizza 2603 W Pleasant Grove Rd, Rogers, AR 72758 (479) 636-0400 $$	**The Rail - A Pizza Company** 218 S 1st Street, Rogers, AR 72756 (479) 633-8808 $$

Sandwiches

Arby's 501 S 8th Street, Rogers, AR 72756 (479) 631-2304 $	Slim Chickens Restaurant 2002 Promenade Blvd, Rogers, AR 72758 (479) 878-2770 $
Atlanta Bread Company 4602 W Walnut Street, Rogers, AR 72756 (479) 936-5800 $	Subway 405 S 8th Street, Rogers, AR 72756 (479) 633-8834 $
Chick-fil-A 2601 W Pleasant Grove Rd Rogers, AR 72758 (479) 246-0003 $	Subway 2511 N 2nd Street, Rogers, AR 72756 (479) 621-8330 $
Center Chick-fil-A 4001 W Walnut Street, Rogers, AR 72756 (479) 636-4664 $	Subway 2301 W Walnut Street, Rogers, AR 72756 (479) 636-6699 $
Crumpet Tea Room 5212 Village Pkwy, Rogers, AR 72758 (479) 899-6322 $$	Subway 2605 Pleasant Grove Road, Rogers, AR 72758 479-899-6415 $
Iron Horse Coffee Company 220 S 1st Street, Rogers, AR 72756 (479) 631-9977 $	Subway Store 2203 Promenade Blvd, Rogers, AR 72758 (479) 631-2727 $
Jimmy John's 2004 S Promenade Blvd, Rogers, AR 72758 (479) 202-5000 $	Subway Store 2710 Rife Medical Lane, Rogers, AR 72758 (479) 633-8850 $

KFC 507 S 8th Street, Rogers, AR 72756 (479) 636-9531 $	Subway Store 5204 Village Pkwy, Rogers, AR 72758 (479) 273-1414 $
KFC 4507 W Walnut Street, Rogers, AR 72756 (479) 636-6881 $	Savoy Tea Company 2203 Promenade Blvd, Rogers, AR 72758 (479) 372-4995 $
Quiznos Restaurants 4505 W Walnut Street, Rogers, AR 72756 (479) 936-7849 $	Tropical Smoothie Cafe 3351 S Pinnacle Hills Pkwy, Rogers, AR 72758 (479) 273-2000 $
Schlotzsky's 2709 W Walnut Street, Rogers, AR 72756 (479) 636-9900 $	

Seafood

Bonefish Grill 3201 Market Street, Rogers, AR 72758 (479) 273-0916 $$	Fish City Grill 2203 S Promenade Blvd, Rogers, AR 72758 (479) 636-8833 $$
Catfish John's 601 W Hudson Road, Rogers, AR 72756 (479) 631-6908 $$	Long John Silver's 1036 W Walnut Street, Rogers, AR 72756 (479) 636-5166 $
Crabby's 1800 S 52nd Street, Rogers, AR 72758 (479) 273-0222 $$	Red Lobster 1710 S 46th Street, Rogers, AR 72758 (479) 636-1648 $

Steaks

Applebee's Neighborhood Grill 528 N 47th Street, Rogers, AR 72756 (479) 936-8989 $$	Outback Steakhouse 4509 W Poplar Street, Rogers, AR 72758 (479) 936-7660 $$
Colton's Steak House and Grill 4700 W Locust Street, Rogers, AR 72756 (479) 636-3336 $$	Ruth's Chris Steak House 3529 S Pinnacle Hills Pkwy, Rogers, AR 72758 (479) 633-8331 $$$
Logan's Roadhouse 530 N 47th Street, Rogers, AR 72756 (479) 986-9100 $$	Texas Land and Cattle 2103 S Promenade Blvd, Rogers, AR 72758 (479) 621-0070 $$
Mister B's Steakhouse 1043 W Walnut Street, Rogers, AR 72756 (479) 636-3122 $$	Theo's Steak 3300 Market Street, Rogers, AR 72758 (479) 657-6720 $$$

SILOAM SPRINGS

Park in Downtown Siloam Springs

As of 2012, Siloam Springs has a population of 15,680. It is the home of John Brown University, a private Christian college, Siloam Springs, AR, located about 35 minutes west from Springdale, AR on U.S. 412, has some surprising attractions for a city of its size. For example, the historic downtown or Main Street Siloam Springs has a number of interesting shops like Occasions, Vintage Accents, Amandromeda, Honeysuckle, Creative Corner and Two Gals Junk.

From April 19 through October 25, Siloam Springs holds a Farmer's Market in its downtown area. The market runs from 8 a.m. to 1 p.m., and you will find all sorts of farm produce, pasture raised meat, artisan crafts and a variety of baked goods at this wonderful locally driven market.

Notable restaurants in Siloam Springs, AR include the Cafe on Broadway, a good place to grab an excellent cup of coffee and the daily special. Enjoy authentic Ozark Plateau cuisine by Chef Miles James at 28 Springs restaurant. The eatery features a rotisserie oven, wood burning grill and handcrafted beverages. It's no wonder it is often mentioned as one of the top five restaurants in NWA. Fratelli's makes a true Italian-style pizza. Homemade dough using finely ground flour imported directly from Italy is hand-tossed, topped and baked in a super hot wood-fired oven.

You see? There are tons of wonderful things to do in Siloam Springs, AR! Before you dive headfirst into this section, however, please note that there is Siloam Springs, AR and West Siloam Springs, OK. This area is one of those areas split down the middle by the state line border. Unless you live there, you won't know which part you were in! I'm going to be talking primarily about Siloam Springs, AR, but we will venture across the state line to Oklahoma, as well, so don't get confused!

MAP OF SILOAM SPRINGS

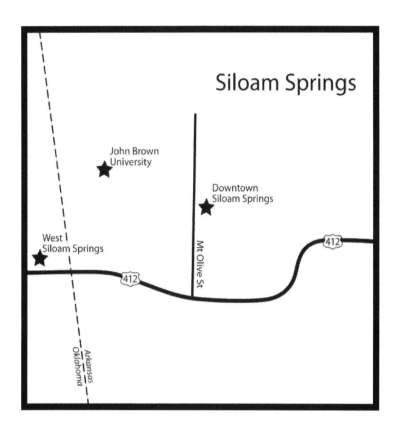

Neighborhoods

Siloam Springs may be small, but it still boasts two main neighborhood areas. You will find most of the restaurants and businesses in Siloam Springs in the historic downtown area and along the U.S. 412 corridor.

What the Locals Say...

Straight from the mouths of this charming community's locals:

Many travelers drive through Siloam Springs without knowing that there are some terrific things to do and fantastic restaurants to try in our small town. In fact, Smithsonian.com named the city as one of the 20 Best Small Towns in

America (May 2012).

Everywhere you look, nature abounds. Our parks, throughout the city, are open to the public and are a great way to spend an afternoon. Sager Creek has rock wall-lined banks and flows through the downtown area. Visitors can relax and enjoy the huge old trees, dogwoods, fountains, green spaces, duck crossings and footbridges. Also, there is the Dogwood Trail, a 2.04-mile paved running trail with some up and down terrain.

Unique specialty and antique/vintage shops in the downtown area are fun to shop. Try Occasions to find just the outfit you are looking for. They have clothing for every occasion and they keep a fresh pot of coffee going regardless of when you come in.

The Farmer's Market, held every Tuesday and Saturday in City Park has everything including farm fresh produce, candles, gluten free bread, scones, perennials and the best chocolate hazelnut cookies you'll find anywhere.

Siloam Springs has some of the best fishing to be found in AR. There are many streams, reservoirs and lakes to fish. Try Fagan Creek, Osage Creek or the Double Bar Ranch Lake. The area is known for Drum, Redear Sunfish and Largemouth bass.

Dependable canoeing, kayaking and rafting is available at the Illinois River's Siloam Springs Whitewater Park. Be sure to wear a life jacket at all times, especially since lifeguards are not present.

Day Trip

Siloam Springs Day Trip

Cherokee Casino West Siloam Springs

Do you like to try your hand with Texas Hold 'Em, Blackjack or Poker? Or do you thrill with the spin of the slot machine wheel? Drive just a few minutes west from Siloam Springs on U.S. 412 to find one of the best Indian-owned and operated Casinos in Oklahoma. Just across the Arkansas and Oklahoma state line is the large, modern, seven-story, Cherokee Hotel Casino. or Cherokee Casino West Siloam Springs, as it's officially called.

This new hotel and casino, located at 2416 U.S. 412 in West Siloam Springs, OK is well suited for business or pleasure. It has a full business center with Internet, is pet friendly, has a restaurant, is wheelchair accessible and has plenty of opportunities for you to dance with Lady Luck.

The casino floor is about 90 percent to 95 percent slots, and the rest is active with exciting table games. There are around 1,500 electronic games; you're sure to find a few that will look lucky and make your day by rewarding you with its jackpot. The popular card table games include Texas Hold 'Em, Omaha Poker and Seven-Card Stud.

The comfortable, quiet rooms are well-equipped with 37-inch plasma TVs, complimentary high-speed wired and Wi-Fi Internet access, complimentary local phone calls, iPod® docking stations, alarm clocks, in-room safes, coffee makers with coffee and assorted teas, refrigerators, two telephones with dual phone lines and voice mail, hairdryers, irons and ironing boards, whirlpool tubs in select suites and express check-out. Who could ask for more? Get your player's card before you check in to receive $10 off the room price per night.

Enjoy live-action cooking at the casino's River Cane Buffet. The pricing is comparable to Las Vegas back in the day when it was really inexpensive. The River Cane Buffet features all of your favorite foods, including Chinese, Mexican, Italian and American, and there is also a full dessert station with a variety of pastries and fresh cakes.

Plan to have an elegant dinner at the Flint Creek Steakhouse, where you can select from high-quality steaks and gourmet entrées, such as lobster and veal marsala. Flint Creek Steakhouse also offers an unusually extensive wine list. Be pampered by the experienced wait staff, and then head on over to Seven to dance the night away.

Thursday through Saturdays there is hot, live entertainment in Seven. Celebrate your wins in the cool atmosphere of Seven. Dance on the largest dance floor in the area and listen to the best local bands. Top national acts also perform at the nightclub. Open until 2 a.m., Seven is a terrific place to close out your day trip.

For more information about Cherokee Casino West Siloam Springs, call (800) 754-4111

ACCOMMODATIONS

There is a full range of modern hotels available in the Siloam Springs, AR area including the Hampton Inn, Quality Inn, Best Western Stateline Lodge, Budget Inn, Super 7 Inn, Super 8 and Stone's Inn. If you are looking for clean comfortable accommodations, you will easily find them in this progressive looking city.

Hotel Amenities

Breakfast: B	*Internet: I*	*Pool: P*
Business Center: BC	*Meeting Rooms: MR*	*Restaurant: R*
Fitness Center: FC	*Pet Friendly: PF*	

Hotels in Siloam Springs, AR with 2 Star Accommodations

Americas Best Value Inn and Suites 1801 U.S. 412 West, Siloam Springs, AR 72761 (479) 524-2025 B, I, P	Quality Inn 1300 U.S. 412 West, Siloam Springs, AR 72761 (479) 524-8080 B, I, MR, P
Budget Inn Siloam Springs 2400 U.S. 412, Siloam Springs, AR 72761 (479) 524-5127 I	Stone Inn 1150 U.S. 412 West, Siloam Springs, AR 72761 (479) 524-5172 I
Cherokee Casino West Siloam Springs 2416 U.S. 412, Siloam Springs, OK 74964 (800) 754-4111 I	Super 7 Inn Siloam Springs 1951 U.S. 412 West, Siloam Springs, AR 72761 (479) 524-5157 BC, I
Hampton Inn Siloam Springs 2171 Ravenwood Plaza, Siloam Springs, AR 72761 (479) 215-1000 B, BC, FC, I, MR, P	Super 8 Siloam Springs 1800 U.S. 412 West, Siloam Springs, AR 72761 (479) 524-8898 B, BC, I, P

THINGS TO DO AND SEE

Gambling at the Cherokee Casino may be the main attraction in Siloam Springs, but if playing poker is not your game, there are other fun things to do in this NWA city. While away your afternoon by shopping at the antique stores and flea markets located in Siloam Springs, AR.

The Parks and Recreation Department hosts many different events throughout the year, weather permitting. As examples, some of the April events scheduled are Kite Day located at the Siloam Springs Municipal Airport and the Dogwood 5K Run at Bob Henry Park Pavilion. Check the Park and Recreation calendar for other upcoming community events.

Arts/Culture
Cathedral of the Ozarks
2000 W University Street, Siloam Springs, AR 72761
(479) 524-7415

Sagar Creek Arts Center
301 E Twin Springs, Siloam Springs, AR 72761
(479) 524-4000
Enjoy music, drama, dance, visual arts, literature and other aspects of theater in this historic 1921 building.

John Brown University Art Gallery
2000 W University Street, Siloam Springs, AR 72761
(479) 524-9500
This gallery hosts prominent shows from nationally and internationally renowned artists, as well as many local artists, faculty and student works.

Local Flair Art Gallery
116 N Broadway Street, Siloam Springs, AR 72761
(479) 524-0424
Stop by to see the fantastic local talent. Browse and buy wall décor, sculptures, jewelry, pottery, stained glass, note cards and collectables.

Siloam Springs Museum
112 N Maxwell, Siloam Springs, AR 72761
(479) 524-4011

Outdoors
Arkansas 59 Canoeing and Rafting
20466 Arkansas 59, Siloam Springs, AR 72761
(479) 524-2223

Bob Henry Park
604 W Benton Street, Siloam Springs, AR 72761
(479) 524-5779

Camp Siloam
3600 S Lincoln Street, Siloam Springs, AR 72761
(479) 524-4565
Camp Siloam is a Christian camp for children, youth and families.

City Park
W University Street, Siloam Springs, AR
(479) 524-5779

Dogwood Springs Walking/Biking Trail
200-298 W University Street, Siloam Springs, AR 72761
The Dogwood Springs Trail is approximately 5 miles connected in the middle by sidewalks running through downtown Siloam Springs. This is a scenic trail to walk or ride, as there is a lot to see as you wind through town, along creeks and through wooded areas.

Green Tree RV Park
1800 U.S. 412 West, Siloam Springs, AR 72761
(479) 524-8898

Natural Falls Oklahoma State Park
West Siloam Springs, OK 74338
(918) 422-5802
This scenic 120-acre recreation area features a 77-foot waterfall with an observation platform, hiking trails, picnic shelters, volleyball, horseshoes, basketball courts, catch and release fishing, playgrounds and a nine-hole disc golf course.

Skydive Skyranch
Hangar 4
Cecil Smith Field, Siloam Springs, AR 72761
(479) 651-6160

Learn to skydive from committed, experienced staff. Skydive Skyranch provides topnotch jumper support and sport parachuting fun. Skyranch can take you from your first jump all the way to the national championship.

SWEPCO Lake
Gentry, AR 72734
SWEPCO Lake is a unique 500-acre heated lake that is great for catching bass. You'll find it 1 mile west of Gentry, AR on Hwy 12.

Twin Springs Park
Broadway and Main Street, Siloam Springs, AR 72761
(479) 524-5779

Wild Wilderness Drive-Through Safari
20923 Safari Road, Gentry, AR 72734
(479) 736-8383

Whitewater Recreation Park
19253 Fisher Ford Road, Siloam Springs, AR 72761
(479) 524-5136
This family-friendly, alcohol-free park along the scenic Illinois River is great for kayakers of all skill levels. It offers 600 feet of engineered river, which expands and creates two distinct rapids. In addition, there is a picnic area, walking trails, rain garden and changing area.

Recreation
Arkoma Lanes
1490 U.S. 412 West, Siloam Springs, AR 72761
(479) 524-6681
Families are sure to love bowling in this Siloam Springs non-smoking, 16-lane bowling facility.

Center Cinema
1102 S Carl Street, Siloam Springs, AR 72761
(479) 238-1506

Shopping
Antique Shops
Farmers Finds
1941 U.S. 412 East, Siloam Springs, AR 72761
(479) 373-1063

French Hen
308 S Mt Olive Street, Siloam Springs, AR 72761
(479) 524-3788

Broadway Antiques
502 S Broadway Street, Siloam Springs, AR 72761
(479) 524-6911

Burlap & Lace
702 S Mt Olive Street, Siloam Springs, AR 72761
(479) 238-1444

Honeysuckle
111 N Broadway St, Siloam Springs, Arkansas 72761
(479) 427-0717

Jenny's Junction
120 Arkansas 59, Siloam Springs, AR 72761
(479) 524-9607

Vintage Accents
114 S Broadway, Siloam Springs, AR 72761
(479) 215-9231

Boutiques
CG Boutique
4985 U.S. 412, Siloam Springs, AR 72761
(479) 601-5737

Petty Cash Boutique
116 S Broadway Street, Siloam Springs, AR 72761
(479) 373-6155

Urban Unique Resale and Boutique
405-B W Tulsa, Siloam Springs, AR 72761
(479) 373-1101

Flea Markets
2 Gals Junk
120 S Broadway, Siloam Springs, AR 72761
(479) 228-1289

Baby & Momma
116 S. Broadway St., Suite 1, Siloam Springs, AR 72761
(479) 373-6153

The Chicken Coop
500 E Main, Gentry, AR 72734
(479) 233-2328

Vintage Heart
4985 U.S. 412 East, Siloam Springs, AR 72761
(479) 366-7693

Specialty Shops
Bathe Siloam Springs
116 N Broadway Suite E
Siloam Springs, Arkansas 72761
(479) 373-6363

Creative Corner
122 S Broadway, Siloam Springs, AR 72761
(479) 228-1236

DaySpring Outlet Store
200 N Progress Ave, Siloam Springs, AR 72761
(479) 549-6315

Dogwood Junction
101 W Tulsa Street, Siloam Springs, AR 72761
(479) 524-6605
This recreational shop rents bikes, kites and more for exploring Siloam
Springs.

Deans Square
16363 Airport Road, Siloam Springs, AR 72761
(479) 238-3035

Occasions
109 W University, Siloam Springs, AR 72761
(479) 524-4366

Sager Creek Quilts & Yarnworks
304 E Central, Siloam Springs, AR 72761
(479) 524-5244

Sassafras
4985 U.S. 412, Siloam Springs, AR 72761
(479) 427-6876

The Chicken Depot
1270 U.S. 412 West, Siloam Springs, AR 72761
(479) 373- 6790

Vintage Shops
Amandromeda
116 N Broadway Street, Siloam Springs, AR 72761
(479) 549-5919

Cottage Haven
3900 U.S. 412 East, Siloam Springs, AR 72761
(479) 549-3600

Spas
Posh Salon and Spa
16363 Airport Road, Siloam Springs, AR 72761
(479) 549-9002

Trends Salon and Spa
1004 S Mt Olive, Siloam Springs, AR 72761
(479) 549-4247

Special Events
Historic Downtown Special Events
There are several festivals and special events in Siloam Springs, AR. For
example, there are the:

- Dog Days of Summer Festival

- Second Saturday Music in the Park

- Movies in the Park

- Wellfest

… and many others!

Farmer's Market (April – October) 8am-1pm
127 N Broadway, Siloam Springs AR 72761
(479) 524-4556
Homemade, homegrown or homespun, the Siloam Springs Farmer's Market
allows venders to showcase their goods and is a great attraction for any guest.

RESTAURANTS

Siloam Springs boasts 51-plus restaurants, including the new and wildly popular 28 Springs restaurant located in the historic downtown neighborhood. The 28 Springs restaurant is one of several outstanding restaurants where you can relax, eat delicious food prepared from scratch, and count on a quality dining experience.

The Café on Broadway, or just "The Café" as the locals call it, is a family eatery where you can eat freshly baked foods and wonderfully prepared entrees. It's hard to believe, but you have a full café, café and teahouse, bakery and a bookstore all under the same roof.

Restaurant Prices

$ - Budget	*$$$ - Upscale*
$$ - Mid-Range	

American

28 Springs Restaurant 100 E University St, Siloam Springs, AR 72761 (479) 524-2828 $$	Callahan's Steak House 210 U.S. 412 East, Siloam Springs, AR 72761 (479) 524-4674 $$
Barnett's Dairyette 111 W Tulsa Street, Siloam Springs, AR 72761 (479) 524-3211 $	City Park Grill 201 W University, Siloam Springs, AR 72761 (479) 373-6301 $
Cafe on Broadway 123 N Broadway St, Siloam Springs, AR 72761 (479) 549-3556 $$	The Wooden Spoon 1000 S Gentry Blvd, Hwy 59, Gentry, AR 72734 (479) 736-3030 $

| Cathy's Corner
1910 U.S. 412, Siloam Springs, AR 72761
(479) 524-4475
$$ | |

Asian

Asian Chef 315-C U.S. 412 East, Siloam Springs, AR 72761 (479) 524-5043 $	Thai City 110 U.S. 412, Siloam Springs, AR 72761 (479) 238-0277 $$
Hunan Village 3402 U.S. 412, Siloam Springs, AR 72761 (479) 524-3979 $$	Thai Cafe 808 S Mt Olive St, Siloam Springs, AR 72761 (479) 427-9223 $

Bakeries

Daylight Donuts 155 U.S. 412 East, Siloam Springs, AR 72761 (479) 524-5884	Fancy Flours Cupcakery 5007 David Drive, Siloam Springs, AR 72761 (479) 553-9459

Bars/Pubs

28 Springs Restaurant 100 E University St, Siloam Springs, AR 72761 (479) 524-2828 $$	Pour Jon's 223 N Wright St , Siloam Springs, AR 72761 (918) 221-8747 $

BBQ

Banjo's BBQ 2125 E Main St #1, Siloam Springs, AR 72761 (479) 524-1888 $$	Dickeys Barbeque 1951 U.S. 412 East, Siloam Springs, AR 72761 (479) 238-1112 $
Hawg City Grill 1004 S Mt Olive St, Siloam Springs, AR 72761 (479) 238-0289 $	

Catering

Edibles by Zoe 1951 North Dogwood Siloam Springs, AR 72761 (479) 459-8105	

Coffee

Pour Jon's 223 N Wright St , Siloam Springs, AR 72761 (918) 221-8747 $	Sweet Stir 2420 East U.S. 412, Siloam Springs, AR 72761 (479) 233-0210 $

Fast Food

Arby's 1001 U.S. 412 West, Siloam Springs, AR 72761 (479) 524-5972 $	Long John Silver's 525 U.S. 412 West, Siloam Springs, AR 72761 (479) 524-2270 $

Hardee's 1625 U.S. 412 West, Siloam Springs, AR 72761 (479) 524-8344 $	Zaxby's 190 N Progress Ave , Siloam Springs, AR 72761 (479) 238-1305 $
KFC 1115 U.S. 412 West, Siloam Springs, AR 72761 (479) 524-4254 $	Sonic Drive-in 1134 U.S. 412 West, Siloam Springs, AR 72761 (479) 524-8510 $

Fine Dining

28 Springs Restaurant 100 E University St, Siloam Springs, AR 72761 (479) 524-2828 $$	Flint Creek Steakhouse U.S. Hwy 412 & State Hwy 59, Cherokee Casino, West Siloam Springs, OK (800) 754-4111 $$$

Ice Cream ~ Frozen Yogurt

CherryBerry Siloam Springs 200 Progress Ave, Siloam Springs, AR 72761 (479) 373-6311 $	

Mexican

Jarritos Restaurant 906 E Main Street, Siloam Springs, AR 72761 (479) 524-9927 $	Taco Bell 1050 U.S. 412 West, Siloam Springs, AR 72761 (479) 524-3920 $

La Hacienda De Los Reyes	Taqueria El Rancho
2010 E Main Street, Siloam Springs, AR 72761	715 E Jefferson St, Siloam Springs, AR 72761
(479) 524-2948	(479) 524-0083
$	$
La Huerta	
1270 U.S. 412 West, Siloam Springs, AR 72761	
(479) 524-0061	
$	

Pizza

Fratelli's Wood-Fired Pizzeria	Mazzio's Pizza
118 S Broadway St, Siloam Springs, AR 72761	906 W Kenwood St, Siloam Springs, AR 72761
(479) 599-9197	(479) 549-4949
$$	$$
Jim's Razorback Pizza	Pizza Hut
1200 N Lincoln St, Siloam Springs, AR 72761	391 U.S. 412 East, Siloam Springs, AR 72761
(479) 549-4800	(479) 524-6401
$	$
Little Caesars Pizza	
200 Progress Ave Ste 200, Siloam Springs, AR 72761	
(479) 238-8900	
$	

Sandwiches

Fatiga's Sub Station	SUBWAY
1004 S Mt Olive St, Siloam Springs, AR 72761	123 U.S. 412 East, Siloam Springs, AR 72761
(479) 524-6277	(479) 524-9643
$	$

Quiznos 3121 U.S. 412 East, Siloam Springs, AR 72761 (479) 524-4403 $	

STEAKS

Callahan's Steak House 210 U.S. 412 East, Siloam Springs, AR 72761 (479) 524-4674 $$	Flint Creek Steakhouse U.S. Hwy 412 & State Hwy 59, Cherokee Casino, West Siloam Springs, OK (800) 754-4111 $$$

SPRINGDALE

Northwest Arkansas Naturals

Springdale, along with Bentonville, Bella Vista, Eureka Springs, Rogers, Fayetteville, Lowell and Siloam Springs, are the eight cities and towns that make up NWA, and each offers its own collection of things to do in the Northwest Arkansas area.

Nestled in the Ozarks, Springdale is a large part of the reason why Arkansas is known far and wide as the "Natural State." Located near Beaver Lake, which provides many opportunities for boating, fishing and kayaking, The city is in the very heart of NWA. If nature is not your thing, however, there are many other things to do in the area, such as ice skating, riding the historic railroad, visiting museums, outlet mall shopping, or checking out a Northwest Arkansas Naturals game if sports is something you enjoy.

With a population of 69,797, according to the 2010 Census, it is the fourth largest city in Arkansas. It is the headquarters for Tyson Foods, Inc., the largest meat producing company in the world, and it is also the headquarters for Fuels & Supplies, Inc., the leading fuel supplier for NWA. These two businesses draw many people to the NWA corner of the state, but once they are here, they quickly discover all the many other wonderful things to do in Northwest Arkansas, which is what keeps them here.

The Shiloh Museum is located in downtown Springdale. The museum focuses on history from the 1850s and features interesting interpretive programs and other historical exhibits. The northeast side of the city used to be John Fitzgerald's station and stable, and was a stop on the famous Butterfield Overland Mail Co. Stagecoach route. Today the Butterfield Overland trail is part of the Arkansas Heritage Trails System.

For a fun-filled experience, and if you are so inclined, you can ride the Arkansas and Missouri Railroad on an authentically restored turn-of-the-century passenger car.

Besides the historical significance of the city, it is also noted for hosting the annual July Rodeo of the Ozarks; for being the home of the Northwest Arkansas Naturals baseball team, currently the Double-A Minor League affiliate of the Kansas City Royals; and for being the home of the world-famous, 1940s-era AQ Chicken House restaurant. You don't want to leave the area without tasting this award-winning chicken or visiting many of the other fine restaurants in the city.

Nearby Beaver Lake provides the opportunity for all kinds of wonderful outdoor activities, such as fishing, boating, canoeing and other water sports. The rivers in the area, all of which are well suited for recreational activities, include the Kings, Buffalo and Mulberry Rivers. Take the family or go with friends on a float trip down the Buffalo River. You will never forget the experience!

Whether business with Tyson Foods or Fuels & Supplies or a long overdue vacation plan brings you to Springdale, you will find plenty of things to do in this Northwest Arkansas city where you can make many lasting memories that you and your family and friends can relive year after year.

MAP OF SPRINGDALE

Neighborhoods

There are four main areas of Springdale that include midtown, the west side, downtown and the south town neighborhood. U.S. 412 runs east and west through the middle of the city. Wagon Wheel Road is north of the city and it too runs east and west. Huntsville Avenue and Don Tyson Parkway also run east and west of the city. I-49, U.S. 71B and Hwy 265 are the major roads that run north and south.

What the Locals Say...

Time to take a listen to what the Springdale locals say about their wonderful neck of the NWA woods! When in Springdale, the locals say:

Don't miss the AQ Chicken House Restaurant over on 71B. With good reason, it is world famous for its tasty-treat-delight fried chicken. It's definitely one of the best restaurants in Springdale, AR!

If you are celebrating a special occasion, you can't beat James at the Mill in Springdale. Current and returning Springdale natives always make it a point to eat at James at the Mill. Everything served there is delicious, but a local favorite continues to be the James at the Mill Caesar salad.

Get the jambalaya pasta and ribs at the MarketPlace Grill. The sweet potato fries are also to die for, the spinach dip is superb and the salmon is terrific. MarketPlace Grill is often mentioned as the best place to eat in Springdale.

If you are a baseball fan, visit the $33-million Arvest Ballpark, the home of the Northwest Arkansas Naturals of the Texas League. If you are visiting May through September, you can catch more than just one of the 70-plus home games and cheer our boys on!

To get a true feel for the essence of the city, take the time to walk Emma Ave in downtown Springdale where you will find shops like the Abbey Antique Shop and Mix and Manor. Also, the Shiloh Museum is on the corner of Main Street and Johnson Ave, and if you have time, you can take a ride on the fully restored A & M Excursion train car, which provides a round-trip to historic Van Buren, AR and then back to Springdale. There is much excitement regarding the recent Walton family investment along with a $1 million gift from Tyson foods to bring Downtown Springdale to a new level of fun.

If your timing is just right, you can see the Rodeo of the Ozarks. This event is four days of wonderful family fun, including the professional rodeo competition with quite a nice purse for the winner and two days of parades and celebration.

The first Saturday of each month from 8 a.m. to noon, the Springdale Chamber of Commerce puts on Coffee and Cars. Located on the corner of Emma Ave and Spring Street downtown, Coffee and Cars is a terrific opportunity to see beautifully restored cars and trucks.

ACCOMMODATIONS

Most people visit Springdale for business with Springdale's largest company, Tyson Foods, Inc. As such, there are numerous top-rated, 4+-star hotels located close to Tyson Foods that cater specifically to the business traveler. However, this should not discourage those from visiting Springdale for pleasure, either. It's a wonderful part of NWA to see!

Whether traveling on business or pleasure, the hotels in Springdale, AR are sure to please. For a consistently exceptional experience, try the Double Tree Club by Hilton, the Value Place Springdale, or Inn at the Mill, which is an Ascend Collection Hotel. If you brought your puppy, try the pet-friendly La Quinta Inn and Suites in Springdale. Additionally, there are several budget hotels that provide no-frills accommodations. Customers generally describe the Springdale hotels as quiet, clean and comfortable.

Hotel Amenities

Breakfast: B	Internet: I	Pool: P
Business Center: BC	Meeting Rooms: MR	Restaurant: R
Fitness Center: FC	Pet Friendly: PF	

Hotels in Springdale, AR with 3 Star Accommodations

Doubletree Club by Hilton 4677 W Sunset Ave, Springdale, AR 72762 (479) 751-7200 B, BC, FC, I, MR, P, R	Inn at the Mill, an Ascend Collection Hotel 3906 Johnson Mill Blvd, Johnson, AR 72762 (479) 443-1800 B, BC, I, PF, R
Fairfield Inn and Suites Springdale 1043 Rieff Street, Springdale, AR 72762 (479) 419-5722 B, BC, FC, I, P	LaQuinta Inn and Suites 1300 S 48th Street, Springdale, AR 72762 (479) 751-2626 B, BC, FC, I, PF, P

Hampton Inn and Suites Springdale 1700 S 48th Street, Springdale, AR 72762 (479) 756-3500 B, BC, FC, I, MR, PF, P	Residence Inn Springdale 1740 S 48th Street, Springdale, AR 72762 (479) 872-9100 B, BC, FC, I, MR, PF, P
Holiday Inn Springdale/Fayetteville Area 1500 S 48th Street, Springdale, AR 72762 (479) 751-8300 B, BC, FC, I, MR, PF, P	TownePlace Suites Fayetteville North/Springdale 5437 S 48th Street, Springdale, AR 72762 (479) 966-4400 B, BC, FC, I, MR, PF, P

Hotels in Springdale, AR with 2 Star Accommodations

Comfort Suites 1099 Rieff Street, Springdale, AR 72762 (479) 725-1777 B, BC, FC, I, MR, P	Sleep Inn Suites 1056 Rieff Street, Springdale, AR 72762 (479) 756-5800 B, BC, FC, I, MR, PF, P
Executive Inn and Suites Springdale 2005 U.S. 71B, Springdale, AR 72762 (479) 756-6101 B, BC, FC, I, PF, P, R	Springdale Inn 660 S Thompson Street, Springdale, AR 72764 (479) 751-4878 B, I
Extended Stay America Hotel 5000 Luvene Ave, Springdale, AR 72762 (479) 872-1490 B, FC, I, MR, PF, P	Super 8 Springdale, AR 4540 W Sunset Ave, Springdale, AR 72762 (479) 751-6700 B, I, P
Heritage Inn Springdale 1394 W Sunset Ave, Springdale, AR 72764 (479) 751-3100 B, FC, I, MR, PF, P, R	Travelodge Inn and Suites 1394 W Sunset Ave, Springdale, AR 72764 (479) 751-3100

Motel 8 1206 S Thompson Street, Springdale, AR 72764 (479) 751-9221 B, BC, I, P	Value Place 4397 Dixie Industrial Dr, Springdale, AR 72762 (479) 770-6611 I
Royal Inn 1042 48th Place, Springdale, AR 72762 (479) 756-0040 BC, I	

Bed and Breakfast in Springdale, AR

Perry's Passin' Thru 21365 Perry Road, Springdale, AR 72764 (479) 841-1900	

RV Parks in Springdale, AR

Pilgrims Rest RV Park 21225 W. Hickory Flatt Road, Springdale, AR 72764 (479) 789-7152	Whisler Mobile Home and RV Park 1101 S Old Missouri Road, Springdale, AR 72764 (479) 751-9081

THINGS TO DO AND SEE

Springdale is home to The Northwest Arkansas Naturals, a Double-A Minor League baseball team, currently an affiliate of the Kansas City Royals and a member of the Texas league. The Naturals play some 70 home games at Arvest Baseball Park on the corner of 56th and Watkins in Springdale. The first home game is played in early to mid April. Premium seating is only $12, much cheaper than any major league baseball park. Great family fun!

If you enjoy wine, you will love the Tontitown Winery located at 335 N Barrington Road in Springdale. The wine, cheese and crackers, atmosphere and service are all wonderful. Grapes from Arkansas and California are used to make the exceptional wine.

History buffs can visit the Shiloh Museum of Ozark History located at 118 W Johnson Ave in Springdale. The owner describes the place as a regional museum of the Northwest Arkansas Ozarks.

You can also take a train ride on the Arkansas Missouri Railroad. Economy seating is available, but for the best experience, get a ticket featuring air conditioning and a meal. Boarding is at 306 E Emma Ave in Springdale, and the train ride takes you on a historical adventure through the Arkansas-Missouri railroad past. Who says there aren't a ton of things to do in Northwest Arkansas!

Art/Culture
Galleries
The Art Exchange, LLC
113 W Emma Ave, Springdale, AR 72764
(479) 751-3003

Arts Center of the Ozarks
214 S Main, Springdale, AR 72764
(479) 751-5441

Established in 1967, the Arts Center of the Ozarks offers opportunities for all creative outlets, including singing, painting, dancing, acting, music and sewing. The Center is known as the heart of the arts in NWA. Its goal is to provide terrific entertainment, while offering excellent educational opportunities in the arts. The hands-on approach to the arts utilizes creative inspiration and provides amazing surprises for the entire family.

This community theater is home to six main stage plays and two children's plays, which highlight the Arts Center of the Ozarks annual schedule.

Museums
Shiloh Museum of Ozark History
118 W Johnson Ave, Springdale, AR 72764
(479) 750-8165

The Shiloh Museum of Ozark History focuses on the history of the Northwest Arkansas Ozarks. It got its name from the pioneer community of Shiloh, which later in the 1870s became known as Springdale.

The museum facilitates a research library, which houses a collection of over 500,000 pictures of the Ozarks. Also on the grounds are six historic buildings highlighting the lives of the ordinary people who lived in the rural communities of the Ozarks. Additionally, there are also many permanent exhibits portraying the lives of these everyday NWA men, women and children.

Tontitown Historical Museum
251 E Henri de Tonti Blvd, Springdale, AR 72762
(479) 361-2700

Sports & Recreation
Baseball
Arvest Baseball Park - Home of The Northwest Arkansas Naturals
Corner of 56th and Watkins
3000 S 56th Street, Springdale, AR 72764
(479) 927-4900

The Class AA Northwest Arkansas Naturals baseball team calls the Arvest Ballpark its home. In the summer, the ballpark is the exciting venue for 70 home games, which provide excellent high quality entertainment for the entire region. The ballpark also hosts a variety of other activities including fairs, car shows and festivals. Be sure to stay around for the spectacular fireworks that illuminate the sky every Friday night the Northwest Arkansas Naturals play at home.

Perfect Timing Baseball and Softball Academy
13241 Puppy Creek Road, Ste 21, Springdale, AR 72762
(479) 595-0551

All Sports

All Star Sports Arena

1906 Cambridge Street, Springdale, AR 72764
(479) 750-2600

The All Star Sports Arena in Springdale is a multiple-use facility offering basketball and volleyball courts, martial arts, wrestling, youth flag football, cheerleading and dance studios, and an all-female roller derby.

This 130,000-square-foot sports complex also offers various adult and youth sport leagues.

Jones Center for Families

922 E Emma Ave, Springdale, AR 72756
(479) 756-8090

The Jones Center, Springdale, AR is a premier multi-purpose center for NWA. It includes an indoor swimming pool, fitness center, gymnasium with volleyball and basketball courts, an ice rink, track, a community park, and showers and locker rooms.

In addition to recreational opportunities, Jones Center, Springdale, AR has a teen center, an onsite chapel and a facility for genealogy research. There are also ongoing programs for kids, teens, families and seniors. Admission and all activities and classes are FREE at the Center.

Rodeo of the Ozarks

1423 E Emma Ave, Springdale, AR 72764
(479) 756-0464

Named one of the "Top 5 Large Outdoor Rodeos in 2011" by the PRCA, the Rodeo of the Ozarks brings the best of cowboys and stock together every year for some top level competition.

Roller City

1007 Century Street, Springdale, AR 72762
(479) 756-3866
Premiere Roller Rink

Golf

Springdale is home to two challenging courses and within easy driving distance to 24 others.

Bush Creek Golf Course
6220 Har Ber Ave, Springdale, AR 72762
(479) 750-0606

Springdale Country Club
608 W Lakeview Drive, Springdale, AR 72764
Office: (479) 872-2166
Pro Shop: (479) 751-5185

Designed by Bland P. Pittman and opened in 1927, the 18-hole course at Springdale Country Club offers plenty of golf. The course features 6,673 yards of golf from the longest tees for a par of 72. The course rating is 72.1, and it has a slope rating of 119.

Hiking, Fishing and More
Springdale Parks and Trails
Springdale offers four great parks, an aquatic center, and the regional Razorback Greenway Trail.

Beaver Lake
Beaver Lake offers 500 miles of shoreline, clear pristine water, and every water sport and outdoor opportunity imaginable.

Arkansas Missouri Railroad
306 E Emma Ave, Springdale, AR 72764
(479) 725-4017

The Arkansas Missouri Railroad in Springdale, AR, offers riders a "window seat to history" of NWA with three different routes through beautiful Ozark countryside.

Shopping

Ozark Center Point Place
I-49 and U.S. 412 Intersection, Springdale, AR 72765

If shopping is your cup of tea, you will not be disappointed by the Ozark Center Point Place shopping center in West Springdale. Ozark Center Point Place is home to over 30 retailers. You'll find plenty of stores offering a wide variety of retail fare, including arts and crafts supply retailers; clothing and shoe stores perfect for finding a great new outfit and matching shoes; home furnishings and furniture stores; handyman stores sure to please any do-it-yourselfer; and candy shops for your afternoon sugar pick me up.

Downtown Springdale

Emma Ave in downtown Springdale is home to Springdale's historic business district. The shopping opportunities here are with retailers who have called Springdale their business home for a very long time. Antique shops and unique boutiques quaintly litter Emma Ave with shopping opportunities you'll be hard-pressed to find elsewhere. It's worth visiting all of the unique specialty stores lining Emma Ave. There are plenty of restaurants to grab a quick bite while you're shopping 'til you drop, and you can commune with nature also by traversing Razorback Greenway Trail via its Shiloh Square Trailhead, which is literally a hop, skip, and jump from Emma Ave.

Ann Marie's Farmhouse Antiques & More
3095 Wagon Wheel, Springdale, AR 72762
(479) 659-4518

Antiques & Vintage
101 W Emma Ave, Springdale, AR 72764
(479) 287-6530

Cellar Door Antiques
132 W Emma Ave, Springdale, AR 72764
(479) 595-8819

Christopher & Co.
101 W Emma Ave, Springdale, AR 72764
(479) 419-9381

Eco Chic Resale
4058 Elm Springs Road, Springdale, AR 72762
(479) 750-2987

Midtown Eclectic Mall
308 S Thompson, Springdale, AR 72762
(479) 750-2987

Warehouse 54 Indie Market
101 W Emma Ave, Springdale, AR 72764
(479) 287-6530

Specialty Shops
Dickey Farms ~ Family Owned Farm
14306 Wildcat Creek Blvd, Springdale, AR 72762
(479) 361-9975

Lewis and Clark Outfitters
4915 S Thompson Street, Springdale, AR 72764
(479) 756-1344

Tattoo Shops
Club Tattoo
3204 S Thompson St, Springdale, AR 72764
(479) 750-1835

Rethink Your Ink
601 W Maple Ave #205a, Springdale, AR 72764
(479) 595-9901

Spas
A Touch of Grace Massage and Bodywork
2201 W Sunset Ave, Ste A1, Springdale, AR 72762
(479) 601-7387
Laser Beauty and Skin Care, Inc.
700 N 40th Street, Springdale, AR 72762
(479) 927-9955

Special Events/Festivals

Coffee and Cars

The first Saturday of each month from April to October, downtown Springdale features beautifully restored automobiles alongside some great java!

Arts and Craft Fairs

Every spring and fall, thousands flock to Northwest Arkansas to see and buy handmade specialties, including visiting the outdoor and indoor arts and crafts shows in Springdale.

Arenacross (Bikes Blues and BBQ)

The entire family can enjoy the excitement of motocross in Springdale each year during September's Bikes Blues and BBQ rally. This event brings motorcycle enthusiasts to Springdale's Parsons Stadium from all corners of the state and beyond.

Buckin' in the Ozarks

In late June, a PBR-sanctioned event takes place in Parsons Stadium featuring real cowboys and some of the orneriest bulls around. See who wins the battle between cowboy and bull at Springdale's Buckin' in the Ozarks; you'll be thankful you aren't the one the bull throws off its back!

Christmas Parade of the Ozarks

The Saturday of Thanksgiving weekend brings Christmas to the Ozarks. Be sure to get into the Christmas spirit early and join this festive holiday parade.

Monster Trucks

Springdale's Parsons Stadium is the venue for the popular, loud and big Monster Trucks annual event.

Rodeo of the Ozarks

This four night action-packed professional rodeo ranks in the U.S. as a top outdoor rodeo.

Rodeo Parades

Come join the fun of the annual Rodeo of the Ozarks parade. This annual parade begins and ends the Rodeo of the Ozarks in classic parade fashion. Springdale's downtown area becomes littered with traditional parade floats, beautiful horses, and, of course, plenty of marching bands providing musical entertainment.

Springdale Farmers Market
Jones Center for Families Memorial Walk,
Hwy 265 and Emma Ave.
Saturdays 7am – 1 pm May 3 - Saturday, November 1

Tontitown Grape Festival

Grape festivals are a unique experience nobody should miss. Springdale's Tontitown Grape Festival is an annual August event. Alongside plenty of grape madness, this carnival gives visitors an enjoyable time with traditional carnival games and rides and full bellies of homemade spaghetti dinners.

Wineries/Vineyards/Breweries

Core Brewing & Distilling Co
2470 Lowell Road, Springdale
(479) 879-2469

Macadoodles
838 N 48 Street, Springdale, AR 72762
(479) 717-2518

Macadoodles Springdale, AR offers patrons fine wine, beer and spirits. You'll find thousands of wines and beers to choose from perusing the selection at Macadoodles, Springdale, AR.

Saddlebock Brewery
18244 Habberton Road, Springdale
(479) 419-9969

Sassafras Springs Vineyard
6461 E Guy Terry Road, Springdale, AR 72764
(479) 419-4999
Winery and Vineyard

Tontitown Winery
335 N Barrington, Springdale, AR 72762
(479) 361-8700
Winery and Vineyard

RESTAURANTS

It's no surprise that the city known as the "Chicken Capital of the Country" is home to *the* superb chicken restaurant AQ Chicken. Local patrons come again and again, and tourists drive out of their way to sample the many different chicken recipes served at AQ. This is a must-stop-and-eat in your quest to sample the fine NWA food offered at the many restaurants in Springdale, AR.

If you are looking for a fine dining experience with your special someone, visit James at the Mill, a locally owned and long established upscale restaurant best known to be *THE* premier dining experience in NWA. Of all the restaurants in Springdale, AR, this one takes the cake in high-end cuisine and superb service.

Restaurant Prices

$ - Budget	*$$$ - Upscale*
$$ - Mid-Range	

American

AQ Chicken House 1207 N Thompson St, Springdale, AR 72764 (479) 751-4633 $$	MarketPlace Grill 1636 S 48th Street, Springdale, AR 72762 (479) 750-5200 $$
Bleu Monkey Grill 1100 S 48 Place, Springdale, AR 72762 (479) 750-1948 $$	Neal's Cafe 806 N Thompson Street, Springdale, AR 72764 (479) 751-9996 $$
Buffalo Wild Wings 6938 W Sunset Ave, Springdale, AR 72762 (479) 419-5374 $	Spring Street Grill 101 Spring Street, Springdale, AR 72764 (479) 751-0323 $

Cracker Barrel Old Country Store 1022 S 48th Street, Springdale, AR 72762 (479) 872-2040 $$	**Susan's Restaurant** 1440 W Sunset Ave, Springdale, AR 72764 (479) 751-1445 $$
Flaps Down Grill 802 Airport Ave, Springdale, AR 72764 (479) 361-8032 $	**Wagon Wheel Country Cafe** 4080 N Thompson St, Springdale, AR 72764 (479) 927-1510 $
James at the Mill 3906 Johnson Mill Blvd, Springdale, AR 72762 (479) 443-1400 $$$	

Asian

Bluefin 4276 W Sunset Ave, Springdale, AR 72762 (479) 717-2877 $$	**Mama Tang Restaurant** 3482 Elm Springs Road, Springdale, AR 72762 (479) 751-8989 $
China Café 2255 W Sunset Ave, Springdale, AR 72762 (479) 751-3188 $$	**Mandarin Bistro** 708 S Thompson Street, Springdale, AR 72764 (479) 756-8369 $
E-San Restaurant 2008 W Huntsville Ave, Springdale, AR 72762 (479) 750-7499 $	**Pattaya Thai Sushi** 1210 W Sunset Ave, Springdale, AR 72764 (479) 750-7755 $$

Far East Chinese Restaurant 812 N Thompson St #11, Springdale, AR 72764 (479) 756-2460 $	Silk Road Thai Restaurant 2576 W Sunset Ave, Springdale, AR 72762 (479) 756-6227 $

Bakeries

Ayala's Panaderia 428 Holcomb Street, Springdale, AR 72764 (479) 927-3986	Shelby Lynns Cake Shoppe 118 W Emma Ave, Springdale, AR 72764 (479) 750-0044
El Progresso Bakery 708 S Thompson Street, Springdale, AR 72764 (479) 872-1003	Shipley Do-nuts 1486 W Sunset, Springdale, AR 72764 (479) 499-2533
Little Debbie Co Store 406 E Henri De Tonti Blvd, Springdale, AR 72762 (479) 361-9100	

Buffets

Golden Dragon Buffet 4101 W Sunset Ave, Springdale, AR 72762 (479) 750-9988 $$	Red Dragon 4101 W Sunset Ave Springdale, AR 72762 (479) 927-3683 $$
Panda IV 3050 W Sunset Ave Springdale, AR 72762 (479) 872-8828 $	

Bars/Pubs/Breweries

Core Brewery	Saddlebock Brewery
2470 Lowell Road, Springdale, AR 72764	18244 Habberton Road, Springdale, AR 72764
(479) 879-2469	(479) 419-9969

BBQ

Rib Crib	
1120 Mathias Drive, Springdale, AR 72762	
(479) 361-8191	
$$	

Burgers

Angus Jack Burgers & Fresh Cut Fries	Neal's Cafe
2638 W Sunset Ave, Springdale, AR 72762	806 N Thompson Street, Springdale, AR 72764
(479) 717-2940	(479) 751-9996
$$	$$
Flaps Down Grill	Patrick's
802 Airport Ave, Springdale, AR 72764	3608 Elm Springs Road, Springdale, AR 72762
(479) 361-8032	(479) 751-9245
$	$

Catering

AQ Chicken House	MarketPlace Grill
1207 N Thompson St, Springdale, AR 72764	1636 S 48th Street, Springdale, AR 72762
(479) 751-4633	(479) 750-5200
$$	$$

| Kruton's, Festivities, & Botanicals of NWA
181 Industrial Circle E, Springdale, AR 72762
(479) 750-8981
$$ | Spring Street Grill
101 Spring Street, Springdale, AR 72764
(479) 751-0323
$ |

Coffee

Anonymous Coffee Roasters 2231 Lowell Road, Springdale, AR 72764 (479) 799-6552 $	Pontiac Coffee House 515 S Thompson Street, Springdale, AR 72764 (479) 751-4654 $
ONYX Coffee Lab 7058 W Sunset Ave, Springdale, AR 72762 (479) 419-5739 $	

Fast Food

Arby's 908 S Thompson Street, Springdale, AR 72764 (479) 756-2503 $	Schlotzsky's 1919 W Sunset Ave, Springdale, AR 72764 (479) 751-9800 $
Burger King 5660 W Sunset Ave, Springdale, AR 72762 (479) 770-3030 $	Sonic 1306 S Thompson Street, Springdale, AR 72764 (479) 756-8050 $
Jimmy John's Gourmet Sandwiches 4276 W Sunset Ave, Springdale, AR 72762 (479) 927-0399 $	SUBWAY 411 S Thompson Street, Springdale, AR 72764 (479) 751-3088 $

Hardee's 401 S Thompson Street, Springdale, AR 72764 (479) 751-1021 $	SUBWAY 4719 Butterfield Coach Road, Springdale, AR 72764 (479) 750-9788 $
KFC Springdale 600 S Thompson Street, Springdale, AR 72764 (479) 872-7311 $	Taco Bell 4322 W Sunset Ave, Springdale, AR 72762 (479) 751-2344 $
Long John Silver's 983 W Sunset Ave, Springdale, AR 72764 (479) 756-1720 $	Wendy's 2000 S Pleasant Street, Springdale, AR 72764 (479) 872-2866 $
McDonald's 520 S Thompson Street, Springdale, AR 72764 (479) 751-3510 $	Zaxby's 400 S Thompson Street, Springdale, AR 72764 (479) 750-3740 $
Panda Restaurant 3050 W Sunset Ave, Springdale, AR 72762 (479) 872-8828 $$	

Fine Dining

James at the Mill 3906 Great House Springs Rd, Springdale, AR 72762 (479) 443-1400 $$$	Marketplace Grill 1636 S 48th St Springdale, AR 72762 (479) 750-5200 $$

Ice Cream ~ Yogurt

Braum's Ice Cream and Dairy Store 4374 W Sunset Ave, Springdale, AR 72762 (479) 751-0305 $	N2 Yogurt 2111 S Old Missouri Rd, Springdale, AR 72764 (479) 419-9897 $
Braum's Ice Cream & Dairy Store 907 S Thompson Street, Springdale, AR 72764 (479) 751-7846 $	Tropical Smoothie Cafe 7022 W Sunset, Ste 1, Springdale, AR 72762 479-361-9999 $

Italian

Mary Maestri's Italiano Grillroom 669 E Robinson Ave, Springdale, AR 72764 (479) 756-1441 $$	Venesian Inn 582 W Henri De Tonti Blvd, Springdale, AR 72762 (479) 361-2562 $$

Mexican

Acalpuco Mexican Grill 1602 E Robinson Ave, Springdale, AR 72764 (479) 750-4740 $	Jose's Southwest Grille 5240 W Sunset Ave, Springdale, AR 72762 (479) 750-9055 $
Acambaro Mexican Restaurant 121 N Thompson Street, Springdale, AR 72764 (479) 927-3822 $	Las Palmas 1084 W Sunset Ave, Springdale, AR 72764 (479) 872-1078 $$
Charly's Taqueria 1830 S Pleasant St, Springdale, AR 72764 (479) 751-7888 $	Taco Bell 4322 W Sunset Ave, Springdale, AR 72762 (479) 751-2344 $

Flying Burrito Co 7022 W Sunset Ave #5, Springdale, AR 72762 (479) 419-9400 $	Taco Bueno 7420 W Sunset Ave, Springdale, AR 72762 (479) 361-9115 $
Las Fajitas Mexican Grill 5266 N Thompson Str, Springdale, AR 72764 (479) 872-1346 $	Taqueria Guanajuato 103 N Thompson Street, Springdale, AR 72764 (479) 750-1949 $
La Huerta Bar and Grill 4901 S Thompson St, Springdale, AR 72764 (479) 750-9700 $$	Tesoro Beach Restaurant 701 S Thompson Street, Springdale, AR 72764 (479) 756-5965 $
La Sirena Restaurant 505 Thomas Blvd, Springdale, AR 72762 (479) 872-1280 $	Taqueria El Cunado 700 S Thompson St, Springdale, AR 72764 (479) 751-9307 $
Las Margaritas Mexican Restaurant 2313 W Sunset Ave, Springdale, AR 72762 (479) 756-1088 $	Ultimate Taco 332 E Emma Ave, Springdale, AR 72764 (479) 750-4480 $

Pizza

Eureka Pizza 1503 S Thompson St, Springdale, AR 72762 (479) 756-3030 $	Joe's Pizza and Pasta 4224 W Sunset Ave, Springdale, AR 72762 (479) 750-4450 $$

Fedele's Pizza 2576 W Sunset Ave, Springdale, AR 72762 (479) 361-8843 $$	Little Caesars Pizza 2682 W Sunset Ave, Springdale, AR 72762 (479) 756-5947 $
Guido's Pizza 4275 S Thompson St, Springdale, AR 72764 (479) 750-7775 $$	Mazzio's 1301 E Robinson Ave, Springdale, AR 72764 (479) 872-9999 $
Guido's Pizza 363 W Henri De Tonti Blvd, Springdale, AR 72762 (479) 361-9101 $$	Pizza Hut Springdale, AR 1772 W Sunset #2-A, Springdale, AR 72762 (479) 751-7700 $$
Jim's Razorback Pizza 149 S 40th Street, Springdale, AR 72762 (479) 725-1216 $	Pizza Hut Springdale, AR 2921 S Old Missouri Rd, Springdale, AR 72764 (479) 756-2228 $$

Sandwiches

Jimmy John's Gourmet Sandwiches 4276 W Sunset Ave, Springdale, AR 72762 (479) 927-0399 $	Subway 4719 Butterfield Coach Road, Springdale, AR 72764 (479) 750-9788 $
Schlotzsky's 1919 W Sunset Ave, Springdale, AR 72764 (479) 751-9800 $	Tropical Smoothie Cafe 7022 W Sunset, Ste 1, Springdale, AR 72762 (479) 361-9999 $

SUBWAY Restaurants	Zaxby's
411 S Thompson Street, Springdale, AR 72764	400 S Thompson Street, Springdale, AR 72764
(479) 751-3088	(479) 750-3740$
S	S

Steaks

Applebee's Neighborhood Grill	Western Sizzlin
3953 W Sunset Ave, Springdale, AR 72762	3492 W Sunset Ave, Springdale, AR 72762
(479) 751-9844	(479) 750-3663
SS	SS
Outback Steakhouse	
4808 S Thompson St, Springdale, AR 72764	
(479) 872-2800	
SS	

Wineries

Tontitown Winery	Sassafras Springs Vineyard
335 N Barrington, Springdale, AR 72762	6461 E Guy Terry Road, Springdale, AR 72764
(479) 361-8700	(479)419-4999

APPENDIX A – TRANSPORTATION

Ozark Regional Transit (ORT): Ozark Regional Transit provides public transportation for Northwest Arkansas. Visit OZARK.org for more information.

Taxi, Limo Services:

Abundant Transportation

(479) 553-8294

AAA Car Service

(479) 644-8469

Down Under Taxi

(479)856-2888

Hotel Executive Transportation/NWA Taxi

(479) 571-TAXI

Jim's Express Shuttle

(479) 205-0011

Car Rental Places:

Avis - 1-800-633-3469

Budget - 1-800-218-7992

Dollar - 1-800-800-4000

Enterprise - 1-800-261-7331

Hertz – 1-800-654-3131 (US/Canada)

National – 1-877-222-9058

APPENDIX B – PLACES TO GET DIESEL

Bentonville

Kum & Go

2811 E Central Ave, Bentonville, AR

(479) 254-0683

Kum & Go

2710 Moberly Ln, Bentonville, AR

(479) 464-0849

Kum & Go

3610 SW Regional Airport Blvd, Bentonville, AR

(479) 254-3759

E-Z Mart 425

I-49/US71 and Hwy 102, 2401 S E 14th St, Bentonville AR

 (479) 273-1562

Fastrip #25

307 S US-71 Business, Bentonville, AR 72712

(479) 273-1354

E-Z Mart #425

I-49/US71 Ex 86 (Hwy102), 2401 S E 14th St, Bentonville, AR 72712

(479) 273-1562

Wal-Mart Supercenter

406 S. Walton Blvd, Bentonville, AR 72712

(479) 273-0060

Eureka Springs

Bunche's Quick Chek (Phillips 66)

134 E. Van Buren/Hwy 62 Easy, Eureka Springs, AR

(479) 253-9732

Riverlake Outdoor Center (Exxon)

14735 Hwy 62 West/Junction of Hwy. 62 & 187, Eureka Springs, AR

(479) 253-5628

Eureka Springs Exxon

102 Passion Play Road/Hwy 62 East, Eureka Springs, AR

(479) 253-6558

Motor Coach & RV Dumping Stations

Eureka Springs KOA – RV Ony $15.00

Kettle Campground – RV $5 – Motor Coach $25

Wanderlust RV Park – RV $10 – Motor Coach $25-$50

<u>Fayetteville</u>

Wal-Mart Supercenter

I-49 Ex 62 (US62), 2875 West 6Th Street, Fayetteville, AR 72704

(479) 582-0428

Tobos 66

I-49 Ex 58, 1200 W. Wilson St, Fayetteville AR

(479) 521-2627

<u>Rogers</u>

Fast Trax 7

I-49 Ex 85, 4601 W Walnut St, Rogers AR

(479) 636-7444

Wal-Mart Supercenter

US71, 2110 West Walnut, Rogers, AR 72756

(479) 636-3222

Kum & Go #403

I-49 Ex 86 (US62), 2400 W. Hudson Rd, Rogers, AR 72756

(479) 986-9403

Fast Trax #7

I-49 Ex 85, 4601 W Walnut St, Rogers, AR 72756

(479) 636-7444

Springdale

Wal-Mart Supercenter

US71, 2004 S. Pleasant St, Springdale, AR 72764

(479) 751-4817

Braich Arrow Express

1298 W Henri De Tonti Blvd, Springdale AR

(479) 361- 9644

Pilot Travel Center

US 412 & 71 Bypass, 5660 West Sunset Avenue, Springdale AR

(479) 872- 6100

Pilot Travel Center

I-49 Ex 72 (US412), 5660 West Sunset Avenue, Springdale, AR 72762

(479) 872-6100

APPENDIX C – URGENT CARE CLINICS IN NWA

Bentonville

MedExpress Urgent Care (Coming Soon)

1995 S.E. Walton Blvd, Bentonville, AR 72712

Ozark Urgent Care
1706 SE Walton Blvd #4, Bentonville, AR 72712
(479) 464-0400

Northwest Medical Center
3000 SE Medical Center Pkwy, Bentonville, AR 72712
(479) 553-1000

Fayetteville

Karas Urgent Care
1057 N Garland Ave, Fayetteville, AR 72701
(479) 966-5088

MediServe Walk-In Clinic
1188 N. Salem, Fayetteville, AR 72704
(479) 442-0006

MediServe Walk-In Clinic
117 E. Sycamore, Fayetteville, AR 72703
(479) 521-0200

MedExpress Urgent Care (coming soon)
2890 N. College Ave, Fayetteville, AR 72703

Washington Regional Medical Center
3215 N. North Hills, Fayetteville, AR
(479) 713-1000

Lowell

Karas Urgent Care
114 Harrison Ave, Lowell, AR 72745
(479) 770-4343

Rogers
Family Medical Walk-In Clinics

1300 W Walnut St, Rogers, AR 72758
(479) 361-5756

Springdale

Family Medical Urgent Care
1306 S. Pleasant St, Springdale, Arkansas 72764
(855) 707-5550

MedExpress Urgent Care (coming soon)
1160 S. 40th St, Springdale, AR 72762

APPENDIX D – NWA VISITOR INFORMATION CENTERS

Bella Vista
Bella Vista Village POA
98 Clubhouse Drive, Bella Vista, AR 72715
(479) 855-8000

Bentonville
Bentonville Convention & Visitors Bureau
104 E. Central, Bentonville, AR 72712
(479) 271-9153

Eureka Springs
Eureka Springs Visitors Information Center
615 Village Circle/Pine Mountain Village
(479) 253-8737

Fayetteville
Fayetteville Visitors Bureau
21 S. Block Avenue, Fayetteville, AR 72701
(479) 521-5776

Rogers
Rogers Convention & Visitors Bureau
317 W. Walnut, Rogers, AR 72756
(479) 636-1240

Siloam Springs
Siloam Springs Chamber of Commerce
108 E. University St., Siloam Springs, AR 72761
(479) 524-6466

Springdale
Springdale Chamber of Commerce
202 W. Emma, Springdale, AR 72765

NWA Arkansas Welcome Centers
13750 Visitor's Center Drive, Bella Vista, AR 72714
(479) 855-3111

Siloam Springs Welcome Center
2000 U.S. 412, Siloam Springs, AR 72761
(479) 524-4445

Have you packed your bags...?

We hope you have enjoyed the Northwest Arkansas Travel Guide. This beautiful and fun part of the country is exploding with growth and unparalleled opportunity. NWA breeds fearless business leaders who generously give back to their home communities ensuring that the NW corner of the state continues to be #1 in the region in so many different areas. Business, world-class shopping, exceptional lodging, award-winning restaurants, unique outdoor adventures, stunningly beautiful museums and other outstanding attractions make this the premier area to visit in the state.

While you are in NWA, you can use the Guide as your constant travel companion. For your traveling convenience, it comes via several different platforms (Kindle, itunes, nook). Be sure to download the ebook version so you can access the Guide on your Kindle, iphone, android phone, tablet or any other reading device.

Since we update all NWA Travel Guide information on a weekly basis, be sure to continually check back at http://NWATravelGuide.com for current deals and listings. While you are there, take the time to sign up for our free reports and amazing weekly deals.

Let Us Know...

Please let us know if we left anyone out or if we need to make corrections. You can contact us via our website at http://NWATravelGuide.com.

Enjoy your visit to Northwest Arkansas!

Made in the USA
Lexington, KY
14 March 2015